Organising White-Collar and Corporate Crimes

This book explores how we can re-constitute our approach to analysing and empirically investigating the organisation of white-collar and corporate crimes, with a view to building fuller theoretical and empirical accounts. The work demonstrates how knowledge can be produced and systematised within a conceptual and analytical framework concerned with understanding how such crimes are organised, why they are organised as they are, who gets involved in them as primary offenders and as facilitators, and the 'real' factors that shape these organisational dynamics over time in particular contexts and under varying conditions. In doing so, the book examines the distal (far-off) and proximal (close) social arrangements and relations that create and shape emergent white-collar crime opportunities and their structures. It also investigates the mechanisms, relationships, processes, and conditions that are necessary for the commission, or the unfolding, of white-collar crimes, or for their non-commission. How these are contingently connected to particular contexts is explored. The work also considers the people who collaborate, connect, and otherwise associate, whether ephemerally or for longer periods, in the pursuit of criminal goals and the actual or potential skills, expertise, and abilities of these people to accomplish or resist particular behaviours that are required of them. Finally, the book assesses the human, social, cultural, and material antecedents that enable white-collar crimes to flourish or fade. The work will be of particular interest to scholars theorising about and empirically investigating white-collar and corporate crimes, or seeking to understand empirical approaches to analysing such behaviours and other types of crime. It is primarily aimed at critical social scientists, including criminologists and sociologists, as well as socio-legal, business, economics, and political studies scholars. The work will also be of interest to practitioners and policymakers keen to learn more about how and why these crimes are organised as they are.

Nicholas Lord is a Professor of Criminology in the School of Social Sciences at The University of Manchester, UK.

Michael Levi is a Professor of Criminology in the School of Social Sciences at Cardiff University, UK.

'In this groundbreaking work, Lord and Levi present a detailed analysis of how complex white-collar and corporate crimes are organized. By focusing on the mechanics of white-collar offenses, they advance our understanding of how and why these multifaceted crimes persist as well as suggesting mechanisms for their regulation and control.'

Michael L. Benson, *Professor of Criminology, University of Cincinnati*

'Lord and Levi, renowned global scholars, take readers on a tour de force into the world of white-collar and corporate criminals. Focusing on the very nature of these crimes – organisation, they lay bare the deep mechanisms on which they thrive. Razor-sharp analyses of juicy cases complement a truly intellectual adventure.'

Susanne Karstedt, *Professor of Criminology, Griffith University*

'This book by two of the most authoritative scholars in white-collar criminology offers a comprehensive account of how white-collar crimes are organized and financed, as well as many case descriptions of seriously harmful white-collar crimes in contemporary organizations. An essential read.'

Judith van Erp, *Professor of Regulatory Governance, Utrecht University*

'Seventy-five years after Edwin Sutherland characterized white-collar crimes as crimes of organization, this book provides the analytical framework to actually study the contemporary organization of white-collar and corporate crimes. This is much needed to advance white-collar and corporate crime scholarship.'

Karin van Wingerde, *Professor of Corporate Crime and Governance, Erasmus School of Law, Erasmus University Rotterdam*

'Most studies apply mainstream theories from criminology to white-collar and corporate crime, with mixed results. This book revitalizes the field with an opposite approach, by directly aiming at the core of white-collar crime. Understanding 'organisation' is key to understanding the true nature and root causes of white-collar and corporate crime.'

Wim Huisman, *Professor of Criminology, Vrije Universiteit Amsterdam*

'Why are white-collar and corporate crimes organized as they are? What conditions give rise to different forms of organisation over time? How do people come together to undertake and accomplish these illegal acts? In this unique and important book, the authors conduct a deep dive into the underlying mechanisms of organisation by connecting diverse literatures (opportunity, white-collar crime scripts, and multi-mode, multi-link network analysis) and applying their integrated perspective to case studies of white-collar and corporate crime. The approach is innovative and illuminating. I heartily recommend it.'

Sally S. Simpson, *Distinguished University Professor (Emerita), Department of Criminology and Criminal Justice, University of Maryland*

Organising White-Collar and Corporate Crimes

Nicholas Lord and Michael Levi

Routledge
Taylor & Francis Group
LONDON AND NEW YORK

First published 2025
by Routledge
4 Park Square, Milton Park, Abingdon, Oxon OX14 4RN

and by Routledge
605 Third Avenue, New York, NY 10158

Routledge is an imprint of the Taylor & Francis Group, an informa business

British Library Cataloguing-in-Publication Data
A catalogue record for this book is available from the British Library

Library of Congress Cataloging-in-Publication Data
Names: Lord, Nicholas, author. | Levi, Michael, author.
Title: Organising white-collar and corporate crimes / Nicholas Lord and Michael Levi.
Description: Abingdon, Oxon [UK]; New York, NY: Routledge, 2025. | Includes bibliographical references and index.
Identifiers: LCCN 2024047738 (print) | LCCN 2024047739 (ebook) | ISBN 9781138296107 (hardback) | ISBN 9781032990019 (paperback) | ISBN 9781315100227 (ebook)
Subjects: LCSH: Commercial crimes—Law and legislation. | White collar crimes—Law and legislation. | Corporations—Corrupt practices.
Classification: LCC K5215.L67 2025 (print) | LCC K5215 (ebook) | DDC 364.16/8072—dc23/eng/20241009
LC record available at https://lccn.loc.gov/2024047738
LC ebook record available at https://lccn.loc.gov/2024047739

ISBN: 978-1-138-29610-7 (hbk)
ISBN: 978-1-032-99001-9 (pbk)
ISBN: 978-1-315-10022-7 (ebk)

DOI: 10.4324/9781315100227

Typeset in ITC Galliard Pro
by Apex CoVantage, LLC

For Helen and Ida, and Tia the cat, all of whom are purrfect.

– NL

To Penny, Julia, and Debbie, our grandchildren Evan and Sidney, and all our animals, whom I have much neglected while writing this and other things.

– ML

Contents

Acknowledgements

This book would never have happened were it not for the generosity and support of my co-author, Michael Levi, who took the time back in 2006 to discuss my potential PhD project and then take me on as a PhD student at Cardiff University in Wales. The kindness, encouragement, and guidance shown significantly altered my career path and trajectory, and, in the following years, influenced my intellectual journey right up to shaping the focus of this book on the organisational aspects of white-collar and corporate crimes. Relatedly, this book would also not have taken the shape it has without the intellectual direction provided by Adam Edwards (my PhD co-supervisor), who introduced me to the philosophical tradition of critical realism in the social sciences, which, in turn, has shaped my approach to theory building and empirical research, and, in turn, the approach presented in this book.

– Nicholas Lord

I fully reciprocate the good fortune that led me to Nick Lord, who has vigorously and rigorously carried the flame that first led me to this area of research many decades ago. He and Adam Edwards propelled me along the path of critical realism as the core perspective of this book. I am also particularly grateful to the late Richard F Sparks for first encouraging my interest in the organisation of crime for gain while at Cambridge, and to my friends and colleagues Susanne Karstedt, Ken Pease, and Peter Reuter, who, though they were not asked to read drafts or to contribute to the writing of this book, have stimulated me to think more carefully and to write less self-indulgently. They bear no responsibility for the outcome. Semper gratus ero.

– Michael Levi

Both authors would like to thank colleagues who took the time to read earlier versions of the manuscript or particular manuscript chapters relating to their expertise. These include Michael Benson, Melissa Rorie, Katie Benson, Jon Davies, Tom Diviák, and Aleksandra Jordanoska. Their feedback was invaluable and improved the final version of the book.

1 An Organisational Perspective
Introduction and Overview

Introduction

This book is about how we can re-constitute our approach to analysing and empirically investigating the *organisation* of white-collar and corporate crimes. By focusing on *organisation* – the 'how' questions that underlie the understanding of crime rates – a fuller theoretical (and empirical) account can be developed of those criminal phenomena associated originally with the privileged, upper socio-economic individual and corporate actors to whom Edwin Sutherland (1983) sought to draw attention in his seminal work in 1930s and 1940s United States: this included price fixing and other collusive corporate crimes, anonymising the offenders until his 'uncut' version appeared in 1983, 33 years after his death. It equally illuminates the crimes of those less elite offenders often analysed within the framework of 'white-collar crime' but who have more diverse demographies, reflecting the changing nature of both the managerial classes and the range/supply chains of business activities compared with that era. The spread of (i) digital and global supply chain vulnerabilities (from data hacking to food contamination and people smuggling/trafficking), and (ii) 'offshore' corporate and trust company mechanisms of financial opacity has created manifold senior-junior insider and also outsider possibilities for the commission of crimes that did not then exist or, in some cases, may have existed but were not then recognised. The book, then, is about how we can think about, produce, and systematise our knowledge within a conceptual and analytical framework concerned with understanding *how* such crimes are organised, *why* they are organised as they are, *who* gets involved in them, both as primary offenders and as facilitators/'crime enablers', and the 'real' factors that shape these *organisational dynamics* over time within particular contexts and under varying conditions.

In the context of white-collar crimes, we mean many things by 'organisation'. We mean the distal (far-off) and proximal (close) social arrangements and relations that create and shape emergent white-collar crime opportunities and their structures; we mean the mechanisms, relationships, processes, and conditions that are *necessary* for the commission, the unfolding, or for the non-commission of white-collar crimes and how these are *contingently*

DOI: 10.4324/9781315100227-1

connected to particular contexts; we mean the people who collaborate, connect, and otherwise associate, whether ephemerally or for longer periods, in the pursuit of criminal goals, and the actual or potential skills, expertise, and abilities of these people to accomplish (or resist/deflect) particular behaviours that are required of them, as well as the human, social, cultural, and material antecedents that enable white-collar crimes to flourish or fade. For instance, as the FTX/Alameda fraud unravelled in 2023, we learned how founder Sam Bankman-Fried moved investors' deposits from his cryptocurrency exchange company, FTX, to his cryptocurrency hedge fund, Alameda Research, to illegally pay off its lenders and make personal 'loans' to himself and others, and directed others to commit crimes and lie to lenders and investors about company finances. The case was able to happen due to the combination of contingently necessary social arrangements, such as the coming together of enduring structural economic relations (e.g., investment by people and institutions for profit – or for expected profits that may not materialise – within venture capitalism, alongside market conditions including non-transparent beneficial ownership, lax independent governance,[1] and so on) that create the conditions of possibility for fraud of this type to occur. Alongside these far-off structures, the close, situational emergence of motivated collaborating individuals (e.g., Bankman-Fried and his close colleagues at FTX and Alameda), who, at some stage – maybe even when they began trading – recognised suitable opportunities to defraud investors (necessary for the fraud but their personal circumstances being contingent – i.e., they may be seasoned high-net worth investors or university professors with an interest in cryptocurrencies). Then, via their poorly regulated corporate structures spanning countries, they created mechanisms with fraudulent *potential*, whose realisation required these individuals to possess the particular capacities, skills, expertise, and confidence to seize the opportunities. Notwithstanding their guilty pleas and jury convictions, Bankman-Fried and some/all colleagues may not have thought they were doing or had done anything morally wrong or that might be treated as criminal. The FTX fraud was organised under conducive conditions, made possible by the coming together of contingently necessary causal mechanisms, and mediated through the actions and mindsets of the particular characters at the centre of the case. One of the effects of having an economy more strongly based around digital products and services than in the past is normalising the extraordinary profitability of businesses run by much younger people with less conventional backgrounds and roles, as well as (however spuriously) the value of intangibles such as digital currencies such as Bitcoin. Though it is important to appreciate the long history of fraud through the centuries and its criminalisation (Balleisen, 2018; Levi, 2008, 2016; Taylor, 2013; Toms, 2024; Turner,

1 Transparency of ownership and governance laxity are not simply binary – they are matters of degree, and judgments about where on the axes they lie may be disputed during and after the fact.

2024), the normalisation of less tangible products such as software and the financialisation of the economy create a range of criminal and licit opportunities for younger entrepreneurs that would not have been possible in earlier eras. They also provide a broader range of challenges for internal compliance officers, regulators, and criminal investigators to intervene early enough to prevent or reduce harm and perhaps deliver justice.

These are the sort of organisational dynamics generated as part of broader configurations of economy and society that can endure over time, such as the distribution of different sorts of white-collar crime opportunities across social strata and systems. If we integrate and systematise the production of knowledge about these dynamics, we gain better insight into the criminal organisation of white-collar crimes. Thinking in terms of 'organisation' is more than semantics. It has implications for how we build theory on white-collar and corporate crimes; for how we develop convincing explanatory accounts of associated behaviours; and also, for how we contribute to operational and policy discourse by enabling those motivated to control these social 'bads' to do so with a keener appreciation of the likely effects of their interventions.

The approach we put forward in this book stems from decades of researching and thinking through the nature, dynamics, and governance of crimes by individual and corporate actors across varying market and institutional contexts. Our own research has drawn attention to the importance of examining organisation. Since his seminal work on *The Phantom Capitalists*, one strand of Levi's research has foregrounded an understanding of the processes inherent to white-collar crimes and frauds of varying types, and encouraging research into the organisation of these serious crimes for gain. (See Edwards and Levi, 2008; Levi, 2008.) This entails investigating the nature of how people identify and collaborate with others, organising their behaviours to realise *some* white-collar crime opportunities; the routine activities or 'scripts' through which they must go to accomplish (or not) their intended behaviours; and the conditions or pre-conditions (necessary, sufficient, or contingent) that link the motivations of individual offenders to the legacies of modern political economies.

Furthering this line of inquiry, at the 2016 annual meeting of the European Society of Criminology in Münster, Germany, and in the follow-up session to a financial crime plenary by Wim Huisman, Lord presented a framework for thinking through these 'real' factors in the form of the 'five Cs' of white-collar crimes: commission, cooperation, capital, capacities, and conditions. These factors encourage us to ask: How and why do would-be offenders recognise and exploit financial crime opportunities or not? How does the presence or absence of 'crime networks' and 'professional enablers' known to and trusted by the willing offender(s) make a difference to 'crime commission'? (This is an issue often neglected in individualised explanations of involvement in crime.) What resources and/or financial and social capital are required for different financial crimes? That is, how are the funds for the crimes acquired and used without raising suspicion from peers or from 'responsibilised' internal and external professionals, who nowadays, in almost all countries, are likely to have an obligation under anti–money laundering legislation to report to their national Financial Intelligence Unit any suspicions of crime ***if and when formed***? And what running costs of crimes emerge, and how much do they vary over time and space? Setting up an impressive façade of wealth and prestige in work and lifestyle – however hip among such as 'crypto bros' – is not cheap, as demonstrated by Sam Bankman-Fried's private plane and office-home in the Bahamas and the 'bling' on Instagram fraudsters like 'Hushpuppi',[2] who are less celebrated in elite circles but highly celebrated in other quarters. What kinds of certification, skill sets, knowledge, and expertise do offenders need (or need to recruit if not already present in their network) to organise different kinds of white-collar crimes, and how difficult is this to put in place? Why do some social, economic, and systemic structures and conditions create environments in different industries and organisations that are more contagious, resilient, and/or immune to opportunities for white-collar crimes and their commission?

The questions we pose here require us to make connections between the underlying factors or structures generating the coming together of the particular mechanisms that constitute the commissioning process of any given white-collar or corporate crime, and the conditions or relations that enable the crime to take place, or produce other outcomes, such as being detected or otherwise failing in a fraudulent scheme. The term 'commissioning' may imply goal-oriented, preconceived offending, particularly in cases with little ambiguity on the criminal nature of the offences or the criminal intent of those involved. But we also use the term to incorporate the ways in which crimes may unfold as part of ongoing business or other practices, such as where offenders may not set out to engage in crime, but their contextual choices result in crime happening. In our view, making the connections outlined here implies a requirement to combine both abstract thinking and empirical analysis to gain insight into what are complex sets of social relations and organisational dynamics. For instance, as outlined here, there is a need to analyse the interactions and social relations within and between (i) remote distal causes (e.g., the contingent geographical and historical antecedents of white-collar crimes), (ii) situational opportunities and proximal factors (e.g., particular settings and routine activities of those involved, including the 'scripts' of the crime commission process), and (iii) (pre-existing) networks of offender cooperation and collusion (e.g., the substantial social relations of connection between different causal groups). All three are needed for a truly comprehensive understanding of these behaviours. This involves identifying how motivated (and cooperating) offenders necessarily interact with criminal opportunities and targets under contingent conditions that are conducive to crime or its control, such as the absence of 'capable guardians' in particular settings who could have

2 https://www.bloomberg.com/features/2021-hushpuppi-gucci-influencer/

stopped altogether or reduced the number and scale of crimes. Understanding how these interactions and settings are shaped by wider social-structural antecedents that may be unobservable therefore requires isolating in thought as part of a more concrete conception of the causal mechanisms of white-collar offending.

But individual offenders are not only social products, as they are also shaped in combination with internally derived mechanisms. For instance, individuals need to have skills and confidence as well as motivation, targets, and offending-conducive situations. There are generative structures such as human capacities (i.e., the cognitive, behavioural, and affective dimensions of individuals, including their knowledge and expertise, skill sets, mental/physical abilities); social capacities (i.e., social structures and relations that shape the interactions of opportunities, individuals, and routine business activities and operations); material capacities (i.e., resources, capital, matériel, or the 'tools' of the crime); and cultural capacities (i.e., the shared experiences, beliefs, and intersubjectivities of individuals in particular situations). We explore these different dimensions in this book as part of our analytical framework.

With this in mind, this book both builds on and moves beyond current academic debates to provide a comprehensive, evidence-based, and realist[3] analysis of the organisation of white-collar and corporate crimes. We import concepts and ideas from critical realism (see footnote 1) to offer fresh ways of thinking intellectually about the multi-faceted nature of crime commission, integrating an analysis of structure with an analysis of causal mechanisms and social relations alongside situational contexts and individual capacities, to help us explain white-collar and corporate crimes. This framework does not provide a 'formula' that all should follow but will allow interested readers to dip into particular chapters to enhance or supplement their research, or perhaps challenge (or reaffirm) their own ways of thinking. The framework unashamedly makes the case for foregrounding complexity and the multi-faceted factors that shape white-collar and corporate offending to encourage us to think also about variations in the nature, organisation, and levels of offending across contexts and cultures, and over time. This is to avoid reducing interpretations or understandings of such phenomena to specific explanations, such as individual

3 By 'realist', we mean our preference for a critical realist approach to analysis and articulation and to the production of knowledge and theory building characterised by processes of abduction, abstraction, and retroduction. (See Sayer, 2010; Edwards and Levi, 2008.) That is, foregrounding the multi-faceted and concrete aspects of white-collar crimes, and how different essential and contingent factors configure in different contexts and times to gain insight into not only the empirical (perceptions and sensed data) and the actual (events), but also the real (deep causal mechanisms). Critical realist approaches offer a fallible and adaptive approach, in contrast to the successionist, positivist hypothetico-deductive testing of theory and variables, or the inductive, interpretivist approach to building theory. We are not suggesting that these other approaches are impermissible or fundamentally flawed, but critical realism is our preference for reasons we think defensible.

psychopathy, internal corporate control policies, or macro-economic structures; variation exists in the social and economic world, and we need to recognise this in our theorising.

'So what?' you might say. How does highlighting the complex, multi-faceted nature of white-collar offending help inform explanations of these behaviours beyond specific contexts? The framework here goes beyond multi-factorial accounts of offending, to distinguish causal mechanisms or factors that are *necessary* for these crimes to occur from those which are merely contingent and, in turn, allow us to identify what is contingently necessary over time and place. This can help us identify common features across analogous white-collar offending. For instance, why are some causal factors activated under certain conditions again and again? Or why do other causal factors not lead to offending under other conditions? Which factors regularly restrict or constrain the realisation of opportunities to offend despite the ease with which they could be exploited? For instance, in June 2023, Stephen Teixeira, a compliance chief at a Chinese fintech company, was charged by the Securities and Exchange Commission (SEC) with insider trading, after passing on to his friend, Jordan Meadow, who worked as a stockbroker, inside information that Teixeira accessed from the computer of his girlfriend, who worked at an investment bank.[4] (They were also charged criminally.) In this case, a combination of mechanisms with causal potential emerged, such as the particular working context enforced by the pandemic at that time (e.g., working from home with others on laptops, rather than in secure offices), that generated new opportunities. Other situational mechanisms present were the poor security/cyber practices of his girlfriend, who left her computer unattended and unlocked; asking Teixeira to monitor for urgent emails; and the installation of a device, bought by Teixeira, to move her mouse to make it appear she was actually working, enabling him to access it without her knowledge. Yet, Teixeira also needed knowledge and motivation to activate this opportunity structure. (Cyber)-fraud levels rose during the pandemic, indicating that this particular condition was exploited again and again across contexts, but, in some cases, more secure working practices at home will have restricted the realisation of the opportunity, or, in this case, would have made Teixeira change the 'script' and access the information using different means if he could, assuming he still recognised that there was an opportunity, or even seek to involve her actively in the scheme, which might have led to her incrimination and removed an innocent defence. We note that such domestic 'pillow talk' cases might have taken place prior to the COVID-19 pandemic – and that these would be a small proportion of insider trading examples anyway – but hybrid working-from-home (WFH) practices have become much more commonplace since the beginning of the pandemic, reconfiguring a range of fraud and 'organised crime' risks. In

4 https://www.wsj.com/articles/compliance-chief-charged-with-insider-trading-on-information-pilfered-from-girlfriend-2ebd9b03

other cases, unauthorised actors with the opportunities to access information would not have had the skills or knowledge to do so (e.g., device installation), meaning 'objective' opportunities elsewhere would not be recognised or, if recognised, would be constrained. Where crimes are attempted, they may fail to be accomplished due to these skills or knowledge gaps, or for other reasons. Failing can be a relative term. Failing in *some* or even the majority of attempts is built into volume frauds like advance fee and phishing emails, which are very low cost at scale. At the other extreme of both gross and net income from fraud, in February 2016, 35 fraudulent instructions were issued by North Korean hackers via the SWIFT network to transfer around US$1 billion from the Federal Reserve Bank of New York account belonging to the central Bank of Bangladesh (White, 2022). Five of the 35 fraudulent instructions were successful in transferring US$101 million. The Federal Reserve Bank of New York blocked the remaining 30 transactions, amounting to US$850 million, due to suspicions raised by a misspelled instruction. (But with US$66 million unrecovered, still a substantial profit for a partial failure!)[5] Understanding how such combinations of conditions and mechanisms come together and lead to crimes unfolding aids insights into the organisation of similar and diverse crimes across analogous and different contexts.

Asking such questions about what is contingently-necessary helps us move beyond describing relevant factors with causal potential to explaining why certain factors contributed to any given case of white-collar crime occurring. By foregrounding complexity in this way, we avoid the temptation of overly reductionist or simplistic accounts of causality (e.g., A leads to B), which defy the contingency of everyday life. Similarly, we avoid the specious seduction of attempting to create general theories or universal laws of offending. Instead, we can identify the mechanisms we consider to be most likely to shape white-collar offending and test these empirically to gain more concrete insights into which factors more plausibly contribute to white-collar crimes occurring in specific contexts.[6] Of course, we cannot always identify all relevant mechanisms that contribute to (or restrain) offending behaviours, or the mechanisms we identify may turn out to be less significant than first thought. This means we can refine our ideas and pursue alternatives until the propositions we identify plausibly represent the key context-specific determinations of different white-collar crimes.

The book is for critical social scientists, including, but not limited to, criminologists, sociologists, and socio-legal, business, economics, and political studies scholars, who have an interest in theorising about and empirically investigating white-collar and corporate crimes, or in understanding empirical approaches to analysing such behaviours. Our main focus is on white-collar

5 The Lazarus Heist: How North Korea almost pulled off a billion-dollar hack, 21 June 2021 https://www.bbc.co.uk/news/stories-57520169

6 A process referred to as retroduction.

and corporate crimes, but the framework is applicable to other crime types and criminological phenomena. The book will also be of interest to practitioners, policymakers, and those from not just public but also private and civil society organisations who have a keen desire to learn more about how and why white-collar and corporate crimes are organised as they are. This is not an introductory book to white-collar and corporate crimes, and we expect readers will already have some knowledge of the nature, concepts, and theories of white-collar and corporate crimes and social reactions to these, but we briefly touch on these aspects next.

White-Collar and Corporate Crimes in the 21st Century: A Brief History of the Present

We began writing this book in the shadow of several corporate scandals in which otherwise non-criminal, legitimate business organisations and their employees and associates have been implicated in a diverse array of criminal and illicit activities. Focus on such criminality and deviance has not always been so forthcoming. Popular stereotypes of serious crimes tended to focus on the *Underworld*, where full-time criminals, originating within the socially deprived, 'dangerous classes', would organise their criminal enterprises as part of more monolithic Mafia-type[7] organisations, or, more loosely, as components in ephemeral or impermanent networks. Such stereotypes were, in part, disturbed by recognition of ostensibly law-abiding *Upperworld* elites who occasionally did bad things. But it was the work of Edwin Sutherland that sought to puncture this bifurcated model intellectually with his stress on criminality as learned behaviour and assertion that white-collar crime *was* also 'organised' crime (Levi and Lord, 2017, 2023). This is an important intellectual point, as it encourages us to think through *how* different sorts of white-collar crimes are organised, *why* they are organised in the ways that they are, and *what* those factors and conditions are that appear essential to their organisation.

Sutherland's Legacy: White-Collar Crimes as Organised Crimes

Sutherland recognised white-collar crimes as 'organised crime', not in the contemporary sense in which organised crime discourse is associated with illegitimate, external full-time criminal gangs and criminal enterprise, but in the need to understand the formal and informal 'organisation' of the white-collar crime activities, rather than being accidental or episodic:

> White-collar crimes are not only deliberate; they are also organized. Organization for crime may be either formal or informal. Formal

7 This is a technical term in Italian legislation, including hierarchical longer-term offender structures that may not be traditional Mafia groups.

> organization for crimes of corporations is found most generally in restraint of trade, as illustrated by gentlemen's agreements, pools, many of the practices of the trade associations, patent agreements, and cartels. Formal organization is found, also, in conferences of representatives of corporations on plans regarding labor relations. They are organized formally also for the control of legislation, selection of administrators, and restriction of appropriations for the enforcement of laws which may affect themselves. . . . The informal organization for crimes by corporations consists in consensus among businessmen. While businessmen, with consensus, give lip service to free competition and free enterprise, they also, with consensus, practice restraint of trade. They are not willing to bear the burdens of competition or to permit the economic system to regulate itself in accordance with the laws of supply and demand, but they adopt the method of industrial planning and manipulation.
>
> (Sutherland, 1983: 229–230)

In these terms, 'offenders' may restrain trade – that is, organise their white-collar crime behaviours collaboratively, through structures such as 'gentlemen's agreements' (usually male), trade associations, cartels, and so on – with the aim of influencing legislation or restricting law enforcement, as well as fixing prices. In less regulated economies, businesses may seek to manipulate or restrain trade in their favour. For instance, a corporation would more likely reward their advertising agencies that increase sales, irrespective of the honesty of their methods. As Adam Smith (1982) put it – at least prior to the regulation needed to save capitalism from itself – in *The Wealth of Nations* (ch. 10): 'People of the same trade seldom meet together, even for merriment and diversion, but the conversation ends in a conspiracy against the public, or in some contrivance to raise prices'. We see such conditions and dynamics in many contemporary corporate scandals. Thus, white-collar crime has invaded areas that were formerly considered discrete, particularly as most activities that people think of as 'organised crime' have white-collar components. (See also Albanese, 2014, for analysis of the similarities and differences between white-collar and organised crime.)

For instance, in 2018, Dutch bank ING agreed a financial penalty of €775 million with prosecutors as part of a settlement for compliance failings that allowed criminal finances to be laundered via 'corporate vehicles', such as shell companies. Chief financial officer Koos Timmermans was forced to resign (an occasional outcome in such cases) after being held individually responsible.[8] This followed the Danske Bank scandal that had come to public attention earlier in 2018, when it emerged that thousands of clients, who ought to have

8 Though, by 2023, he was authorised by the Dutch Central Bank as fit and proper for senior appointments in Dutch banking: https://www.nn-group.com/news/nn-group-nominates-koos-timmermans-for-appointment-to-the-supervisory-board/

been viewed as suspicious, were able to launder €200 billion via the bank's Estonian branch, made possible through internal compliance mechanisms whose inadequacies were, at best, highly negligent. Chief executive Thomas Borgen resigned, despite claiming he 'lived up to his legal obligations',[9] though he was retained until a replacement was found and was entitled to collect a year's pay.[10] In April 2021, all charges were dropped against him and other Danske executives because the Danish prosecutors could find insufficient evidence to justify 'gross' negligence; a later civil suit against him also failed in 2022, though the appeal by investors has not yet been heard as we write.[11] In April 2023, six former Danske Bank staff were charged in Estonia with laundering $1.6 billion and €6 million euros in a professional operation that hid the true ownership from clients and others in the bank.[12] To date, two of them have been convicted and sentenced to a combined total of 16 years' imprisonment; others remained on trial in 2024.[13] In December 2022, Danske Bank reached a combined settlement (including pleading guilty to money laundering charges in the US) of $2.06 billion with the US and Danish authorities, which also involved three years of probation for the bank.[14]

In the last decade, we also saw Volkswagen and its corporate associates committing globally massive deliberate falsification of toxic diesel emission levels to enhance corporate sales targets and profits, while Mitsubishi also falsified data in Japan for similar motives: this would normally be analysed as white-collar crime, but it is also properly labelled as 'organised crime'. There is no reason managerial classes cannot be organised criminals, even if they also largely engage in licit activities! In addition, car industry political lobbyists successfully (and legally) sustained inappropriate lab-based testing to make European emissions and fuel consumption look much better than they really

9 https://danskebank.com/news-and-insights/news-archive/company-announcements/2018/ca19092018a

10 https://www.theguardian.com/business/2018/sep/21/is-money-laundering-scandal-at-danske-bank-the-largest-in-history

11 https://www.reuters.com/legal/danske-bank-investors-appeal-court-clearance-ex-ceo-borgen-report-2022-12-12/

12 https://www.reuters.com/world/europe/estonia-charges-six-ex-danske-bank-branch-staff-money-laundering-case-2023-04-17/

13 https://globalinvestigationsreview.com/article/two-convicted-in-danske-bank-linked-money-laundering-case-in-denmark

14 https://danskebank.com/news-and-insights/news-archive/company-announcements/2022/ca13122022. The chairman of Danske Bank stated: 'The resolutions mark the end of the investigations by US and Danish authorities. We have cooperated since we were approached by the authorities and accept the terms of the resolutions. We offer our unreserved apology and take full responsibility for the unacceptable failures and misconduct of the past, which have no place at Danske Bank today. We have learnt from our mistakes and we have taken the steps necessary to ensure that Danske Bank has robust measures in place to do everything possible to prevent these failures taking place again'.

were, reducing the scale of illegality and the risks of cheating, but not doing much for the environment.

In the political sphere, the Brazilian president, Dilma Rousseff, was impeached in 2016 and replaced by others also accused of corruption, voted out of power by many Brazilian parliamentarians awaiting trial for far more serious corruption and other offences than hers; the conviction of her predecessor Lula has since been quashed by the Brazilian courts, allowing his return to power in 2023 as elected president. In 2015, the Romanian prime minister was forced to resign following anticorruption protests, which continued periodically as parliamentarians sought to protect themselves from criminal charges; similar anticorruption protests in the EU led to leaders being replaced in the Czech Republic, Malta, and Slovakia, though other subjects of protests were elected to high office. The South African president Jacob Zuma was driven from power and has been embroiled in a range of corruption allegations relating to personal enrichment and the purchase of inappropriate aircraft for the air force, and, in 2016, was ordered by the Constitutional Court to repay $400,000 of personal benefit in refurbishment of his home, which he later did. State Capture in South Africa received a thorough analysis by the Zondo Judicial Commission (2022), but the problems of systemic corruption there remain.

In sport, FIFA had a well-merited reputation for corruption, and was, until 2015, safe from criminal justice interventions; in 2022, Sepp Blatter and Michel Platini were acquitted in Switzerland on charges of fraud against FIFA. The case is an exemplar of how, once the veil of secrecy is penetrated by arrests and/or whistle-blowers, incentivised by offers of immunity or sentence bargaining, a mass of revelations (and sometimes prosecutions) can follow. Motivated more by national prestige than money, systemic state-sponsored Russian athletics doping scandals led to the suspension of the track and field team and some other Russians from the 2016 Rio Olympics, and all athletes from the Rio Paralympics. This ban on the Russian flag and anthem continued in Japan, well before Russia's second invasion of Ukraine. In April 2023, the International Testing Agency imposed two-year sanctions on nine Russian wrestlers based on data retrieved from the Moscow anti-doping laboratory. Sixteen of twenty-two voting Exco members present when the football World Cup was awarded to Russia and to Qatar have been implicated in or investigated over some form of alleged corruption or bad practice.[15] This is merely a selection of recent high-profile cases, and we expect them to continue.

Tombs and Whyte note that, in addition to the dramatic cases that make headline news (such as those mentioned here), corporations are responsible for wide-ranging and cumulatively substantial 'routine, everyday harm' (Tombs and Whyte, 2015: 37). They document this with respect to four key areas:

15 https://www.theguardian.com/football/2022/oct/08/football-corruption-and-the-remarkable-road-to-qatar-world-cup

corporate theft and fraud (particularly in the retail financial services sector), crimes against consumers (e.g., food unsafety), crimes against workers (workplace safety crimes), and crimes against the environment (e.g., air pollution) (Tombs and Whyte, 2015: 37–50). It is argued these crimes reflect conditions of state-corporate symbiosis whereby regimes of permission are created, enabling corporations to thrive and be treated differently to individuals (Whyte, 2014). In addition, there is a range of 'middle-class crimes' or 'shady practices' in which tax and other frauds are committed by people who regard themselves as respectable and are so regarded by others, even when the others know about the quotidian offending (Farrall and Karstedt, 2020). Social attitude surveys show increasing cynicism about political and other leaders.

Dominant representations and constructions of the crime phenomenon often reflect common-sense conceptions of criminality associated with the 'street' or 'serious and organised' criminal who is characterised by an inherent propensity to offend and is presented as an external threat to moral society, whilst simultaneously being inherently embedded within the larger social context. Yet 'crimes' and misconduct by those in elite political and economic positions can de-legitimate the system politically (Levi, 2013) and may harm firms, groups, and individuals both within and outside their socio-economic class. Shifting analytical focus away from 'crimes on the streets' and 'organised crime' towards 'crimes in the suites' disturbs popular stereotypes about the composition of 'threats to society' and attempts to represent criminality with a single type of person driven by risk appetites and social pathology. Accounting for such a diverse range of criminal actors, acts, and responses to them – criminal, civil, and regulatory – poses a fascinating set of research questions, including the conditions under which at least *some* forms of white-collar crime become or fail to become social problems that 'require' the intervention of *criminal justice* rather than *regulation* (Katz, 1980; Levi, 2009). That regulation may come from state bodies or from enhanced corporate governance, including court-appointed monitors.

In the book, to make the framework more concrete, we analyse case studies of white-collar and corporate crimes that can happen in a range of contexts. There are differences between (i) ostensibly stable, enduring, and legitimate corporations with viable products/services that engage in episodic or routine offending, such as the LIBOR market manipulation (whose criminality is still in 2024 a matter of dispute) or the Volkswagen emissions scandal; (ii) corporations that base their activities on unviable business products or models and turn to fraud to keep the lie and income stream going, such as the Theranos product fraud, in which failure was inevitable (though a different corporation may yet develop a viable product); and (iii) those corporations that turn from seemingly stable corporations into criminal enterprises, such as Wirecard's accounting deception, in which senior employees siphoned funds from viable products/services and covered this up with fabricated transactions at scale in Germany and Singapore. (Though a 2022–2024 criminal case in Germany may decide whether or not there is sufficient proof that this was a fraud from the outset and, if so, who was a knowing party to it. See also McCrum, 2022.)

In these terms, if we are to analyse diverse and sometimes qualitatively different behaviours within the conceptual framework of 'white-collar crime', we need a set of connecting concepts and themes that enable comparison in order to produce meaningful empirical, analytical, and theoretical insights. Thinking in terms of 'organisation', and of the approach we put forward in this book, enables such meaningful analysis. By analysing 'organisation', we can identify those structures, relations, practices, or other mechanisms that come together to constitute the necessary aspects of white-collar crimes, and how these are contingently connected to particular contexts during the commissioning, or unfolding, of these behaviours. But how does this depart from other approaches to theorising and researching white-collar crimes? We first revisit key themes from the literature as a means of framing our own approach.

Dominant Approaches to Theorising and Researching White-Collar Crime

There is an abundance of scholarship expositing key conceptual and theoretical arguments in the area of white-collar crimes. For a more extensive overview of these debates, readers can visit our chapter on 'White-Collar and Corporate Crimes' in the Seventh Edition of the *Oxford Handbook of Criminology* (Levi and Lord, 2023; see also Van Slyke et al., 2016; Levi, 2019; Rorie, 2020). In brief, we consider the term 'white-collar crimes' as best viewed as a flexible sensitising concept rather than as a definitive concept (Blumer, 2009). There is no definition that has proven to be satisfactory to all, but the label of 'white-collar crime' nonetheless retains its appeal in the academic community, and for the public more widely also. We are in favour of retaining the concepts of white-collar and corporate crime for their political and social value, while acknowledging that there are many offender-victim status and full-time/part-time and regular/one-off criminality combinations that are concealed within the term. In contemporary debates, the division between white-collar crime and 'organised crime' also generates increasing tension, especially in relation to fraud. The emergence of cybercrime as a sub-discipline complicates the issues further, not least because some frauds are a hybrid mixture of online and offline: especially if we take into account the movement of funds, there are very few activities in contemporary life that are entirely 'off grid'. Thus, the range of things to which our analysis could relate are shifting sands, as the denotation of what exploitation relates to (e.g., fair wages, the environment, modern slavery, border criminology) strains the divisions between 'organised crimes' and white-collar and corporate crimes, because what activities (including financial transfers) do not need some kind of corporate engagement?

A brief analysis of associated behaviours highlights the centrality of supposedly legitimate actors in the context of otherwise legitimate business, institutional, and market environments in undertaking inherently harmful and exploitative behaviours. For instance, Edward A. Ross's 'criminaloid' characterised the inherent business duplicity of legitimate actors alongside a pretence of respectability and piousness, driven by the same motivations as others (Ross, 1907: 47–50). In a more Marxist European than populist American tradition, Bonger (1916) argued that lower- and upper-class offending alike are explicable as products of opportunities of the 'capitalist economic production regime'.

The integration of these key themes led Edwin Sutherland to define white-collar crime 'approximately' as 'a crime committed by a person of respectability and high social status in the course of his occupation' (Sutherland, 1949: 9). Sutherland's empirical focus was on the violations of the 70 largest US corporations at that time and of elite executives within these, though much of his actual research incorporated a diverse array of offences, such as workplace theft, fraud by mechanics, and deception by shoe salespersons. As Slapper and Tombs (1999: 4–5) summarise, Sutherland's concept demonstrated (i) that the common image of typical crimes and typical criminality (i.e., the preoccupation with volume crimes) was inaccurate, (ii) that a reductionist criminology explaining criminality in terms of lower-class pathology (e.g., general theories foregrounding strain or social/individual pathology) was inadequate, (iii) that criminology needed to include a wider range of criminal behaviours and also the process of criminalisation (i.e., the offences of elite actors and their integration with political processes), and (iv) that one must explain both the predatory crimes by the wealthy against the poor and the abuses of power by the wealthy (i.e., recognise in whose interests laws are created and enforced or not). However, Sutherland's definition is clouded in various ambiguities (see Nelken, 2012) and 'has itself become an imprisoning framework that confuses the offender with the offense and inadequately attends to the structural aspects of white-collar crimes' (Pontell and Geis, 2007: xiv). Furthermore, as we noted earlier, since the Sutherland era, the nature of international business with its long supply chains and the financialisaton of all commerce, socio-economic status, and the interplay between national and transnational regulation and criminalisation have been transformed.

As with many debates in white-collar crime research and theorising, we see binary distinctions frequently used as a rhetorical device to reinforce different approaches. For instance, distinctions between the nature of offender and the nature of the offence; the concern with individual, in contrast to organisational, corporate offenders; or ideologically driven preferences for more regulatory or more crime control responses are commonly presented. These debates have yielded many insights but have sometimes created a restrictive conceptual iron cage within which we can lose sight of realist accounts of these phenomena in favour of pushing particular political positions.

For instance, the extent to which social status ought to be a defining element of white-collar crimes is often cited to illustrate how it limits and/or enhances explanatory accounts (Benson et al., 2024: 7). The deficiencies associated with Sutherland's definition led some to render the concept 'impotent for theory building' (Braithwaite, 1985: 3), stimulating alternative conceptualisations in terms of the nature and features of the offences. (See Edelhertz, 1970; Shapiro, 1990.) This, in turn, has been argued to neglect the elite component and expand public policy challenges (Geis, 2016: 35; Pontell, 2016: 39). A more useful approach would be to analyse how elite occupational positions and high social esteem provide access to opportunities to commit particular financial offences; to possess the knowledge, techniques, networks, locations, and skills needed to carry them out; and to disarm or even deter the *potential* suspicions of auditors, media, police, and regulators. Thus, Felson and Boba (2010: ch. 7) refer to white-collar crime as a crime of specialised access. In any event, since the 18th century, Ponzi and other schemers have always included an element of entrepreneurs of aspiring status, sometimes leavening their boards with high-status people who are selected on the basis that they are unlikely to exercise critical governance, a trend which has continued with the rise of Silicon Valley and cryptocurrency 'pioneers'. Relatedly, research from Galvin et al. (2022) indicates that the US public have a clear vision of what a white-collar criminal/crime looks like (i.e., offenders of seeming 'high status' with occupational access, financial means, and consequences) and that definitions should incorporate practically relevant dimensions of these.

Definition is, of course, important. The definitions of 'white-collar crime' that we construct have theoretical, empirical, and policy implications. (See Pontell, 2016.) How we define and conceptualise our research focus shapes how white-collar crime is represented, measured, explained, prevented, regulated, and sanctioned. Various conceptualisations of white-collar and corporate crimes have been advanced over the years, which have significant differences of nuance. (For an overview, see Levi and Lord, 2023.) Yet terminological disputes may, in multi-paradigmatic fields, last indefinitely. The key point is that across these conceptualisations there are common analytical features, such as the focus on unlawful acts and omissions in the course of an occupation and/or in an organisational setting (public or private), the foregrounding of a violation or abuse of trust characterised by some form of deception or dishonesty, and the misuse of otherwise legitimate business or institutional procedures and practices to conceal behaviours.

Extant research into white-collar and corporate crimes reinforces the relatively elastic scope of these concepts, as diverse behaviours are integrated into the scope of analysis,. from embezzlement to fraud to environmental harms. In turn, white-collar and corporate crimes as analytical constructs have reified particular features or parameters of the phenomena under study, with arguments in favour of doing so pointing to the potential to generalise commonalities across diverse crime types, such as offender-victim-regulator dynamics, or offending locations and nature. However, in doing this, important differences in the *actual* organisation of white-collar crimes and the underlying relations and practices that constitute these behaviours under different conditions become obscured. By shifting focus to an organisational perspective on white-collar crimes that is built on contingently necessary social relations, we can move away from the recurring endeavour of attempting to demarcate in terms of common features attributed to offenders or offences and pursue more concrete conceptions of white-collar crime offending. That said, questions do remain of what criteria we actually do use and properly can use when distinguishing, for instance, legal from illegal organisational acts, and whether we include in our construct all acts in which corporations are used as tools in crime. For example, the corporate entity is becoming a ubiquitous feature of many crimes and frauds, many of which we would not traditionally consider 'corporate crimes'. Given the low cost of buying a company in the UK, for example, the creation of corporations as tools or instruments of criminal behaviour – for example COVID-19 loans or grants – is now within reach for all but the poorest of people, but does the involvement of a corporate entity imply that the criminal behaviours ought to be analysed within the framework of corporate or organisational crime? The concept of the corporation needs to be further thought out in relation to the notion of crimes committed by, or on behalf of, the corporation.

In these terms, it is not always helpful to focus on what 'it' (i.e., the offending behaviour) or 'they' (i.e., the offenders) look like, as we lose sight of why the crimes are organised in certain ways under particular conditions. Instead, a more sensible and realist question, and a distinguishing contribution of this book, is to analyse those factors and conditions that shape the ways in which crimes of certain types are organised over time and how those who get involved in them cooperate to accomplish their goals or fail to do so. This includes considering substantively the underlying 'real' factors that influence these crimes (e.g., generative structures, capacities, social relations, resources, capital, and so on). But while much may be known on the organisational aspects and conditions of these, at no point have they been comprehensively integrated, as we do in this book. Our organisational perspective offers a pragmatically useful but theoretically fresh framework that can step by step, study by study, illuminate the nature of white-collar crimes.

Structure of the Book

The organisation of white-collar crimes remains intellectually underconceptualised. This book reconstitutes the debate around white-collar crime, providing an advanced analytical framework for comprehensively making sense of how such crimes are organised, why they are organised as they are, and the key factors and conditions that shape their 'organisation' over time and in particular places. To do this, the explicit narrative around organisation is addressed across seven chapters. This first chapter, by way of introduction, has set out the need to examine organisation. It is our contention that such an approach can generate fresh empirical insights into white-collar and corporate crimes that contribute to fuller explanatory accounts of these behaviours. In making progress through the book, readers may prefer to draw on the particular modes of analysis presented in Chapters 2 (scripts), 3 (networks), 4 (finances), and 5 (geographies), as each can provide a useful framework for empirical research and also conceptualising and theorising substantive white-collar and corporate crime topics. However, in Chapter 6, we integrate these varying approaches as part of a 'capacities model' that thinks through how we can bring together these layers of analysis for fuller explanatory accounts, before providing suggestions of research programmes geared towards illuminating the organisation of white-collar and corporate crimes. We provide further details on each chapter next.

Central to understanding white-collar and corporate crimes is a comprehensive and detailed understanding of the procedural dynamics of the crime commission process: that is, the particular mechanisms that come together to enable these crimes to flourish, and their interaction with opportunity structures. In Chapter 2, we present a process model for understanding the 'scripts' of white-collar crimes: that is, the sequence of events that offenders must go through in order to accomplish their activities and the various permutations that may exist during these processes. In other words, what does it take to carry out white-collar and corporate crimes? Which tasks are necessary for white-collar crimes of different types, and where and how do they need to be performed? How do actors organise around some perceived opportunities for white-collar crimes, and how are such opportunities distributed socially? That is, we must understand the sequence of events or stages that offenders must go through in order to accomplish their activities and to realise opportunities as they arise as part of routine social patterns of activities in the professional environment. Here, we explore further what this integrated script-opportunity framework consists of, foregrounding key dimensions such an analytical approach and identify some key features of a high-level or more universal script analysis of white-collar crimes. We then distinguish between the 'necessary' and 'contingent' aspects of such scripts. That is, we identify those relations, practices, and mechanisms that must necessarily come together for the crimes to take place, and how these are contingently connected to particular contexts and conditions, shaping the particular configurations of offending behaviour in particular situations. In social scientific terms, this distinction is useful for developing a fuller theoretical account of the fundamental aspects of white-collar crimes. Whilst identifying generalisable themes or regularities and patterns is difficult due to the inherent diversity of the offending behaviours, all such crimes involve situated actions and social interactions and relations.

Chapter 3 analyses network approaches to white-collar and corporate crimes. A recurring theme in the preceding chapter is the significance of networks that enable or restrict opportunities for white-collar and corporate crimes, and influence how the crimes are accomplished. The relations that exist within the social networks of white-collar criminals are central to the organisation of their criminal activities and have implications for the scripts of the crime commission process. We analyse the nature of these relations, or ties, mostly between different people, but also between people, organisations, or other units of analysis. This, of course, includes an analysis of offender cooperation and how offenders' social networks or legitimate employment connections enable them to identify and recruit willing co-offenders they can trust, in some way rely on, or utilise as unwitting cooperators to carry out their crimes. In this way, we can reorganise our analysis to understand the dynamics of offender cooperation in order to appreciate the functioning of (ready-made or pre-existing) illicit networks within licit markets and how such (ephemeral) groups flexibly, efficiently, and, if necessary, secretively, organise their behaviours and/or diversify in response to certain stimuli. This links white-collar crime to developments in analysing organised crime networks. If we can analyse relational data to provide insight into which actors are core to the functioning of a criminal network or enterprise, or into commonalities that exist in the structures of different white-collar crime networks, for instance, a fuller explanatory account of white-collar crimes can be developed.

Even where individuals seemingly act alone, their relations with other people, products, or places remain significant. While there may sometimes be only one primary offender, wilfully blind or unwitting facilitators or cooperators are always involved in some way. In other words, people can cooperate in an illegal enterprise without anyone being able to show they did so intentionally or even without their *actually* doing so intentionally. Networks precede and emerge from offender cooperation and collaboration, and understanding how offenders use their social networks or legitimate employment connections to identify and recruit willing co-offenders they can trust or in some way rely on to engage in their criminal enterprise, is a key aspect of the organisation of white-collar crimes. In this chapter, we therefore consider what a social network analysis framework can bring to an understanding of white-collar crimes. As part of this analysis, we foreground some key themes pertinent to the organisation of white-collar crimes: brokerage relations in terms of those who connect or liaise between actors or nodes involved in criminal enterprise; secrecy, efficiency, and resilience of white-collar crime offending networks; and flexibility and adaptability to changing conditions, usually following external enforcement stimuli. In our view, integrating dynamic network analyses with the crime script approach offers valuable insights into the functioning and vulnerabilities of networks of white-collar and corporate crimes.

In Chapter 4, we analyse the financial aspects of white-collar and corporate crimes. To undertake many white-collar crimes, resources are required (e.g., how are the funds for the crimes acquired and used without raising suspicions and interventions from peers), and costs may emerge (e.g., opening secret bank accounts or front companies in offshore locations to conceal the movement of illicit finances). Furthermore, the finances of crime may also need to be concealed and/or converted into usable assets in the legitimate economy. This chapter thus presents a framework for understanding the *finances for* and *finances from* white-collar and corporate crimes. We first analyse the finances for and from white-collar crimes before exploring mechanisms and strategies for conversion, control, and concealment of any illicit finance. That white-collar and corporate crimes require finance in some way is well known, but these financial aspects have not been sufficiently conceptualised. We address this gap by asking key empirical questions that need to be addressed to understand the financial components of white-collar and corporate crimes. For instance, what needs to be financed; how much finance is needed; and how are the finances generated, managed, and distributed? Similarly, what are the different forms of proceeds (cash, electronic transfers, cryptocurrencies, minerals) that emerge; how can offenders conceal the derivation of funds from these crimes while also retaining control over them; and how do they overcome particular obstacles and problems posed by corporate and regulated sector controls (such as anti–money laundering and anti-bribery)? This chapter addresses such core questions. Furthermore, we foreground an analysis of the role of third-party facilitators and enablers (e.g., lawyers, bankers, accountants) who intentionally, incompetently, or unknowingly facilitate a range of white-collar and corporate crimes. While there is often an assumption that profits made through white-collar crime are absorbed as profit in the licit economy, we examine how such financial gain can also be reinvested back into criminal enterprise, more commonly associated with 'organised crime'. A focus on the money component of white-collar and corporate crimes can not only help us understand the organisation of these crimes, but also offer a plausible situational route to intervention.

Chapter 5 focuses on the geographical components of white-collar crimes, in particular the 'beyond-state' dynamics. White-collar and corporate crimes take place in (interacting) local, national, beyond-national, and global contexts; however, white-collar crime scholars only rarely refer to the *inter*national, *multi*national, *trans*national, or *global* aspects of the crimes they study, even if these are predominantly national in nature. Consequently, the corresponding features and components of these 'beyond-national' dynamics have not been comprehensively unpacked or conceptualised. Similarly, conceptualising and interrogating the dynamics of white-collar crimes that go beyond national boundaries as part of their organisation and nature, while recognised as significant, are often not a core analytical concern. Understanding the varying characteristics and features, as well as the differing configurations, interrelations, and organisational dynamics of those white-collar crimes that, in some way, transcend jurisdictional boundaries, is significant for white-collar crime theory and research. This chapter examines these issues in further detail and thinks through the implications of the beyond-national aspects of white-collar crimes, bearing in mind the conditional relationships of the white-collar crime commission process that overlay common patterns of routine business activities. These relationships shape the organisation, distribution, and concentration of white-collar offending across jurisdictional boundaries. With this in mind, this chapter explores white-collar crimes that have beyond-national scope with a view to questioning how useful it is, or can be, to understand how different white-collar crimes pertain to, are associated with, or are restricted to particular 'territories' at the domestic (i.e., nation-state), international, transnational, multinational, supranational, and global levels. This should contribute to sceptical thinking about 'country risk' measures in anti–money laundering and anti-corruption public and private sector policies.

Chapter 6 builds on the preceding chapters to put forward a realist perspective towards understanding white-collar crime capacities. In the chapter, we consider and analyse the connections between social structures that generate the combining of those mechanisms with causal potential for commissioning white-collar crimes and the conditions that determine the outcomes that follow. This represents a concrete conception of organisation. It includes analysis of the capacities for the commission of white-collar and corporate crimes. That is, there are human, social, material, and cultural capacities that create the pre-conditions for white-collar offending – we consider these as mechanisms of white-collar and corporate crime commission. These capacities interact with the opportunity structures, 'scripts' (Chapter 2), and networks (Chapter 3) of white-collar and corporate crimes and allow different offending behaviours under different circumstances to flourish or fade. We deconstruct these capacities to demonstrate what are multi-faceted and complex social relations that underpin white-collar and corporate crime commission as varying capacities generate varying opportunities for offenders who possess different attributes and who are a product of societal conditions. Understanding this variation is key for building theory on the generators of offending. We then focus more specifically on the individual offenders. An often under-researched and under-theorised area of criminal behaviour generally, and white-collar and corporate crimes more specifically, is how we understand the skills, knowledge, and expertise required of individual offenders to undertake what can be complexly organised behaviours. White-collar crimes often require a certain level of 'know-how' in order to be accomplished, but the different kinds of expertise, knowledge, and skills required for different white-collar offences have not been conceptualised and often not even researched explicitly. As mentioned earlier, the skill sets, expertise, and knowledge of different actors can enable or restrict offending, and this has implications for the need to collaborate with others or to refuse opportunities. In these terms, we develop a framework for understanding variations in certification, expertise, skills, and knowledge and how these variations can stimulate, permit, or constrict offending behaviours when opportunities arise.

In Chapter 6, we also examine the cultural embeddedness of white-collar crimes, specifically considering how particular organisational and institutional practices and environments are conducive or not to criminality, representing necessary and contingent relations in the commissioning process. For instance, considering the measurement problem surrounding unreported and unrecorded crimes, why is it that (given uncertainties about 'true' levels of offending), certain industries, sectors, and/or organisations are more resilient or immune to white-collar crimes, whereas in others, there is contagion (or at least coterminous mutual adoption)? Relatedly, a key distinguishing feature of white-collar and corporate crimes is that they take place in the context of otherwise legitimate institutional and/or organisational environments, though some may 'weaponise' apparently legitimate organisations as 'fronts' to commit planned frauds. How is it possible for them to do this? We consider the organisational lens as central to understanding how opportunities arise in organisational settings, how offenders are able to undertake their criminal behaviours as part of their normal routine activities and business/employment practices, and how organisational cultures can facilitate or inhibit these offending behaviours. We explore these issues to understand how offenders use their specialised access to undertake crime and how and why it is more or less pervasive across different contexts.

Furthermore, we also analyse how legitimate markets provide a 'ready-made' structure and network for the organisation of illicit behaviours, and how this enables offenders to conceal their relations and behaviours behind otherwise (or apparently) legitimate business and/or employment practices, making detection difficult. We consider these dynamics between the illicit and licit as part of the crime commission process and foreground the importance of understanding market structures and different market types (e.g., certain product markets have different levels, such as premium or (sub-) standard quality, and certain structures create dysfunctionality and criminal opportunities) at local, transnational, and global levels. We examine how the features and conditions of these markets permit white-collar crimes to be organised, and also the ways in which licit and illicit markets intersect and overlap.

Chapter 7 reviews the central narrative around 'organisation' and goes on to present a vision of how future criminologists and social researchers can progress concrete research and theorising. ***Inter alia***, we discuss how intensive and extensive[16] research methodologies and strategies that offer different accounts of the social world can be used – independently, mixed, or combined – to collect and analyse data on the key factors and issues outlined in the book. We also examine current and potential data sources that can inform our understanding of the key ideas addressed in the previous chapters. We use this to propose a programme of further research in the area of white-collar and corporate crimes to advance the area empirically, conceptually, and theoretically.

Finally, in Chapter 8, we reflect on the framework we have put forward and consider how it fits with existing research in the field and reinforcing what we think the framework offers for social scientists investigating white-collar and corporate crimes. We start by considering four issues that are touched on implicitly throughout the book that we do not engage with in detail: (i) accounting for change (over time and place), (ii) implications of an organisational perspective for regulation and control, (iii) white-collar and corporate crimes in more ***digital*** economies and societies, and (iv) problematising issues left unresolved in the book. By reflecting on these four issues, we are able to position our framework in the current white-collar and corporate crime scholarship. We then, as is customary, think about what research is needed in future to help us better understand how and why white-collar and corporate crimes unfold as they do in different contexts, and how such research insights can more broadly speak to a wider array of behaviours and phenomena.

16 See Figure 7.2 for a detailed examination of 'intensive' and 'extensive' research strategies.

2 Scripts

Introduction

In this chapter, we examine a theme central to analysing the organisation of white-collar and corporate crimes: the breaking down of the elements of criminal organisation into their component parts, a process that has been operationalised through 'script analysis' (Cornish, 1994; Cornish and Clarke, 2003). In other words, what does it take to carry out white-collar and corporate crimes? Which tasks are necessary for white-collar crimes of different types, and where and how do they need to be performed? How do actors organise around a range of perceived opportunities for white-collar crimes? Crucial to understanding white-collar and corporate crimes is a comprehensive and detailed understanding of these scripts, or procedural dynamics, of the white-collar crime commissioning or unfolding processes, and their interaction with specific opportunity structures. That is, we must understand the sequence of events or stages that offenders must go through in order to accomplish their activities and the various permutations that may exist during these processes to realise opportunities as they arise as part of routine social patterns of activities in the professional environment.

In the first part of this chapter, we explore further what this integrated script-opportunity framework consists of, foregrounding key dimensions of such an analytical approach. Here, we identify some key features of a high-level, or more universal, script analysis of white-collar crimes. We then distinguish between the 'necessary' and 'contingent' aspects of such scripts: that is, we identify those relations, practices, and mechanisms that are essential (i.e., necessary) for the crimes to take place, and those conditions and dynamics that are contingent, and are liable to vary across contexts and situations, but which nonetheless shape how the behaviours are organised in the ways that they are. In other words, the 'scripts' of white-collar crimes represent contingently necessary manifestations of social objects, mechanisms, and relations that lead to particular crime events occurring when sufficient conditions come together. (See Chapter 6.) Furthermore, the 'scripts' of context-specific white-collar crimes are a product of deeper underlying structures and routinised patterns of business activities. In social scientific terms, this framing is

DOI: 10.4324/9781315100227-2

useful for developing a fuller theoretical account of the fundamental aspects of white-collar crimes and for gaining insight into the organisation of these crimes. In policy terms, this can assist us in understanding how we can identify critical points of vulnerability with a view to intervention. In the second part of this chapter, we demonstrate what some of these specific scripts would look like, drawing on our empirical research to give insight into the scripting process and the theoretical and policy implications of this.

Scripting White-Collar and Corporate Crimes: Opportunity and Process

Some white-collar crimes and harmful behaviours can appear relatively sophisticated to organise and accomplish, while others may require less preparation and fewer resources. For instance, corporations pursuing tax 'efficiency' by shifting profits to lower-tax jurisdictions to erode their tax base in higher-tax jurisdictions must pre-plan this and are likely to require expert assistance to set up vehicles via which to construct these financial arrangements.[1] To artificially separate taxable income from the activities that generate the monies in particular locations involves a series of steps and processes, such as utilising professionals (e.g., lawyers, notaries, accountants) with the capacity to create 'shell companies' for controlling monies and entering into contrived contractual arrangements. In contrast, businesspeople providing cash incentives to win local business contracts – that is, engaging in bribery – may not need to go through an extensive set of steps to do so, though identifying potential bribees, obtaining and offering the cash for the bribe (or some alternative form of reward or medium of bribery), and keeping this arrangement concealed still do nevertheless require some organisation. Getting large sums in cash or setting up some non-cash transfer process may require some falsification of accounts, which might subsequently be questioned. In any case, a mode of thinking and analysis for deconstructing the processes involved is beneficial for how we understand the organisation of the crime or the 'scripts' of the crime commission process.

The 'scripting' approach was first developed in the 1990s as a framework for

> 'generating, organizing and systematizing knowledge about the *procedural aspects* and *procedural requirements* of crime commission: It has the potential to provide more appropriately crime-specific accounts of crime commission, and to extend this analysis to all the stages of the crime-commission sequence'.
>
> (Cornish, 1994: 160, emphasis in original)

1 The OECD has identified 'base erosion and profit shifting' (BEPS) by multinational enterprises as a priority tax concern: http://www.oecd.org/tax/beps/

It is an analytical framework that enables 'a careful and comprehensive analysis of the nature of the problem to be addressed, including developing a clear understanding of the various crime scenes, actors and their resources' (Levi and Maguire, 2004: 457). Analysing the procedures and processes that form part of white-collar crime organisation informs us of 'what' these crimes consist of and 'how' these crimes are carried out, telling us about the routine activities and situations that characterise offending environments. In our view, understanding the 'scripts' of white-collar and corporate crimes should be a component of more explanatory models of those crimes than it currently is.

The framework builds on theories of routine activity, placing attention on the circumstances and situations of criminal acts and the necessary convergence of likely offenders, suitable targets, and the absence of capable guardians, and analysing how social structure and patterns of social activities produce these convergences (Cohen and Felson, 1979; Felson and Eckert, 2019). For instance, the nature of financial markets, the ways of operating in different industries and sectors, the societal structures that provide access to occupations for some but not others, amongst other factors, all shape the routine daily activities of occupational actors; it is as part of these routinised and structured patterns of behaving that opportunities can be perceived. In these terms, the starting point for any crime script analysis must be an understanding of opportunity, the nature of the 'problem', and how actors organise around these structures. This implies a shift towards focusing on the opportunity structures of white-collar crimes (Benson et al., 2024), which, like script analysis, are influenced by theories and observations of routine activity, crime patterns, rational choice, and situational crime prevention (Benson et al., 2009).

For white-collar crimes to occur, an *opportunity* must be present. This is self-evident and arguably tautological, though an 'objective' opportunity is a necessary but not sufficient condition of crime occurrence. However, it is not the mere presence of an opportunity that is important but the particular characteristics of the opportunity; as Benson et al. (2024) demonstrate, all white-collar crimes have a specific *opportunity structure* that differs between different types of crime. The *opportunity structure* refers to the set of conditions or elements that must be in place in order for white-collar crimes to be able to take place. Different settings naturally create different opportunities that vary in accessibility and attractiveness to would-be-offenders. When intervening with the structures of white-collar crime opportunities, certain core components must be recognised. Specifically, the nature of these offences is such that: (i) the offenders usually have legitimate, 'specialised access' to victims and targets and the offending environment; (ii) the offender remains spatially distant from victims at the time of the offence; (iii) deception or concealment enables offenders to hide the offence; and (iv) criminal intent is often ambiguous or made to seem ambiguous as the acts may closely resemble routine, legitimate activities. (See Benson and Madensen, 2007: 613–614.) In contrast to 'ordinary' crimes, the nature of the target of offending is more esoteric, there is (at least sometimes) a lack of identifiable victims, and the concept of a physical offending location is less relevant (Huisman and van Erp, 2013) whilst, in terms of personal characteristics, these actors appear legitimate and respectable, at least in the context in which they are operating. (Someone advising on cryptocurrency 'investments' might not need the same demeanour as someone selling pensions or funeral plans: that is, their appearance, emotional tone, etc. need to be suitable for the context to obtain legitimacy in the eyes of their target investors.)

Once an opportunity has been recognised and the decision made to attempt to realise this, actors must figure out how they will go about their deviant intentions, and this will vary depending on the nature of the opportunity and the individual and social contexts. Thus, discrete types of white-collar crimes will each have discrete 'scripts'. These scripts are characterised by 'event' schema that help us organise our knowledge about how to understand and enact commonplace behavioural processes or routines (Cornish, 1994: 158). In these terms,

> scripts can be divided up into scenes involving smaller units of action, or plans required to achieve major sub-goals. Indeed, the term 'scene', in everyday parlance, suggests episode, location, background, and plan of action all at the same time. Scripts also have roles associated with them; require props, such as setting 'furniture' and facilitators; and take place in a variety of specified locations.
>
> (Cornish, 1994: 159)

White-collar and corporate crimes, like all crimes for gain, have steps and stages, not necessarily linear and sequential, but flexible and adaptable in response to changing conditions and actor innovations. These steps take place across different scenes within the crime script. Each of the different scenes that make up the steps of the white-collar crime can be carried out in different ways and so have different permutations of the 'facets' that make up the different ways the behaviours can be undertaken. That is, actors can accomplish the goals and purpose of particular scenes in different ways. Underpinning the script approach is an assumption of rational choice for understanding offending behaviours and decisions that can be prevented by intervening with the situations in which they take place (Clarke and Cornish, 1985), and this is useful for regulation. If we accept that white-collar and corporate crimes are most often rational, goal-oriented, and purposive behaviours, then by understanding the procedural aspects of these behaviours, suitable intervention mechanisms can be mapped onto their scripts.

Crime script analysis can involve different levels of abstraction or of generality and specificity. For instance, as Leclerc et al. (2011: 212) demonstrate, we can distinguish between (i) 'meta-scripts' (i.e., all crimes within a classification: e.g., corporate frauds), (ii) 'proto-scripts' (i.e., different subgroups within an offence: e.g., for corporate frauds, those offences that focus on accounting frauds specifically), (iii) 'scripts' (i.e., subdivisions of specific offences into categories according to a specific dimension relevant for situational prevention: e.g., particular victim types, situations, modus operandi), and (iv) 'tracks' (i.e., detailed accounts of offending within particular circumstances). Essentially, for any given offence, the crime commission process, or the ways in which crimes unfold, become more specific as we move from the meta-script to the track level. Systematising knowledge at the specific level of 'tracks' to inform more general 'scripts' can encourage theory building and comparison between how specific or general scripts are at the 'proto-script' and 'meta-script' levels to identify common patterns across different white-collar crimes in order to gain insights that go beyond the idiosyncrasies of any given offence.

While criminal behaviours, including some white-collar crimes, can appear simple, this may be a function of their routinised production, which serves to conceal important features of their organisation, sequencing, and acquisition (Cornish, 1994: 157). For instance, using the example of bribery in business, at its most basic level, the bribery can be reduced to an illicit transaction between at least two actors – a bribe giver and a bribe receiver – in the course of routine business engagement. While this may indicate those fundamental necessities of bribery, the underlying organisational dynamics can be lost if we become preoccupied with the moment(s) of criminality, rather than considering the preparatory and post-event components which are often present in commercial bribery, but usually not in street bribery of police, et cetera. (Targeted seduction and intimidation may also be present in 'organised crime' corruption of law enforcement and prisons, which has a different planning logic from spontaneous or endemic street policing.) There may also be significant lifestyle factors or group/network dynamics that shape or facilitate actor decisions to engage in crimes (Hancock and Laycock, 2010); see Chapters 3 and 6). Of course, how white-collar crimes are organised is also partly a function of control responses. For instance, we might look to the impact of the emergence of the transnational anti–money laundering and anti-bribery frameworks, the increasing scrutiny of corporations that in some way enable 'modern slavery' within their organisational structures, or the more recent focus on crimes against ecosystems and the planet. The corresponding legal frameworks, public and private enforcement activities, formal and informal social control strategies, and so on, all shape how offenders may need to organise their white-collar crimes. Additionally, whilst much attention is often placed on how offenders think and behave as part of script analytic approaches, it is important we also integrate a focus on the affective or emotional aspects of white-collar offending. For instance, Langton and Piquero's (2007) work on strain theory and white-collar crime drew attention to the potential negative emotional aspects of strain for white-collar actors, and how these may differ from other criminal populations. Similarly, Pusch and Holtfreter (2021) considered the negative emotional aspects of strain as part of their meta-analysis of individual and organisational predictors of white-collar crime. But the role of emotion remains underdeveloped and under-researched, and although white-collar offenders are often assumed to be highly rational, this emotive component can play a very big role; emotions have the potential to overwhelm (or at least interact with) 'rationality', which may be viewed as the selection of methods to achieve goals that are not themselves sensibly thought of as being purely the product of reason.

Script analysis has seen most success in developing analytical and prevention-focused thinking to disrupt the behaviours of organised criminals (Levi and Maguire, 2004: 429). The script analysis approach has been persuasively applied to a range of serious criminal enterprises, such as drug manufacturing in clandestine laboratories (Chiu et al., 2011) and drug importation (Morgenthaler and LeClerc, 2023), the online stolen data market (Hutchings and Holt, 2015), human trafficking for sexual exploitation (Savona et al., 2013), infiltration by Mafias of the public construction industry (Savona, 2010), investment and mortgage fraud (Gilbert, forthcoming), ransomware attacks (Matthijsse et al., 2023), the switching of vehicle identification numbers from wrecked to stolen vehicles (Tremblay et al., 2001), illegal waste activity (Tompson and Chainey, 2011) and in conjunction with social network analysis in relation to stolen-vehicle exportation operations (Morselli and Roy, 2008), the distribution of counterfeit alcohol (Lord et al., 2017), the illegal taking of deer (Goodall, 2019), theft of oil from pipelines (Alonso Berbotto and Chainey, 2021), tiger poaching (Skidmore, 2021), money laundering (Gilmour, 2023), contract killings (de Korte and Kleemans, 2022), transnational computer fraud (Van Nguyen, 2022), counterfeit identity document procurement (Holt and Lee, 2022), and fisheries crimes (Svorken et al., 2023). The approach has also been used to unpack the mechanics of the LIBOR market manipulation (Jordanoska and Lord, 2020), corruption in public procurement (Zanella, 2013), and mortgage frauds (Gilbert, 2024). The increasing use of this approach in relation to serious and complex organised crime reflects the simple yet effective way in which the complete sequence of actions and decisions before, during, and after a crime and across all stages of crime commission can be identified, thereby giving a fuller range of possible intervention points that has clear crime reduction and disruption potential for law enforcement and regulatory authorities. However, by focusing on the specifics and mechanics of the crime commission process, the approach does not fully inform an understanding of wider market drivers and social conditions (e.g., supply and demand, including consumer preferences; market competition) or the heterogeneity of offender motivations (e.g., whether financially motivated by greed or fear of failing at an individual level or structurally shaped by business pressures), and therefore deep, 'real' causal mechanisms. Similarly, the approach does not sufficiently illuminate the organisational and institutional pressures and factors that shape variations in offending behaviours by actors in the course of their occupations over time, though we can begin to understand why certain choices might be made under differing conditions. (See Chapter 7.) Nevertheless, despite its increasing use in relation to serious and organised crime, crime script analysis has remained at the margins of white-collar crime thinking. We seek to address this gap by encouraging research into the procedural dynamics of white-collar and corporate crimes, integrated with an 'opportunity structure' perspective.

The Dynamics of Opportunity

Whether a white-collar crime opportunity is recognised as such is determined by varying dynamics that relate to more *proximal* factors, such as the individual characteristics of the offenders or the cultural narratives of the occupational, institutional, or organisational offending contexts, and more *distal* factors, such as the geo-historical antecedents or drivers and the social patterns of opportunities. For instance, ways of doing business have developed over time, with certain practices, such as free tickets for events, elaborate holidays, or shopping trips (sometimes disguised as or combined with conferences), the provision of sex services, and so on, becoming common and routine in many industries and sectors in at least some countries: the universality is often difficult to determine due to partial evidence. Analysing how these emergent social structures and patterns of social activities produce the necessary convergence at the micro level of motivated offenders, suitable targets, and an absence of capable guardians informs an understanding of the circumstances and situations of criminal acts (Cohen and Felson, 1979; Felson and Eckert, 2019). But whilst opportunities reflect the coming together of these multi-faceted layers, opportunities to offend only become available to different individuals after they obtain certain occupational positions. For instance, only some actors have access to 'high-end' opportunity structures (e.g., major corporate frauds compared with embezzlement potential, the latter being possessed by most if not all accountants) that are unevenly distributed by virtue of social-political-economic position in society. Understanding how and why different actors encounter different opportunities gives insights into the capacities of different individuals to engage exclusively in particular sorts of crimes. However, with reference to Clarke (2012), opportunity alone does not 'make the thief', but if the cultural conditions are conducive, then offending is more likely, and their motivation to offend is more likely to be activated if the individual(s) experience some crisis in their personal or occupational life. Table 2.1 outlines the key aspects of objective opportunities.

Setting aside motivation, that 'objective' opportunities for white-collar crimes may arise is not enough in itself for a white-collar crime to occur. In addition to variations in being tempted (e.g., levels of both greed and offers/pressures to defraud), opportunities need to be recognised by those who encounter them. For instance, the purchasing executive may not recognise the ease with which they could inflate the prices of contracts in collusion with preferred bidders in order to obtain kickbacks until offered/pressurised to

Table 2.1 Key Aspects of Objective White-Collar and Corporate Crime Opportunities

Opportunity Variables	*Opportunity Recognition*	*Opportunity Realisation Shaped by:*	*Examples*
Proximal Factors (Individual)	Cognitive (how white-collar offenders think)	Risk assessment, cost-benefit analysis of elements they think about, evaluation of required process and procedure for crime commission.	Embezzlers may recognise, thus possessing the relevant knowledge, that siphoning funds from business accounts is a solution to a non-shareable financial problem (e.g., Cressey, 1950).
	Affective (how white-collar offenders feel)	Judgments of morality and normative expectations in line with shared beliefs, inter-subjective interpretations, underlying values, and assumptions. Emotive responses.	Corporate bribers may feel uneasy about providing prostitutes or indeed cash to public officials and so must neutralise these feelings.
			Intra-organisational and external fraudsters may feel empathy with at least some potential victims of their frauds.
	Behavioural (how white-collar offenders behave)	Seeing opportunities can influence people's routines and ways of behaving as they seek out or avoid such encounters: for example, to reduce temptation.	The bankruptcy fraudster may actively seek out failing businesses to take over, load them with credit, and then disappear with the funds (e.g., Levi, 2008).
Proximal Factors (Situational)	Technical	Business practices and procedures that represent daily routine working environments.	The emergence and role of relationship managers in banks whose unscrupulous clients go about normalising poor due diligence practices over time.
			Cybercrime and crime-as-a-service offer opportunities that lower the skills entry point to crime, whether this involves access to specialist hackers or to company service providers.
	Cultural	The institutionalised practices that drive ways of behaving and the available rationalisations in the offending context.	The credit lender with embedded organisational reward policies that incentivise the learning of high-risk, high-reward behaviours irrespective of the consequences for others, rather than pro-social, ethical approaches.
	Social	The nature of interactions with others, including how individuals are socialised into different settings.	The new tax advisor who learns aggressive avoidance or evasion techniques from established co-workers or professional firms.

(*Continued*)

Table 2.1 (Continued)

Opportunity Variables	*Opportunity Recognition*	*Opportunity Realisation Shaped by:*	*Examples*
Distal Factors (Structural)	Stratification	Structural patterns of different opportunities that only some actors can access, dependent on position in the social strata and, in some cases, possession of professional licences.	The pathways into certain career types (e.g., politics) is more readily accessible for those from privileged backgrounds. This reflects wider societal imbalances, providing access to certain kinds of fraudulent opportunities for some groups.
	Variation	The dispersal of specific opportunity structures: i.e., opportunities for some crimes are more numerous than others.	Opportunities for theft at work are more numerous than opportunities for accounting fraud as more people occupy positions amenable to the former than the latter. However, each fraud may be easier to conceal than each theft.
	Geo-historical antecedents	Systemic and structurally embedded political and economic patterns of behaviour in given contexts over time.	Wide-scale consumerism encourages individualist pursuit of status goods that may, in turn, encourage criminal innovation.

collude by them. Or the manager at a meat processing plant might not see that possessing legitimate licences for the processing of different meats (e.g., beef and horse) provides scope for adulteration and/or substitution. In the 'arms race' between intentional fraudsters and (mostly private-sector) crime controllers, barriers to entry into criminality are raised, which intentional or opportunist fraudsters have to overcome even if they see opportunities. Such threshold-raising efforts are less common in other areas of corporate crime, though that may be because greater scrutiny is applied to supply chains of migrants and products, or to product safety (as following Boeing 737-Max crashes and blow-outs around the world – perhaps especially in North America – or the powdered milk scandals in China). Such issues may be technical, or they may result from different cost-benefit weightings being applied in response to scandals, regulatory or criminal justice interventions, or shifts in organisational or wider shareholder/stakeholder moralities (Van Erp and Levi, forthcoming).

At the proximal-individual level, how individual actors subjectively perceive these objective encounters (and their moralities) shapes whether they will seek to realise the opportunity or resist it. The cognitive processes of rational individuals, including how they interpret and calculate opportunities, may involve an assessment of risk and potential benefits or losses and an evaluation of what needs to be done and how they would do it should they decide to do so. For instance, if managers of meat processing plants see minimal risks of detection for mixing horse mince with beef mince, they would need to consider how to label and pack the product, how to incentivise plant workers to comply, and how to circumvent any potential product testing before the point at which it would become untraceable. How white-collar offenders and potential whistle-blowers feel about such opportunities and potential deviance (should they recognise it as such) is also significant. Most human actors recognise the moral component in behaviour, so they may judge the normative expectations of their potential or contemplated actions in line with shared beliefs within the organisation or industry, or society more widely (if they have any idea what those are), and this is likely to influence their choices (unless they are psychopathic or find some imaginative ways of squaring their principles with their immediate financial interests). There may also be an emotive dimension to these encounters, as the opportunity may invoke excitement or dread, which, in turn, can shape a person's response, or the individual(s) may lack the confidence to engage with the opportunity. Potential white-collar offenders who encounter opportunities may also change their ways of behaving as they seek out more analogous opportunities, waiting for the conditions to be more conducive to perceived success, or avoid these opportunities so as not to drift into deviance. A senior central bank official in charge of determining the technical qualities of bids to print banknotes may see opportunities for receiving bribes from bidders, but they may not wish to risk their highly paid, high-prestige secure jobs. Whether (groups of) individuals go about realising opportunities is, of course, also shaped by skill sets, knowledge, and expertise they possess and whether these are sufficient for the crime, or, if not, whether they are able to recruit those with the necessary capacities. (See Chapter 5.) For example, as Cressey (1955) noted, all accountants can embezzle, and the same applies to other professionals with the capacity to defraud or to launder money (Middleton and Levi, 2015; Benson, 2020; Levi and Soudijn, 2020), yet we need to better understand why such actors accept or decline to make the most of these opportunities, which decisions may be malleable in different circumstances.

At the proximal-situational level, an understanding is needed of the technical requirements of particular occupations, including the business practices and procedures that represent the daily working environments of employees. Particular occupational behaviours are better suited to different types of crime. For instance, working in sales increases the frequency of interactions or associations with others outside the organisation who may request or be conducive to accepting inducements for preferential treatment, depending on the state of the market and the product. The cultural drivers within the organisation represent ways of behaving that have become institutionalised and ways of thinking or rationalising deviance in the offending context. For instance, policies that generate unreasonable targets over time can influence employee behaviour, whilst 'groupthink' dynamics enable employees to amorally assess what is best for the organisation (and often themselves). This may be affected by whether people discuss this sort of behaviour in the workplace or observe others, behaviour. Additionally, a culture of passive implementation: see the case of Nick Leeson and the downfall of Barings Bank, in which the reluctance of his Singaporean and other South Asian subordinates to question high-status personnel was used to enable his activities. The social dynamics of situations are also germane here. That is, the nature of interactions within peer groups and between employees and middle and senior managers, as well as processes of socialisation in working environments, all impact whether criminal behaviours are learned or incentivised. Allied with these dynamics, and requiring further empirical research, is the nature of inter-subjective (dis)agreement within organisations. This relates to the existence (or not) of shared experiences, social conventions, and interpersonal relations in different offending contexts and environments. For instance, if collaboration is needed, there must be other actors who share the primary offender's perception of the opportunity and are willing and able to offend with them, or perhaps can be controlled and relied on by the offender. Thus, inter-subjective beliefs and experiences may dictate whether an opportunity can be realised or not. If those other actors do not tolerate certain ways of behaving, this can create obstacles to the offending, unless they can be side-lined or dismissed.

At the distal level, we can see that opportunities are patterned structurally in relation to the different occupational, institutional, and organisational environments individual actors can access. For instance, a person's position in their occupational or more general social strata influences their education, social network, skill set, and employment prospects, in some cases restricting access to elite environments on the basis of wealth, power, and social connectivity.

These structural relations, which are often enduring arrangements but could be more ephemeral, determine which actors encounter which opportunities as part of their legitimate occupational positions. Macro social patterns of business, organisational, and institutional routines shape opportunities. For instance, only some actors have access to 'high-end' opportunity structures, which are unevenly distributed by virtue of social-political-economic position in society. There is also variation in the frequency and accessibility of opportunities associated with particular offence types, contexts, and strata.

Understanding how and why different actors encounter different opportunities gives insights into the capacities of different individuals to engage in some crimes only. For example, a medical practitioner is unlikely to encounter an opportunity for manipulating the financial markets by virtue of the distinct routines in different professions, though they might receive tip-offs from patients or colleagues, and they can prescribe medicines that generate benefits to them as well as (at a huge scale) to pharmaceutical companies like Purdue for (over)prescribing OxyContin. Similarly, the opportunities that arise for medical practitioners of different types are also likely to differ. That said, some crimes have more dispersed opportunity potential than others, enabling a higher range of actors to engage. Embezzlement of organisational funds, for example, may be available to actors from different professions. Very little is known about the variation that exists in the types of opportunity that arise under more or less different conditions. Understanding the dispersal of opportunity structures presents an interesting area for future white-collar crime research. Intertwined with all the aforementioned dynamics are geo-historical conditions that shape individual, organisational, and structural components. That is, systemic and structurally embedded political and economic phenomena vary over time across different contexts, but these shape criminal opportunities. There is scope here for useful cross-cultural empirical investigation to gain insight into the causal potential created by different political or economic systems, and the fundamental legal, cultural, and social principles that characterise different systems.

Opportunity Distribution

We can think about the distribution of opportunities in terms of variance and frequency (how many times opportunities arise). Variance relates to the concentration or dispersal of the opportunities for different white-collar crime types in a particular situation: that is, the range of opportunities that are available to any given offender. Frequency relates to how often opportunities for those different crime types emerge: that is, whether opportunities are constantly or rarely available for offenders. Figure 2.1 visualises the dynamics between variance and frequency. The vertical arrow represents the spectrum from a high concentration of different white-collar crime type opportunities (top) to a high dispersal of white-collar crime opportunities of different types (bottom). The horizontal arrow represents the spectrum from a high frequency to a low frequency of opportunities arising.

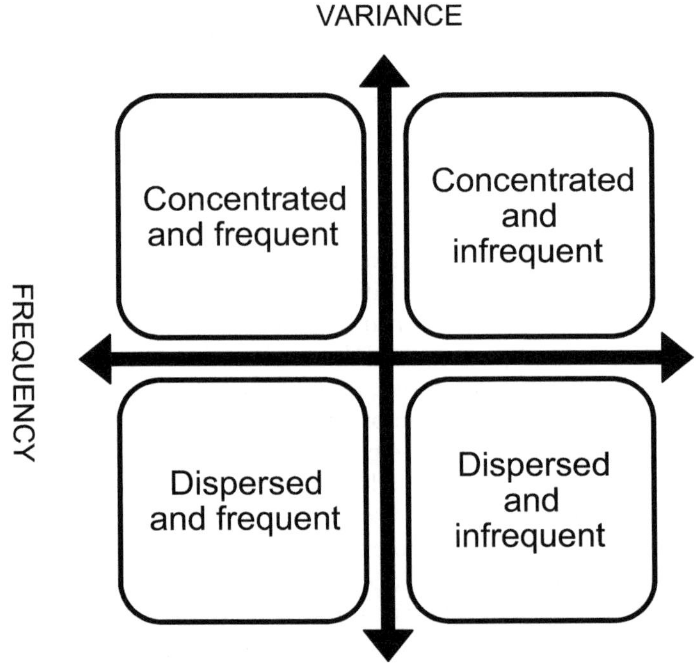

Figure 2.1 Variance and Occurrence of White-Collar Crime Opportunities

The first key analytical point is that some white-collar crime types have more dispersed opportunity structures and potential than others, and this enables a higher range of white-collar actors to engage. The second key analytical point is that the opportunity structures of different white-collar crime types appear more frequently and are more accessible than others. For instance, the embezzlement of organisational funds is highly dispersed in that there are likely to be opportunities for such theft in most organisations with varying levels of potential for crime commission, depending on levels of internal/external regulation and oversight, and other contingency factors. In addition, frequency (if not severity) is also likely to be high, as most employees possess the capacities to carry out such crimes, and the routines of organisations (e.g., expenses claims, use of equipment, etc.) generate patterns of opportunities provided they do not 'get out of hand' and attract serious counteraction. Thus, actors from different white-collar professions will have access to embezzlement opportunity structures. In contrast, if we think of the VW emissions fraud, then the development of defeat devices to cheat emissions regulations represents a more concentrated form of white-collar crime in that it can only occur within particular business types, such as car manufacturers. However, once this road has been taken by those actors involved, the fraud is extremely frequent, as the emissions software is repeatedly installed in many cars. The development of such software therefore has a lower level of dispersal but is frequent (or there would be no point in the commission of that particular crime type). Another example would be that of a general medical practitioner who is unlikely to encounter an opportunity for manipulating the financial markets by virtue of the distinct routines in different professions, though they may find such opportunities (and insider tip-offs) via their patients and friends, depending on their sporting, gambling, and sex interests. That said, they will have the opportunity for abusing patients, making this a highly concentrated opportunity structure for this particular form of white-collar crime, but it's likely to be infrequent due to the high risks of being detected unless patients and fellow workers are deterred from reporting or are disbelieved/ignored. (Although, depending on jurisdiction, medical doctors will likely encounter different healthcare fraud opportunities that reflect the routines and systems of healthcare operation.) Finally, as an example of dispersed and infrequent crimes, white-collar actors will frequently encounter opportunities for tax evasion (and avoidance); this is likely to be infrequent (when intentional) as it comes with higher risk due to the usual involvement of third-party professionals, such as accountants and lawyers, unless the latter are willing to conspire or have ways of mitigating their own professional and personal risks.

The key argument here is that we need to analyse the embeddedness of white-collar offenders in particular social relations alongside the individual human capacities in order to understand how causal powers of offending are activated or causal constraints suffered. Causal potential will exist over time and, under certain conditions, will contribute to decisions to offend. Alongside this, we can also analyse how social patterns of routine activities influence the emergence of opportunities, and their concentration or dispersal, as well as their frequency of availability, to help us better understand where white-collar crimes are more or less likely to occur. But when opportunities are in place and offenders possess appropriate skills and knowledge, they may also need material capacities to realise the crime commission process.

We can also reverse the question to consider individual or business opportunities for good, pro-social behaviour or compliance with laws and rules. In some cases, businesses may be obliged or compelled to prevent harms by their firm and others, and to prevent other forms of non-compliance that may occur within their organisational structures or by their employees and associated persons. (The UK's 'failure to prevent' model of corporate liability shifts the focus towards such organisational faults – see Lord and Broad, 2017.) If corporations that fall within these regulatory landscapes do not take action, they may be viewed as non-compliant, and thus liable for organisational omissions (e.g., with financial and anti-money laundering reporting). The presumption of such approaches is that regulated businesses and organisations are not just willing to comply but also possess the requisite capacities to comply. As Parker and Nielsen (2011: 14–15) have argued, '[M]otivation to comply is of secondary importance if a firm does not possess the capacity to comply'. There is notable variation in the capacities of businesses to comply or to go beyond compliance and behave pro-socially. Organisational compliance, then, is a product of the

> interaction between the adoption of formal systems for compliance management (one component of structure), the perceptions, motivations and strategies of individuals within the corporation in relation to compliance (agency), and the local norms and habituated practices (culture or cultures) that mediate between corporate structures and individual agency.
>
> (Parker and Gilad, 2011: 172)

Necessity and Contingency in the Crime Scripts of White-Collar and Corporate Crimes

As discussed earlier, script analysis integrates micro-level situational contexts and mechanisms with macro-level patterns of activities, as we see in routine activities perspectives, and this informs us about the emergence of opportunities and how actors realise these some of the time. To extend this framework further, much can be gained by distinguishing between those relations, practices, and mechanisms that are ***necessary*** to white-collar crime commission (i.e., the crimes cannot take place if specific relations and mechanisms are not present, such as a willing offender, lack of controls, etc.) and their ***contingent*** connections to varied conditions (i.e., the contextual antecedents that either enable the crime to take place or hinder it from doing so, and, in turn, shape how the behaviours are organised in the ways that they are). (See Edwards, 2016.) To assist with identifying those necessary and contingent aspects of the organisation of any given white-collar crime, a useful set of questions to consider includes the following (adapted from Levi, 2007):

- How and why do those engaging in white-collar and corporate crimes perceive a situation as a 'crime' or 'profit-generating' opportunity?
- How do they obtain whatever finance, precursors, equipment, or data needed for the crime?
- How and why do they find people willing and able to offend (if this is necessary for the crime contemplated) and who are controllable and reliable? What roles do these co-collaborators play (e.g., laundering, storage, etc.)?
- Are the offences carried out in domestic and/or overseas locations and with or without physical presence in jurisdiction(s)?
- In which ways are immediate enforcement/operational risks minimised? Especially if planning to repeat crimes, how do actors neutralise law enforcement by technical skill, by corruption, and/or by legal arbitrage, using legal obstacles to enforcement operations and prosecutions which vary between jurisdictions?
- Is it necessary to convert the fruits of crime into money or other usable assets in desired currencies? How are these illicit finances used (e.g., reinvested in

crime, for personal benefit) and managed (e.g., within otherwise legitimate financial systems or in other ways) over time?
- How do actors decide which jurisdiction(s) offers the optimal balance between social/physical comfort and the risk of asset forfeiture/criminal justice sanctions? This may vary over time. Indifference in any one state or sub-state arena may suffice to neutralise an investigation, and staffing inadequacies as well as corruption may be the cause of official inaction.

By addressing these questions, we can begin to identify the structures, mechanisms, and conditions that together inform an explanation of particular white-collar crimes, including which different mechanisms and relations are necessary or contingent to the white-collar crime commission process. As we have argued elsewhere, thinking in these terms allows us to move beyond simplistic situational accounts that focus on motivated or likely offenders, suitable targets, and a lack of guardianship, as being 'motivated' is alone not enough (Lord and Levi, 2017; see also Edwards, 2016). In our view, these questions require considering substantively the underlying, real, and multi-dimensional factors that influence white-collar crimes. This, of course, invites questions of explanation and causal relations, and we consider these issues in terms of the varied capacities, structures, mechanisms, and conditions that shape the organisation of white-collar crimes in more detail in Chapter 6.

Research into actual white-collar crimes over time has consistently identified certain regularities or common properties and referents that constitute some of the necessary aspects of these behaviours that appear across varied contexts. For instance, key features or relations of white-collar crimes include:

- The offenders have legitimate access to the location(s) where the crimes take place as well as to business or occupational resources/finances as part of their daily activities and employment – this is a necessity since, without a legitimate occupational position, the white-collar crime, by definition, cannot occur.
- The offenders are spatially separated from the ultimate victims, meaning that, as they operate in their corporate subsystems, they are able, if necessary, to 'neutralise' and/or 'rationalise' concerns over any potential victims, such as the unknowing public in those countries where funds are diverted to private hands or where inferior products end up.
- The actions of the offenders have a superficial appearance of legitimacy because white-collar crimes can be easily concealed as an otherwise legitimate financial transaction, which increases the ability to circumvent routine detection mechanisms. (See Benson et al., 2024.)

These features are central because white-collar crimes would be unsuccessful if they did not look sufficiently like legitimate activity not to stand out as 'out of place' to even slightly capable and motivated guardians,[2] and this gives some business offenders a structural advantage over other types of offenders (Levi, 2015: 11). However, within this high level of generality, more concrete accounts of white-collar crime commission can be analysed through script analysis as this mode of thinking provides a framework for establishing and capturing the necessary mechanisms of particular white-collar crimes, in particular the concrete 'tracks' of these crimes. To use the example of insider trading in the UK as analysed by Zeng (2021), we can identify the following mechanisms (and sub-mechanisms) that constitute the varying components (i.e., pre-activity, preparation, activity, post-activity) of the crime process:

M1: Entering inside (primary entry, temporary entry, exogenous entry, improper entry)
M2: Procuring resources (trading capacity, security measures, human resourcing)
M3: Tipping (opportunistic, repetitive, organisational)
M4: Transaction (buying/selling stocks, short selling and derivatives, organisational trading)
M5: Retaining proceeds (transferring and dividing proceeds, concealing proceeds)

These particular mechanisms (M) represent the necessary aspects of insider trading, but whether or not they come together in order for the white-collar crime to successfully take place is contingent on various context-specific conditions. The particular configuration of the script is also contingent on context, meaning varying tracks, or sub-mechanisms, may occur. Figure 2.2 visualises these varying necessary and contingent aspects of Zeng's insider dealing script.

For instance, in the case of 'entering inside', offenders may have legitimate access to the inside environment in either a primary capacity (for instance, as an official employee), temporary capacity (such as a professional service provider like an accountant), or exogenous capacity (such as outsiders who will be aware of their pending large investments in a particular company) or illegitimate access in an improper and perhaps inherently unlawful capacity (such as when so-called 'Chinese walls' between departments of the same firm are unlawfully breached). In the case of 'procuring resources', offenders need to have trading capacity to capitalise on non-public information (often drawing on pre-existing personal wealth or institutional accounts to trade), to implement security measures to minimise detection (such as using encrypted communication tools), and, in terms of human resourcing, find co-offenders (such as via kinship or friendship networks or simply from observing the potential co-offenders' behaviour). In the case of 'tipping' – that is, of communicating

2 In our view, the capability of guardians should be seen as a matter of degree rather than as a binary capable/incapable.

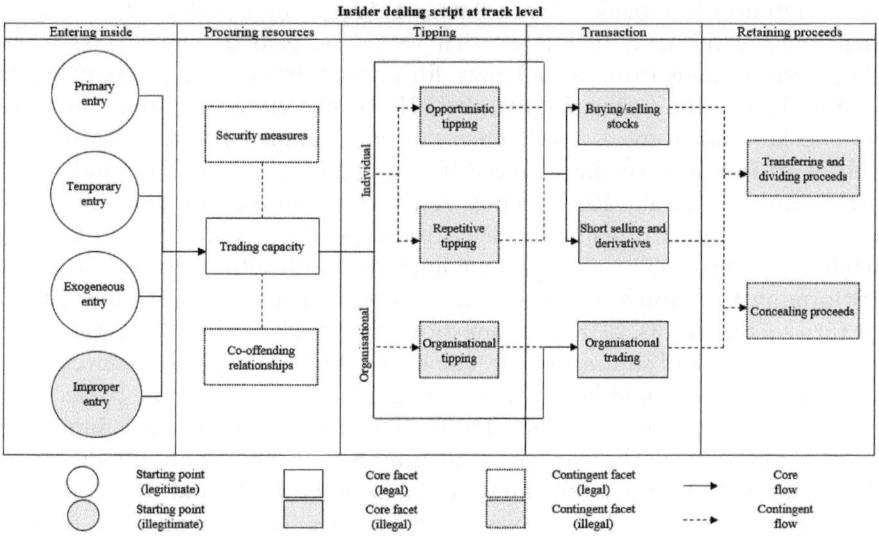

Figure 2.2 Insider Dealing Script at the 'Track' Level

Source: Zeng, 2021: 85

the insider information to others outside the organisation – this might be opportunistic (e.g., notifying friends and family after a fortuitous encounter at work), repetitive (usually pre-planned intention where inside information is routinely accessed and shared), or organisational (such as where the 'tipper' would indirectly influence colleagues to trade on a particular financial event for the benefit of the business). In the case of 'transaction', whereby the actual trading activity takes place, offenders may buy or sell particular stocks, engage in short selling or derivative contracts, or undertake organisational trading, usually involving a form of wall crossing. In the case of 'retaining proceeds', offenders may need to transfer or share the profits made for personal spending or paying off co-offenders, or otherwise conceal the proceeds/savings generated, utilising variously sophisticated schemes, such as shell firms, to do so.

Thinking in terms of the necessary and contingent aspects of white-collar crimes enables focus to be placed on the processes inherent to crime commission and through which these behaviours are organised.

Applying the Framework in Empirical Research: Market Manipulation

How could this integrated script, opportunity structure, and capacity analysis of high-level white-collar crimes be carried out in practice? We provide an example here, drawing on empirical research by Jordanoska and Lord (2020) into market manipulation, more specifically, the 'scandal' involving the fixing of the London Interbank Offered Rate (LIBOR). The LIBOR is a set of rates that indicate the level of interest that would be paid by large banks when they borrow funds from other banks, for a given period, in a given currency. At the time of the financial crisis, the LIBOR was closely scrutinised due to its two key functions: as a reference rate for a range of financial contracts, and as an indicator of the financial health of major banks (Hou and Skeie, 2014; Koblenz et al., 2014). Thus, retail loans, mortgages, and derivatives contracts, amongst other financial instruments, were dependent on the rate while it was also used to indicate the liquidity and health of banks – a poorly performing bank must pay higher rates to borrow money from other banks, in turn increasing its LIBOR submission. Essentially, the LIBOR was based on calculations and submissions by the banks about what they perceived their borrowing rates should be, with an average number from all the banks' submissions used to determine the LIBOR. The highest and lowest submissions were discarded from the average calculation, but through collusion, dishonest submissions could move the rate upwards or downwards, and this was where those involved were able to achieve illegal profits. The case involved the rigging of these rates to create financial gains, that, without deception, would not have otherwise been possible for the financial institutions involved.

The impacts of the LIBOR scandal were evident across Europe and the US, and, in terms of scripts, mechanisms, and routine activities, demonstrated how finance capitalism, and the dominance of financial institutions in capitalist markets, created opportunity structures accessible to particular elite actors who, due to their occupational positions and expertise, were able to encounter, recognise, and realise them. Banking practices had become routinised and standardised across institutions globally, with actors in banks interacting with these patterns daily, seeing opportunities arise. To better understand the scripts of the manipulation, Jordanoska and Lord (2020) analysed enforcement decisions from a range of social control agencies from across the globe where regulatory and/or criminal actions had been taken against the banks and those individuals involved, and supplemented this analysis with interviews with former regulators and defence lawyers. They sought to illuminate the following questions:

1. What were the procedural aspects of the benchmarks manipulation, and what were the organisational dynamics of these processes in different 'scenes'?
2. Which actors (individual and corporate) were central to the manipulation, and how did they cooperate across the manipulation 'script' in their occupational roles?
3. In what ways did regulatory and organisational conditions, with a focus on supervision and capable guardianship, create opportunities and potential for manipulation?

They analysed the range of interactions between the relevant actors, these actors' behaviours, and the resources essential to allowing the manipulative behaviours to occur. By analysing the *how* of the LIBOR rigging, they were able to gain insight into the procedural aspects and organisational dynamics of the manipulations in different 'scenes' of the script, to identify which actors (individual and corporate) were central, how they cooperated across the script, and the ways in which regulatory and corporate conditions created opportunities and potential for the manipulations. This analysis provided insights into those *necessary* mechanisms of white-collar crime commissioning. As Figure 2.3 visualises, their analysis delineated the rigging into four essential scenes: (i) calculated positioning and identification of co-collaborators, (ii) recruitment of collaborators, (iii) (ephemeral) manipulation, and (iv) recompense and solicitation. Furthermore, their analysis illuminated a paradox in regulatory and organisational actors' acting as both 'capable guardians' as well as 'facilitators of misconduct'. We can extend this script analysis of the LIBOR rigging to think also in terms of the capacities for LIBOR rigging, or market manipulation more broadly.

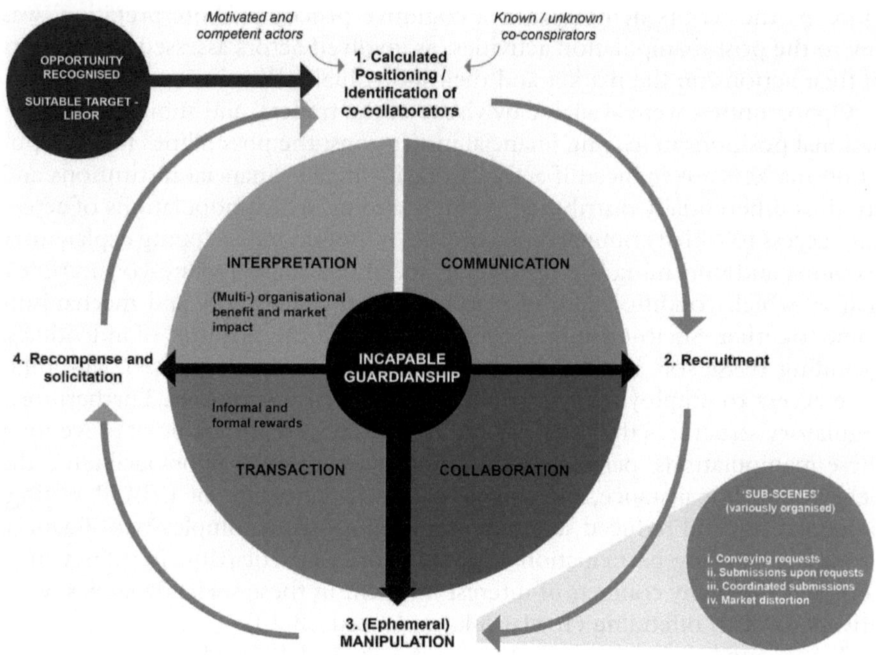

Figure 2.3 The 'Scripts' of LIBOR Manipulation

Source: Jordanoska and Lord, 2020[3]

3 Jordanoska, A. and Lord, N. (2020) 'Scripting the mechanics of the benchmark manipulation corporate scandals: The "guardian" paradox', *European Journal of Criminology*, 17(1), pp. 49–64. Copyright © 2020 by (Sage Publications). Reprinted by permission of Sage Publications.

In terms of the proximal-individual level, the actors in these occupations require a certain, high-level expertise in and knowledge of the functioning of markets and rates, including relevant training and qualifications, which provides them the appropriate cognitive capacities for seeing a profit-generating possibility and the self-confidence (and motivation) to take these on. They would also know appropriate ways of behaving and appropriate practices for the submission process through this professional expertise and competency, enabling them to conceal their manipulations as routine business practice. In other words, pre-existing structures shaped the coming together of the necessary aspects of the crime process. For example, 'scene 1' contained activities that formed part of the actors' daily profession: the opening of trading positions in derivatives tied to the movement of LIBOR currencies, and research into the effects of their movement on existing positions. Thus, the predicting, assessing, and hedging of risks, including LIBOR movements, are common aspects of trading in financial instruments: legitimate, routine activities. These calculations were necessary precursors to the manipulation activities. Furthermore, as the scripts demonstrate, a cognitive process of 'interpretation' was key to the post-manipulation activities, as involved actors assessed the impacts of their actions on the market and their individual institutions.

Opportunities were available by virtue of the traders' and submitters' occupational positions in leading financial institutions; the possibilities for manipulating markets are reduced if actors work in smaller financial institutions and are thus differentially distributed. Understanding which populations of actors have access to which criminal opportunities is useful for developing explanatory accounts and informing the contingent social relations of white-collar crimes: that is, which conditions are in place when articular actors and mechanisms come together. Socio-economic backgrounds and the 'habitus' of individuals, including those soft social skills that may be unevenly distributed, can influence access to employment in banks and financial institutions. Furthermore, regulatory structures that had evolved over time were incapable of preventing these manipulations, particularly as these structures and actors facilitated the behaviours. For instance, the shift toward self-regulation of LIBOR setting, deregulation, and reduced state intervention; growing complexity of financial products; growing participation of panel banks as participants in money markets; and the many conflicts of interest inherent in these social dynamics, were drivers towards offending (Jordanoska and Lord, 2020).

To accomplish the 'script', data were required by traders/submitters to calculate their positions and potential gain from movements in the market. Access to and understanding of these data were vital, necessary precursors to the actual manipulation (scene 1). Access to computerised systems for submission, to communications devices to collude with others (scene 2), and to tangible gifts/rewards (scene 4) were all part of the scripts. For instance, in scene 4, direct rewards for individuals included free travel, entertainment and meals, and payment of a set bonus, and for organisations, they included directing commission-generating business towards whole trading desks. In scene 2, email exchanges, instant messaging, and phone calls, along with face-to-face interactions, were all required to communicate the potential opportunity for manipulation and the specifics of how this was to be done.

Given the extensive collaboration within and across institutions between actors, a shared, inter-subjective belief in how the system worked was necessary to ensure recruitment to the manipulations. These beliefs and values that enabled actors to rationalise their actions extended beyond specific locations and into multiple sites, embedded as part of the 'system'. However, in scene 1, during the identification of co-collaborators, this depended on the particulars of the trading strategy as only those traders whose predicted submission was not beneficial were needed, making these networks flexible and adaptable, and determining the requirements of the particular script. Most interestingly, insights into the organisational cultures of the banks demonstrated how, in some of the manipulations in scene 3, actors talked openly about manipulating the LIBOR submissions with the level of self-censorship notably low. Actors were socialised into these environments, ways of behaving were institutionalised, and an array of rationalisations existed in terms of these shared cultures. Thus, 'the benchmark manipulations differ from other complex networked corporate crimes where extensive measures are undertaken to conceal the illegal activity' (Jordanoska and Lord, 2020: 21). The criminality of LIBOR manipulations and the extent to which they were officially indulged remain contested to the present day, with some American convictions being overturned and one key British offender – Tom Hayes – appealing his conviction after his release from prison, in an ambience in which there is increasing distrust of official claims about the integrity of markets and regulators.

This discussion demonstrates some of the insights gained from analysing the scripts of the LIBOR manipulation. What is clear is that the detailed analysis of the necessary mechanisms and components of the LIBOR rigging was able to identify contingent routinised activities where oversight was lacking or problematic, whilst also recognising these necessary mechanisms alone are not sufficient. For instance, in some cases, the close physical proximity of traders and submitters enabled traders to regularly 'shout out' their preferred rates of submission, demonstrating the routine nature of the manipulation and frustrating social control efforts by regulators as such exchanges would be undocumented, but these actors also possessed relevant knowledge and expertise to know what was needed to shift rates. These open manipulations demonstrated the vulnerabilities evident in the organisational environment and the potential for altering these dynamics to remove the opportunity.

Similar, multi-layered insights were identified by Fligstein and Roehrkasse (2016), who focused on the financial crisis of 2007 to 2009 and the corresponding widespread fraud in the mortgage securitisation industry. They found that theories emphasising the impact of deregulation or technical opacity identify only necessary, not sufficient, conditions. They argue that changes in competitive conditions and firms' positions within and across markets also contributed to the landscape that enabled such behaviours. For instance, as the supply of mortgages began to decline around 2003, mortgage originators lowered credit standards and engaged in predatory lending to shore up corporate unit profits (and, in our view, to generate their personal performance-related bonuses). In turn, mortgage-backed securities issuers and underwriters who were part of giant banks and building societies committed securities fraud to conceal this misconduct and to enhance the value of other financial products. Patterns of mortgage fraud in the UK contained elements of the same behaviour, but also some differences (Gilbert, forthcoming).

Absent large-scale social and economic intervention, law enforcement authorities can draw on such insights when devising evidence-based measures for immediate reductions. Drawing on the principles of situational crime prevention (see Clarke and Cornish, 1983; Cornish and Clarke, 2003), attempts can be made to increase the effort, increase the risks, reduce the rewards, reduce provocations, and remove excuses in relation to highly specific white-collar crime types (Benson et al., 2009). For instance, as in the LIBOR example, had conflicts of interest within single organisations been removed by ensuring so-called 'Chinese walls' were in place between those departments setting and trading on benchmarks, then the effort required to commit the fraud would have increased. Similarly, ensuring clear internal policies were in place that clarified how the benchmark rates ought to be set would have removed excuses. Notwithstanding, affecting those underlying structures that generate the coming together of mechanisms should be part of the dialogue for longer-term prevention approaches, but understanding particular crime scripts and mechanisms can inform potential vulnerabilities that might prove more useful for enforcement actors and other 'guardians'.

Concluding Thoughts

This chapter has sought to demonstrate how an integrated understanding of opportunities and scripts can be beneficial for the production of knowledge and explanatory accounts of white-collar crimes, as well as for purposes of policy interventions. These contingently necessary manifestations of social objects and relations represent the mechanisms of white-collar offending that, when activated, produce criminal events under the right conditions. (See Chapter 6.) In these terms, the 'scripts' of context-specific white-collar crimes are produced by underlying structures and routinised patterns of business activities. By organising our thinking to consider white-collar crimes in terms of the 'skill sets, contacts, start-up capital, and running costs that they require' (Levi, 2009: 231), we can recognise how necessary it is to have convergence in space and time of a specific situation (e.g., a vulnerability in how interbank lending rates are established), a target (e.g., the ease with which offenders can manipulate this), and the absence of capable guardians (e.g., where they may paradoxically act as facilitators or at best be *in*capable). If law enforcement authorities consider how potential offenders organise their behaviours – including confronting problems of gaining finance, gaining access to crime opportunities, and retaining their freedom and crime proceeds (Levi, 2009: 225) – they can intervene in, prevent, or reduce the potential for the crimes to take place.

3 Networks

Introduction

A recurring theme in the preceding chapter is the significance of networks that enable or restrict opportunities for white-collar and corporate crimes, and influence how the crimes are accomplished. The relations that exist within the social networks of white-collar criminals are central to the organisation of their criminal activities and have implications for the scripts of the crime commission process. (See Chapter 2.) These relations are mostly between different people, such as personal, work, or communication relationships, but might also be between people, organisations, or other units of analysis, such as an individual person having a connection to information, equipment, or a particular location. If we can analyse relational data to provide insight into which actors are core to the functioning of a criminal network or enterprise or commonalities that exist in the structures of different white-collar crime networks, for instance, a fuller explanatory account of white-collar crimes can be developed. Even where individuals seemingly act alone, their relations with other people, products, or places remain significant. Networks precede and emerge from offender cooperation and collaboration, and understanding how offenders use their social networks or legitimate employment connections to identify and recruit willing co-offenders they can trust or in some way rely on to engage in their criminal enterprise is a key aspect of the organisation of white-collar crimes. In this way, we can reorganise our analysis to understand the dynamics of offender cooperation in order to appreciate the functioning of (ready-made) illicit networks within licit markets and how such (ephemeral) groups flexibly, efficiently, and, if necessary, secretively organise their behaviours and/or diversify in response to certain stimuli. In this chapter, we therefore consider what a social network analysis framework can bring to an understanding of white-collar crimes.

We start with an overview of the social networks perspective before considering the application of the approach in relation to crime, organised crime, and then white-collar crime specifically. We then put forward two particular approaches within the vast social networks analysis area as being especially relevant for analysis of white-collar crimes: multi-mode, multi-link (multi-time)

DOI: 10.4324/9781315100227-3

analysis, and ego-net analysis. At this point, we also demonstrate the utility of a criminological network analysis for better understanding the connected roles of actors across different scenes of white-collar crime scripts and their centrality to the success or failure of the white-collar criminality. As part of this analysis, we foreground some key themes pertinent to the organisation of white-collar crimes: brokerage relations in terms of those who connect or liaise between actors or nodes involved in criminal enterprise; the secrecy, efficiency, and resilience of white-collar offending networks; and flexibility and adaptability to changing conditions, usually following external enforcement stimuli. In our view, integrating dynamic network analyses with the crime script approach offers valuable insights into the functioning and vulnerabilities of networks of white-collar and corporate crimes. Our key argument is that the extent to which 'crime networks' and that ambiguous term 'professional enablers' are available to the willing white-collar offender affects crime commissioning (see Chapter 5); in our view, though intelligence on criminal networks is often incomplete, theoretical models based on context-free explanations of white-collar crimes have not sufficiently considered the networked dynamics of such offending.

Social Network Analysis and Criminology

In this section we (very) briefly review the literature on social network analysis in order to inform those not familiar with the methodology and theory of the key principles and added value of this analytical approach. We then examine how social network perspectives have been utilised in criminology before analysing the (marginal) use in white-collar and corporate crime research specifically to date.

What Is Social Network Analysis? A Very Brief Overview

Social network analysis has a long history in sociology (Scott, 1988), but only since 1990 has interest in social network methodology and theory rapidly increased as behavioural science recognised that the social contexts of actions matter (Wasserman et al., 2005: 1).[1] Social network analysis, then, is a perspective that encourages focus 'on *relationships* among social entities, and on the patterns and implications of these relationships' (Wasserman and Faust, 1994: 3, emphasis in original). As Crossley et al. (2015: 3) note:

> Connection is a constitutive fact of social life. A social world comprises not only a plurality of social actors, both human and corporate (e.g. firms or governments), but also interaction and enduring ties between those actors. Actors influence one another and exchange resources, becoming

1 This may also coincide with the development and spread of computers and software, without which non-trivial social network analysis cannot be carried out (Borgatti et al., 2013).

> interdependent. They cooperate, compete, conflict, support and seduce one another. And these interactions and ties make a difference.

The social networks perspective foregrounds links between two or more nodes (e.g., individuals, organisations, nation-states, amongst other types of node that possess different characteristics or attributes) and their ties, where the unit of analysis is the collection of individual nodes and their linkages (e.g., friendship, kinship, etc.), rather than any given individual actor alone. At its most basic level, single ties (e.g., person to person, or person to business connections, etc.) exist and where multiple ties are present and these become the building blocks of more complex configurations of nodes. Figure 3.1 visualises these dynamics:

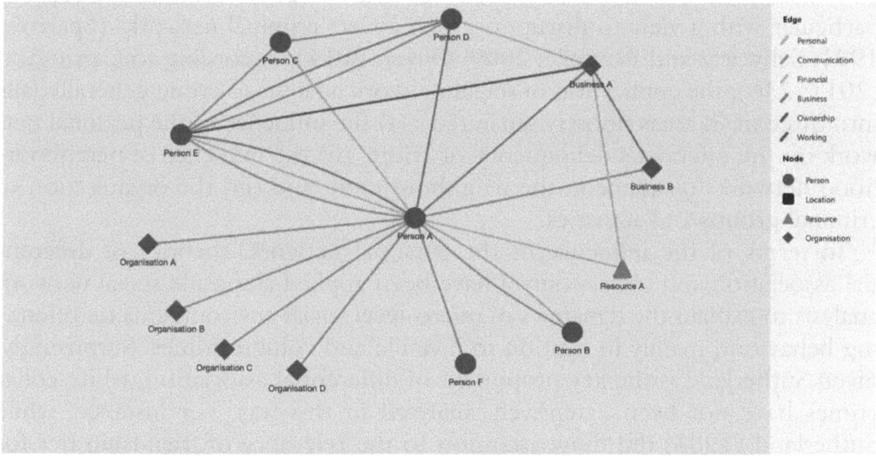

Figure 3.1 Basic Network Visualisation Using ScriptNet
Source: Lord et al., 2020

In these terms, the social networks approach is underpinned by the several key principles (Wasserman and Faust, 1994: 4): that actors and their actions are viewed as interdependent rather than independent, autonomous units; that relational ties (linkages) between actors are channels for transfer or 'flow' of resources (either material or nonmaterial); that network perspectives focusing on individuals view the network structural environment as providing opportunities for or constraints on individual action; and that network models conceptualise structure (behavioural, social, economic, or political) as lasting patterns of relations among actors. Thus, the approach facilitates insight into the nature of ties between actors (network structure and composition) and corresponding patterns or regularities, the variables that relate to these features, and how these features change over time. Various levels and units of analysis exist with social networks, such as the centrality or density/connectedness of different actors within the network, the reciprocity or resilience that exists within the network, and the structural equivalence between groups, amongst many others. In other words, network analysis can describe the structure of the network as a whole; it can identify the most prominent or marginal actors, groupings of tightly connected nodes in the networks, and the mechanisms that give rise to network structure and dynamics. (For an in-depth introduction to the history and nature of social network analysis, see the seminal Wasserman and Faust, 1994; Carrington et al., 2005; Borgatti et al., 2013.)

Social Network Analysis, Crime, and Criminal Networks

Criminologists and those interested in understanding crime and deviance have recognised the potential of empirically analysing the varying relational structures and features of criminal groups (see (Varese, 2013; Campana, 2016), in particular with a view to disrupting such covert criminal networks (Sparrow, 1991; Schwartz and Rouselle, 2009; Oliver, 2014). According to Carrington (2011: 236), the application of social network analysis to crime generally falls into three main areas (loosely separated): (i) the influence of the personal network on the offender's delinquency or crime, (ii) the influence of neighbourhood networks on crime in the neighbourhood, and (iii) the organisation of criminal groups and activities.

In terms of the influence of the personal network, theories of differential association and social control have been applied alongside social network analysis to explain the dynamics of micro-level social environments on offending behaviour, mainly in relation to juvenile and volume crimes. Surprisingly, given Sutherland is the key proponent of differential association, white-collar crimes have not been extensively analysed in this way. For instance, while Sutherland (1983) did draw attention to the relevance of friendship ties for how white-collar crimes are organised, and this was reinforced in his account of the nature of individual associations with pro-crime narratives, a specific network analysis of such ties has not emerged. If variations in the attributes of the personal network, such as the types of social ties, the composition of the network, and the features of the network structure, have contributed to an understanding of individual deviance at the level of 'street crimes' (Carrington, 2011: 241), then an analysis of the personal networks of white-collar offenders might also be informative. In general, ego-net analysis is concerned with (i) the structure of the network: that is, whether the ego is embedded in a dense network of relationships or it is brokering between otherwise-unconnected nodes (alter-alter ties are key in describing the latter) and (ii) the homogeneity of the network: that is, whether the attributes of egos and alters are homogenous or heterogeneous. For instance, in the case of a high-end Ponzi scheme, as we saw with Bernie Madoff, it could be said that Madoff essentially acted as a broker between otherwise unconnected investors, with these investors being unaware of the identities of others, but whose funds were connected for the purposes of the scheme. (Though some investors did know each other directly or by repute, since this was a technique used by affinity fraudsters to attract other victims, also a characteristic in the Theranos fraud.) Similarly, we could say that Madoff and his investors shared certain attributes and characteristics, such as particular status in investment communities, or shared economic, social, and cultural capital and thus represented a more homogenous network.

At the neighbourhood level, social network analysis has been used to identify variations in the attributes of corresponding networks and explain rates of crime by drawing attention to the structural conditions in neighbourhoods (e.g., disorganisation, disadvantage, mobility, etc.) that shape personal networks or the influence of networks of pro-social residents (Carrington, 2011: 243). As stated earlier, this research has tended to prioritise volume crimes and is beset with difficulties in establishing which neighbourhood actors are pro-social and what the composition of the 'neighbourhood' actually is. This line of inquiry foregrounds spatial proximity and the diffusions of particular crime events, such as violence, between adjacent neighbourhoods and gangs operating within and across these boundaries, and the conflict or cooperation that emerges (e.g., Papachristos and Bastomski, 2018; Bichler et al., 2019). Whilst this strand of research may not seem directly relevant to white-collar crime, there is clear value in thinking in terms of the 'corporate/organisational neighbourhood' and integrating the structural conditions of the workplace to understand the occurrence of white-collar crimes.

Finally, social network analysis has focused on the organisation of criminal networks specifically. That is, it seeks to understand the collaborative and mostly covert networks of those already involved in criminal activities (Oliver, 2014). The focus here is on the group, rather than individual and personal networks per se (though the former is often based on the latter); it has tended to produce static and dynamic representations of criminal groups and activities, and has been more exploratory and descriptive than theory driven (Carrington, 2011: 244). More specifically, research has analysed homophily (i.e., shared characteristics), structure (e.g., between actors, size of (sub-)groups, roles, etc.), and inter-network relations (e.g., member affiliations, contagion across groups) of gangs, groups, and criminal networks (Carrington, 2011). Criminal networks differ from other networks due to the need for concealment of the networks actors, ties, and activities, and rich empirical insights have been gained into the area of 'organised crime' specifically (See von Lampe, 2009; Morselli, 2009).

Four key findings have emerged out of the network literature on organised crime that are of significance for white-collar crime network analysis. First, such networks and associated criminal activities are embedded in the broader social context, interacting with the social environment (Kleemans and Van de Bunt, 1999). For instance, Smith and Papachristos (2016) analysed 'multiplexity' (i.e., where more than one relationship type exists between a pair of actors) in organised crime networks in Chicago. They found that although the overlap of criminal, personal, and legitimate networks is sparse within organised crime networks, dependencies between these networks exist and are structurally important, gluing the legitimate and illegitimate worlds together. Similarly, Diviák et al. (2019) analysed the multiplex structure of a Czech political corruption network, assessing the overlap of three relationship types: pre-existing ties, resource transfer, and collaboration. They found that pre-existing ties (e.g., co-membership of a party) were rare but did underpin and reinforce the ties of resource transfer (e.g., bribe paying) and collaboration (e.g., communication). The key point is that there is significance in the overlaps of different ties, such as personal friendships and working relationships, of the different network actors involved. This includes an understanding of the need for social capital: that is, the need for trust of cooperating/collaborating actors, and access to the resources of others, such as connections and linkages to suppliers or specific skill sets (Krebs, 2002). It can be expected that similar pre-existing relationships are important for white-collar crimes, particularly as the criminal activities take place in legitimate environments to which those involved have legitimate access. For instance, the Zondo Commission of Inquiry into the case of South African state capture concluded that it 'evolved as a project by which a relatively small group of actors, together with their network of collaborators inside and outside of the state, conspired systematically . . . to redirect resources from the state for their own gain' (Ramaphosa Response, 2022: para. 3.2.2). Political elites in public office utilised their legitimate access and ties with trusted witting, wilfully blind, or at best negligent private sector actors and beyond to engage in extensive corruption over time. They actively introduced prestigious consultants from Bain & Co (Williams, 2021) and KPMG to help them remove obstructive officeholders and hollow out those with the capability to prevent corruption and fraud (though there is no evidence of active conspiracy by the consultants). As President Cyril Ramaphosa commented in his address on the response to the commission's findings,

> Few could have imagined that this group of people would infiltrate key departments, state-owned companies, private companies, law enforcement bodies and security services to loot vast amounts of public funds; that they would weaken and destroy state institutions and thus undermine the capacity of the state.[2]

Second, insights have been gained into the structural aspects of criminal networks including the strategic positioning of actors within them. For instance, there have been extensive analyses of the structure of organised crime groups: whether more hierarchical and monolithic, or more ephemeral and flexible, and the implications for crime commission and social control. (See Morselli, 2009; Varese, 2013.) A frequent line of inquiry is to analyse the centrality of particular actors in the criminal network to identify how they

2 https://www.stateofthenation.gov.za/assets/downloads/State%20Capture%20Commission%20Response.pdf

are connected to others in the network, or, indeed, broker the connections of other actors, in turn playing a key role in the functioning of the network and associated criminal activities. For instance, Diviák et al. (2019) analysed core-periphery structures in a corruption network: that is, the extent to which there is a densely interconnected group of nodes co-existing (core) with a set of nodes connected to this core group (periphery), but having few connections to each other. (See also Borgatti and Everett, 2000.) They found a fully connected core alongside a more sparsely connected periphery, raising questions about why the politicians at the heart of the case made their interactions so centralised and frequent, despite the vulnerability this creates for the entire network. Relatedly, actors in other criminal networks have sought to strategically position themselves away from the core to reduce the risk of detection and disruption, whilst retaining influence through brokerage. Morselli (2010) focuses on the vulnerable or strategic positioning of network actors to understand how differential positions during enforcement investigations relate to judicial outcomes. Important actors may deliberately choose to be less directly central (less visible) in order to cover themselves, although this is not universal. In addition, the trade-off between network efficiency and network secrecy in criminal networks has also featured prominently (Morselli et al., 2007).

Third, the adaptability of networks in response to certain external (e.g., enforcement intervention) and internal (e.g., changing of actors) stimuli has been shown to be important to how networks deal with change and continue to survive and profit (e.g., Morselli, 2010; Bright et al., 2017). Concepts of 'efficiency', 'capacity to act', and 'longevity' have been used to analyse how networks can adapt and continue (Oliver, 2014). However, Bouchard (2007) focuses on the concept of resilience as a way of empirically representing the extent to which a criminal network can retain its capacity to act. That is, the resilience of a criminal network is determined by how well the network can respond to 'external shocks' such as repressive enforcement interventions (e.g., removing network actors or products such as drugs). The resilience is determined by the network's vulnerability (i.e., will the functioning of the network be damaged from these external shocks or not), elasticity (i.e., if damaged, how well can the network return to its previous states, such as by replacing actors and ties), and adaptivity (i.e., whether it can modify its circumstances to continue functioning rather than recover to its previous state). In terms of secrecy (or covertness), it is likely that network structures differ depending on the type and level of secrecy required, as well as the time the actors or activities need to remain covert and from whom they need to be concealed (Oliver, 2014). As Oliver (2014) summarises, it is often argued that resilience is most likely in networks that are adaptable and flexible (Krebs, 2002), in networks that are decentralised with functionally or structurally equivalent central nodes (Klerks, 2001; Krebs, 2002; Koschade, 2006), and, perhaps of most relevance to white-collar and corporate crimes, in overt networks within which covert networks are embedded (Gimenez-Salinas, 2014).

Finally, there is also scope to empirically analyse how criminal networks grow over time in relation to structure (e.g., density, centrality, size, etc.)

and function (e.g., resilience, capacity to act, etc.). For instance, individuals may change their roles over time in line with the network needs and focus, whilst density remains stable, but the network becomes more decentralised (Bright and Delaney, 2013). Stevenson and Crossley (2014) analysed changes in the network of the Provisional Irish Republican Army between 1969 and 1988. They found that there was a high rate of turnover of nodes in the network – that is, people leaving and entering – and that those who stayed in the network longer tended to be those with more central positions, meaning the structural properties of the network remained quite stable despite the high turnover. However, they also identified a steady rise in network centralisation, with those longer-term network members forming a close core. Temporal dynamics may be a strong explanation of structural variance. Finally, some networked criminal activities are coordinated in online spaces, but 'freelance' cyber networks may be less stable than corporate/state-sponsored ones, as the Russia-Ukraine conflict and its aftermath have shown, although research has shown many cybercriminal business models to be relatively stable (Lusthaus et al., 2023). Understanding those white-collar and corporate crimes cases, like many corruption cases we see, in terms of their network development over time can offer rich insights into the resilience, longevity, adaptivity, structure, and function of such criminal networks.

Social Network Analysis and White-Collar and Corporate Crimes

In addition to its use in crime and criminology more generally, social network analysis has also been applied to white-collar and corporate crime more specifically, although such scholarship remains rare:[3] 'social network analysis has been increasingly utilized to analyse the structure of illicit networks that emerge out of and through legitimate economic activity and to embed individuals and organizations within social structures' (Simpson, 2013: 319). For this reason, Simpson (2013) highlights social network analysis as a promising new direction for white-collar crime research, particularly in relation to empirically connecting different levels of analysis (i.e., micro-meso-macro) to help test the relations of organisational behaviour in particular industries (Rorie and Simpson, unpublished). To this, we would add that we also need to understand why these positional changes and stabilities across white-collar crime networks actually happen, using the relational data to do so – the data alone cannot explain anything.

Early studies of the networks of white-collar crime sought to understand the features and structures of such networks (though, in some cases, in methodologically different ways to contemporary conceptions of social network

3 There is some social network analysis of corporate behaviour generally but not with explicit focus on criminal and deviant conduct. We do not explore this literature here, but it may inform any future research in this area (i.e., what can be learned from legal corporate networks?).

analysis). One early study by Baker and Faulkner (1993) analysed the social organisation and network components of three well-known price-fixing conspiracies in the heavy electrical equipment industry. Using archival data, they analysed actual communication networks in the collusion and found that the structure of these illegal networks was primarily driven by the need to maximise concealment, rather than efficiency, but this was also contingent on information processing requirements (i.e., are the network aims more complex or simple?) determined by market and product characteristics. That is, in the conspiracies, it was expected the need for secrecy was a core consideration due to the high stakes involved and the careers and reputations of the managers and executives who were implicated. However, they suggested the networks structures were also shaped by the coordination of efficient (i.e., quick) and effective (i.e., accurate) information exchange between colluders, not just the need for secrecy. Consequently, the authors hypothesised that 'the need for secrecy should lead conspirators to conceal their activities by creating sparse and decentralized networks' (Baker and Faulkner, 1993: 844). However, their findings were inconsistent, with only two of three cases constituted of sparse and decentralised networks. Notwithstanding the inconsistencies, the study did draw attention to secrecy and efficiency as desirable features for illegal networks in white-collar crimes. For instance, the swift diffusion of investment frauds has been evidenced to be key in alleviating the interest burden[4] and improving illicit profits for those managing the fraudulent scheme (Zhu et al., 2017).

Similar empirical questions about the functioning of covert criminal collaborations and the need for secrecy and efficiency have been analysed in relation to covert networks in organised crime and terrorism (Morselli et al., 2007). It is often assumed that such criminal groups aim to remain hidden from public/private interventions and conceal their activities (i.e., remain secret) but not insofar as such secrecy hinders the goals of their criminal enterprise. However, which side of this trade-off is prioritised depends on the nature of the criminal objectives, such as whether the criminal enterprise is for profit generation or terrorism, while activities requiring shorter timeframes might require efficiency more than secrecy (Morselli et al., 2007). We might also infer that similar considerations are made by networks of cooperating white-collar criminals, but such criminal behaviours are inherently different, as the actors involved are directly visible, rather than hidden outside legitimate markets and systems. Jordanoska and Lord (2020), in their analysis of the LIBOR manipulation (see earlier in this chapter), identified that the rigging was openly discussed and organised within financial institutions with little attempt to conceal the behaviour from colleagues. (The apparent absence of effort to maintain secrecy may also reflect the fact that they simply did not think that what they

4 That is, people are recruited to such schemes through the promise of high-yield, low-risk returns, but investment funds are used to cover the initial interest owed to early investors. In formulaic terms, earnings before taxes divided by earnings before interest and taxes.

were doing was wrong, perhaps additionally that they engaged in concerted self-deception about its wrongfulness. (See Benson and Cullen, 2018.) This reflects how behaviours can be defined in different ways within organisations when an external observer would recognise the deviance. If there had been more active prosecution of this type of market rigging, the view that what they were doing was acceptable would have been harder to maintain. It may be that other network features, such as efficiency and centrality, are more significant than secrecy in the sphere of white-collar and corporate crimes. But this raises questions about how we determine what efficiency actually looks like, how we measure it, and whether it is more useful analytically to foreground concepts of resilience and network vulnerability, elasticity, and adaptivity (Bouchard, 2007), in relation to white-collar and corporate crimes.

Social network analysis has also given empirical insight into investment decisions and victimisation. Baker and Faulkner (2003) later analysed the diffusion of fraud victimisation amongst investors in the case of the Fountain Oil and Gas Company, an example of an 'intermediate fraud' whereby the business was at first entirely legitimate but then turned to investment fraud. They investigated the extent to which investors who became victims were influenced by their social networks (ties to sellers and prior investors), impersonal methods of communication (e.g., direct mail, advertising, etc.), or both. They found that 'the factors that contributed to the success of the business in its legitimate stage are the same factors that contributed to the success of the fraud in its illegitimate stage' (Baker and Faulkner, 2003: 1201). That is, their research indicated that many of the investors were closely connected through their social networks, but investment information was not shared via these networks as the business expanded, even when they were pressured to do so by the company, as investors were keen to 'keep a good thing to themselves' (p. 1198). Instead, the business used impersonal methods such as renting prestigious offices and driving expensive cars to give credibility to the business. However, this lack of information sharing via word of mouth when the business was legitimate was actually beneficial to the perpetuation of the later fraud, as investors did not talk to each other.

This raises questions about the protective or harmful nature of social networks and ties in corporate crimes, such as investment fraud. Baker and Faulkner (2004) explored this dynamic further, empirically testing, in the case study of Fountain Oil and Gas Company, whether social networks were beneficial, in that they help reduce the probability of loss of capital, or exploitative, in that they increase the probability of loss of capital. They found that the harmful and exploitative role of social networks is limited to pre-planned frauds – 'if sellers have only criminal intentions, then social ties facilitate economic crimes' (Baker and Faulkner, 2004: 106). When the business engaged in an 'intermediate fraud', pre-existing social ties to the seller had a protective and beneficial impact, reducing losses. Relatedly, Nash et al. (2018) analysed the role of trust in social ties and due diligence in investment decisions and the ways in which these can protect investors from fraud or cause their fraud victimisation as information is passed through their personal networks. In their case study of the pre-planned Enron Ponzi scheme, they found that trust, specifically institution-based trust (of industry professionals), and due diligence, both increased initial investments and increased net loss. Trust in friends and family has also been shown to be influential in the diffusion of fraud through populations of victims (Nash et al., 2018, contradicting Baker and Faulkner (2003) and to be associated with the types of harm reported by victims (Nash et al., 2018). In a more than tautological sense, trust is central to many white-collar crimes, often accompanied by an element of deception and dishonesty (Shapiro, 1990; Benson et al., 2024), and its role in social networks of white-collar crime perpetration is key. An individual appearance of being successful in business strengthens investors' trust and facilitates recruitment to investment frauds (Zhu et al., 2017).

Social network analysis has also been used to understand the impacts of engaging in unethical behaviour on corporations, in particular on their inter-organisational networks. Sullivan et al. (2007) evidenced that following the commission of an unethical act, the quality of a company's network partners decreases (declining legitimacy results in higher-quality firms leaving the network, and lesser-quality firms are needed to replace them), and the more unethical or illegitimate the behaviour, the greater the deterioration in network partner quality. Consequently, a company's prominence in the network also declines as does its network cohesion. Thus, the perceived legitimacy of a corporation following unethical behaviour influences its future profitability.

These studies represent social network analyses at difference levels of abstraction – individual/personal, organisational, inter-organisational. Rorie and Simpson (unpublished) suggest the social network perspective provides a framework for empirically testing and modelling the direct and indirect linkages between these levels, such as between individuals and organisations at different 'criminogenic tiers' of an industry, in order to understand the consequences of network relations for corporate behaviour throughout the industry. Their discussion of social network analysis related to mortgage fraud in the US specifically, and the need to empirically understand the nature and change of interdependent relationships over time across mortgage industry tiers, the centrality of certain actors and institutions, the strength of ties, and how fraud emerges and moves through the network (Rorie and Simpson, unpublished; Simpson, 2013).

Of course, a key caveat in social network analysis is the issue of unknown network boundaries (Oliver, 2014). Consequently, where possible, network analysis of white-collar crime ought also to include not only offenders and victims or those directly implicated, but also those who were exposed to white-collar crimes but consciously disregarded them (Nash et al., 2018: 86). In addition, empirical analyses of criminal networks have tended to focus on only one type of actor or node: individuals (Bellotti et al., 2020). Furthermore, analyses of centrality may identify individuals as structurally equal in the network, but these can lack an appreciation of the significance of their network function (e.g., possessing high-level information or low-level information) (Bright et al., 2015). Whilst analysing the individuals involved in white-collar crime networks is key, we also see value in integrating multiple node and link types to understand if new insights can be gained in terms of how individuals organise around similar or different objects or locations.

Corporate Bribery and Social Network Analysis

To demonstrate the insights gained through social network analysis, we draw here on a study of corporate bribery networks by Diviák and Lord (2022). They analysed relational data taken from statements of fact published alongside deferred prosecution agreements in the UK with the aim of exploring the structure and dynamics of bribery networks. They first isolated particular mechanisms that are thought to constitute the organisational aspects of the bribery network: namely, the nature of the core-periphery structure (i.e., a densely connected core of key actors), the existence of disassortativity (i.e., the collaboration of actors with different skills and contributions), the repetition of interactions (i.e., indicating trust and compliance), and temporal escalation (i.e., the concentration of interactions at key points in the 'script'). They utilised SNA to make sense of three bribery cases. We present the case of Sarclad Ltd to illuminate this further.

Sarclad Ltd[5] is a UK company incorporated in 2000 that designs and manufactures technology for the metal industry, selling products internationally. Between 2004 and 2012, the company and associated employees and agents systematically paid bribes to win contracts overseas, generating profit of £6.5 million. Sarclad used a network of intermediary agents working in foreign countries to offer bribes on its behalf to public officials thought to have influence and control over the awarding of contracts. Of the implicated contracts, 17 involved a single agent (Dr Guang Jiang) operating through a company called Castmasters, seeking contracts in China. Six other agents were involved in the remaining contracts. Essentially, Sarclad entered into agreements with these agents that stipulated remuneration on the basis of commission expressed as a percentage of the contract value secured. Sarclad the company was charged with 'conspiracy to corrupt' and 'failure to prevent bribery', entering into a DPA for these charges in 2016. Three Sarclad individuals were charged with 'conspiracy to bribe' in relation to 27 overseas contracts: Michael Sorby, Adrian Leek, and David Justice. All three individuals were acquitted at trial. Thus, whilst the *company* was implicated in the crime commission, the *individuals* involved were separately not proved to be guilty (a common issue in Serious Fraud Office prosecutions to date, attributed to the particularities of inference in Anglo-Welsh law).

5 https://www.sfo.gov.uk/cases/sarclad-ltd/

The Sarclad network, depicted in Figure 3.2, comprises 27 actors, and its specific feature is that the statement of fact was detailed enough to allow the authors to distinguish the direction of each tie, making the network directed.

In terms of core-periphery structure, the correlation of the empirical network with an idealised one is 0.78, suggesting a very strong correspondence of the network with a core-periphery structure. The disassortativity was calculated on the attribute denoting whether the actor worked for Sarclad or not because the employees of Sarclad were manipulating the contracts with other actors from a multitude of other companies, depending on the particular contract at hand. The assortativity index of -0.08 suggested disassortative tendencies, but only weak ones. The value of the Gini index is extremely high at 0.96, which substantiates the mechanism of repeated interactions as there are some dyads within which the interactions tend to disproportionately accumulate.

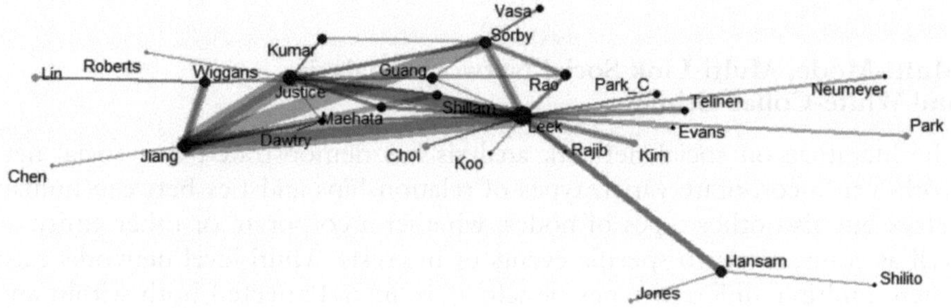

Figure 3.2 Sarclad Sociogram[6]

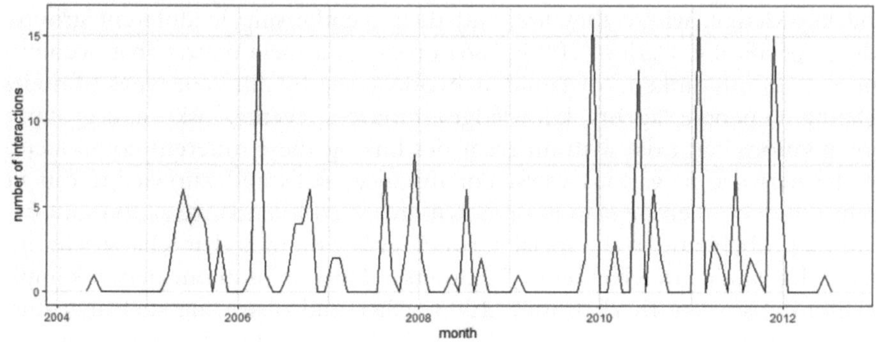

Figure 3.3 Sarclad Temporal Analysis[7]

6 Source: Diviák and Lord (2022: 12). Reprinted under a Creative Commons Attribution 4.0 International License: http://creativecommons.org/licenses/by/4.0/

7 Source: Diviák and Lord (2022: 13). Reprinted under a Creative Commons Attribution 4.0 International License: http://creativecommons.org/licenses/by/4.0/

Lastly, Figure 3.3 depicts the timeline in relation to temporal escalation. There are multiple spikes in the number of interactions in certain months, followed by periods of relative inactivity in the timeline of the Sarclad case. This gives evidence of temporal escalation. In summary, the Sarclad case network exhibits a clear core-periphery structure, and there is evidence in the operation of the mechanisms of repeated interactions and temporal escalation.

Across the cases analysed, Diviák and Lord (2022) found that bribery networks resembled core-periphery structure networks with ties predominantly concentrated between a few very central actors (core), who ad hoc engage with actors from the periphery. Moreover, the authors also identified a strong tendency of actors to repeat interactions and to accumulate interactions within certain dyads. In terms of temporal dynamics, they observed periods of relative inaction alternating with periods of frequent and repeated contacts triggered by the presence of contracts susceptible to corruption.

Multi-Mode, Multi-Link Social Network Analysis and White-Collar Crimes

The literature on social network analysis has demonstrated that social networks can incorporate varied types of relationships and ties between human actors but also other types of nodes, whether a corporate or other entity, as well as connections to specific events or interests. Multi-level networks exist where multiple different types of actors are interconnected both within and across these different types. (See Lazega and Snijders, 2016.) Most notably, Carley (2003) emphasised the contribution of a multi-mode approach to dynamic network analysis that accounts not only for ties between individual actors and their centrality, but also for which actors possess which skills and knowledge, where they are, and their membership in different groups. More specifically, Carley (2003: 136) proposes a meta-matrix that accounts for a set of interlinked, 'dynamic' networks whereby different types of nodes relating to people/agents, knowledge/resources, events/tasks, and groups/organisations can exist with different ties linking these different components of the network in various ways. For instance, skills and knowledge can be transferred; co-membership in organisations or co-attendance at an event can imply a probable tie in the social network. A key point is that 'changes in one network cascade into changes in the others; relationships in one network imply relationships in another' (Carley, 2003: 135), and observing such dynamics can inform how we understand the tendencies of networks to function. In these terms, individuals can be seen as adaptive, capable of learning and taking action (i.e., process), rather than static nodes in the network (i.e., position), allowing networks and agents to co-evolve. This approach to network analysis informs an understanding of relational structures alongside lifestyle features provided by each part of the network together with geographical location as part of the criminal process (Bellotti et al., 2020). Thus, the overall structure of criminal networks can be viewed as an amalgamation of underlying networks or sub-networks and their different layers, whereby each network layer is characterised by ties that enable the exchange of a particular resource, such as information, money, or drugs, resulting in a 'merged multi-relationship network' (Bright et al., 2015: 222). In these terms, networks can emerge from the system of linkages across the required resources for a particular criminal enterprise, and there can be variation in the different network layers in which different actors participate (Bright et al., 2015: 233). Consequently, in contrast to the predominant network analyses of single types of connections, 'the analysis of multiple link types within a criminal network provides a more nuanced understanding of the structure of the network, and of the strategic position of actors in the network' (Bright et al., 2015: 233).

It is at this point that clear overlap can be seen between the (white-collar) crime script analysis (Chapter 2) and multi-mode, multi-link network analysis as:

> Both observe the crime process as a set of organized tasks that evolve over time and adapt to the contextual contingencies. Crime scripts can be deconstructed to identify vulnerabilities in the crime commission process; likewise, criminal networks can be mapped to detect weak (or strong) links and actors. Both crime scripts and criminal networks are crime specific, but at the same time can produce generalizable repertoire and behavioural scripts and relational structure.
>
> (Bellotti et al., 2020: 378)

Integrating these two analytical approaches can be empirically insightful, but at the time of writing, doing so is rare and exceptional.

Towards an Integrated Script-Network Analysis for White-Collar Crimes

There are only two studies within our purview to date that have sought to implement an integrated crime script–social network analysis: Morselli and Roy (2008) and Bellotti et al. (2020). Morselli and Roy (2008) analyse the role of brokers in maintaining flexibility in stolen vehicle exportation operations. They identify that networks with loosely structured processes connected through central actors occupying brokerage positions are more likely to be resilient due to the increased degree of flexibility in accomplishing the collective goals. They argue that the removal of these interlocutors of disconnected others would decrease flexibility and lead to the crime script no longer being functional. Methodologically, an original contribution is made in the integration of the crime script analysis and social network analysis. They analyse betweenness centrality (Freeman, 1978) and brokerage roles (Gould and Fernandez, 1989) in order to identify which actors operate across different scenes, facets, and permutations of the crime script and the key role of these actors in these scenes.

Bellotti et al. (2020: 378–379)[8] extend Morselli and Roy's approach further by substituting the social network analysis with a more dynamic multi-mode, multi-link network analysis that incorporates analysis of not only individuals but also the organisations, resources, and locations where criminal activities take place. (See also Lord et al., 2017.) The analysis included various types of ties, including personal (familial or kinship), transport and logistics (movement of goods), selling and buying goods (trade relations), business (owning or having access to resources), and other types of tie, such as funding, otherwise linked to the cases. The multi-mode, multi-link approach enabled analysis group structure, criminal lifestyles, location, and time. The temporal analysis demonstrates how the same criminal system can organise around substitutable facets of the same crime script, and this, in turn, increases network resilience. (See also Bright and Delaney, 2013.) We present this analysis in further detail next.

Applying the Analytical Approach: Distributing Counterfeit Goods

Though this is not a conventional white-collar crime case, the example here relates to the distribution of counterfeit goods, alcohol in particular, transnationally, with a focus on the role of ostensibly legitimate businesses and occupational actors as knowing conspirators and unknowing facilitators of the criminal enterprise. The insights draw on research from Lord et al. (2017) and Bellotti et al. (2020), in which the authors integrated the previously discussed script analysis with a dynamic network analysis to understand the distribution of counterfeit alcohols between two European jurisdictions, Ireland, and the UK. The analysis was based on enforcement case files and interviews with involved regulators. In this criminal enterprise, legitimate business actors were implicated as primary offenders, and the movement of the illicit products was concealed within legitimate logistics networks (i.e., networks involved in the transportation of goods) and sold via legitimate wholesalers and supermarkets. The behaviours involved an array of knowingly involved and unwitting (and possibly incompetent) legitimate occupational actors and businesses of varying sizes.

Counterfeiting is a form of intellectual property crime that is 'committed when someone manufactures, sells or distributes counterfeit or pirated goods . . . for commercial gain' (Europol, n.d.). The goods are often of inferior quality but presented under a trademark that is identical to, or indistinguishable from, a registered trademark; thus, '[i]n simple terms, counterfeits are imitations of real products that are manufactured without approval from the owner of the brand' (International Trademark Association, 2024). The case studies analysed in this research involved the distribution of counterfeit vodka and counterfeit wine from Ireland to the UK. The researchers sought to understand how this distribution process was organised locally and transnationally, including investigating the core behaviours, actors, and locations that were necessary

8 Lord is a co-author of this study.

to the enterprise. In brief, central to the distribution 'script' were ostensibly legitimate occupational actors and businesses that had different roles in the distribution (e.g., coordinators, gatekeepers, consultants, liaisons), alongside an array of concealment practices to circumvent routine detection measures, such as using shrink-wrapping to disguise the alcohol, fabricated invoices, and paper trails (e.g., for the transport of bottled water). Thousands of litres of alcohol were distributed first via local networks in Ireland, then via transnational logistics companies and routes, and finally via local networks in the UK, where the alcohol was sold via off-licences, restaurants, and wholesalers.

Before undertaking the script analysis, certain assumptions of the crimes were made. For instance, it was assumed that a process of concealment of the illicit alcohol had already taken place. That is, at some point prior to the distribution, the illicit alcohol must have been produced (distilled and packaged) to make it look like the authentic product as well as physically hidden for transportation (e.g., obscuring the contents for legitimate business facilitators by shrink-wrapping the bottles). Following this, the illicit alcohol must also have been stored at a legitimate or illegitimate location before being inserted into legitimate logistics networks. It was also assumed that the illicit alcohol consignment was maintained as a single consignment until 'scene 3', in which it was broken down into multiple consignments.

As visualised in Figure 3.4, the distribution was deconstructed into five scenes (collection, logistics, delivery, disposal, proceeds/finance), and the analysis identified underlying and routine activities connecting each scene at the intersections of licit and illicit markets and networks as they saw the 'integration', 'incorporation', 'de-integration' and 'allocation' of the illicit product at various stages and under particular conditions. In scene 1, a local transport business was paid by one of the business actors to collect and transport the counterfeit alcohol from the point of storage to two legitimate firms. From these locations, other legitimate logistics firms were contracted to collect and deliver the products to the transnational transportation firm. Official paperwork is provided, and a paper trail created to ensure no questions from the legitimate firms involved. Once the consignment has been taken on by the transnational transportation company, a process of integration into a legitimate logistics chain has occurred, as the illicit product is no longer under the direct control of the criminal enterprise. This represents the first stage of deception. In scene 2, transportation occurs via three phases: local in Ireland, transnational, local in the UK. At this point, several companies have been contracted and subcontracted to transport the illicit products; these business appear to be unwitting facilitators utilised to conceal the movement of the illicit alcohol via their subcontracting practices that layer and distance the product from the source. Such business practices are part of normal logistics operations and simply reflect routine procedures and patterns, thus enabling the product to be incorporated into the legitimate system. There is a clear interdependency between illicit and licit networks and criminal enterprise in this case. In scene 3, the illicit product is de-integrated back into the hands of the criminal enterprise. The product was delivered locally in the UK to

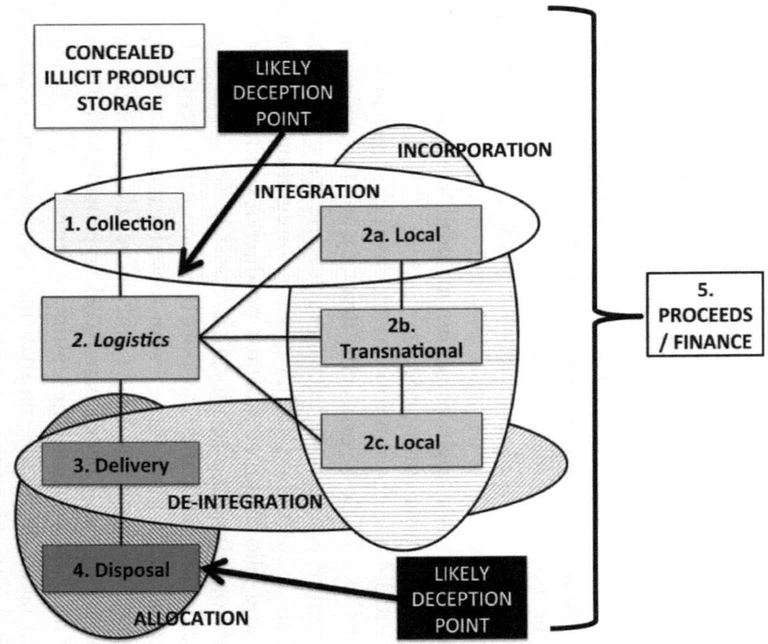

Figure 3.4 The 'Scripts' of Counterfeit Alcohol Distribution.

Source: Lord et al. (2017)[9]

9 Source: Lord et al. (2017: 263). Reprinted under a Creative Commons Attribution 4.0 International License: http://creativecommons.org/licenses/by/4.0/

logistics depots and then to other businesses that represented trusted sources. For instance, in one case, the alcohol was delivered to a Ministry of Transport (MOT) vehicle test centre where the employees there would then re-divert the delivery to a food wholesaler location in the rear of the premises. In scene 4, the products are collected from these delivery locations and disposed of via multiple consumer outlets (e.g., pubs and clubs), usually via unmarked vans and vehicles. It might be that some form of concerted ignorance or wilful blindness occurs as vendors, purveyors, and consumers seek to buy cheap alcohol. Scene 5 refers to the finances required for paying for logistics contracts and the finances generated from final sales of the products and how they are managed and controlled throughout the enterprise. This involved both cash and electronic payments, the smuggling of cash across borders, the purchase of assets for individuals, and reinvestment back into the enterprise.

Following the identification of the scripts, the actors involved, the geographical locations, and the products were integrated as individual nodes into the researchers' multi-mode, multi-link network of counterfeit alcohol distribution. This analysis enabled the researchers to identify the necessary roles that different actors played across the different scenes and their connections to the product and product locations. Figure 3.5 visualises this analysis. The network has 68 actors and 129 ties. Different shades of grey indicate the type of tie and the scenes that nodes belong to, while shapes differentiate between types of actors. Table 3.1 provides the legend for the scenes, ties, and nodes.

Table 3.1 Legend for scenes, ties, and nodes in Figure 3.2

Nodes' Scenes	*Colour*
Collection	*Lightest grey*
Logistic	*Lighter grey*
Delivery	*Grey*
Disposal	*Darker grey*
Proceeds	*Darkest grey*
No scene	*White*
Ties	**Colour**
Personal	*Black*
Transport/logistic	*Darker grey*
Sell	*Grey*
Business	*Lighter grey*
Other	*Lightest grey*
Type of Actor	**Node's Shape**
Person	*Circle*
Logistic/transport business	*Square*
Storage/selling business	*Up triangle*
Place	*Down triangle*
Website	*Rounded square*
Alcohol	*Diamond*

Source: Bellotti et al. (2020)

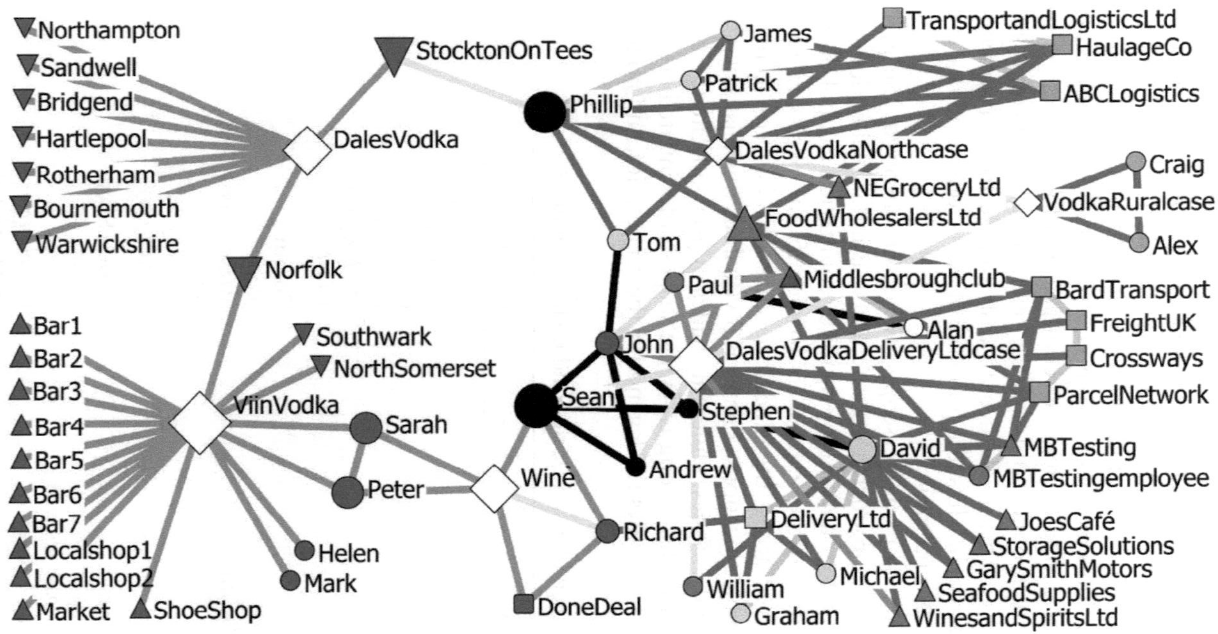

Figure 3.5 The Social Network of Counterfeit Alcohol Distribution[10]

10 Source: Bellotti, E. et al., 'Counterfeit alcohol distribution: A criminological script network analysis', *European Journal of Criminology*, 2018, 17(4), pp. 373–398. Copyright © 2018 by (Sage Publications). Reprinted by Permission of Sage Publications.

Analysing the role of particular network actors in different scenes enabled the researchers to see how opportunities arose and the resources and skills the actors required to realise these opportunities. Extending this further to think in terms of varying capacities, Bellotti et al. (2020) identified that the actors involved needed knowledge of how logistics, locally and transnationally, function in order to be confident that the illicit product would not be detected when no longer under their control. These actors also needed to understand what official documentation looks like in order not to arouse the suspicion of third parties. The layering of contracts assisted here, as due diligence over trusted sources was less likely. The case also demonstrates how opportunities arise due to market structures. For instance, the necessity of demand, the inadequate regulation and guardianship, and the ability to supply, all enabled the actors to be market competitive. Furthermore, opportunities were made possible due to the routinised nature of logistics and transportation that facilitated the straightforward movement of the products. Networks of transnational relations were also established, sometimes short lived (e.g., when using particular firms), but, in terms of core actors to the enterprise, more long-standing. In terms of the knowingly criminal actors, the enterprise was held together by a shared belief in profit generation over time as the illegitimate actors parasitised the legitimate process.

Bellotti et al. (2020) also focused on the brokerage roles of actors that were evident in linking different network layers and scenes of the crime script. Following Morselli and Roy (2008), the authors calculated betweenness centrality (i.e., how many times an actors lies on the shortest path between each network dyad) and brokerage roles (i.e., to observe which actors are better positioned to connect the network, including which scenes each actor was involved in and the type of role they played). For instance, Gould and Fernandez (1989) identify five types of brokerage roles dependent on the direction of the ties and the groups the actors belong to: that is, seeking to understand how one actor (broker) connects two others where no ties exist between them. The five roles are:

- *Coordinator*: All three people belong to the same scene. Coordinators are brokers who manage people and resources within the same scene (e.g., coordinating delivery or collection of the illicit alcohol).
- *Consultant*: The two unconnected actors belong to the same scene, while the broker belongs to a different scene. Consultants are able to move resources across scenes (e.g., funding the costs of logistics without being directly involved in the movement of the goods).
- *Gatekeeper* and/or *Representative*: The broker and one actor belong to the same scene, while the third actor belongs to a different scene. The gatekeeper or representative controls the incomings/outgoings of resources and/or information within the scene they belong to.
- *Liaison*: All the actors belong to different scenes. Brokers carrying out liaison are likely to need an extensive overview of all the procedural steps of the crime script.

The analysis of brokerage roles indicated that liaison was the most frequent type of brokerage role and that one actor, David, carried out 200 brokerage roles across as coordinator, consultant, gatekeeper, and liaison. He was in charge of collection and delivery, presented the highest number of brokerage roles within and between these two scenes, but he also acted as a gatekeeper and liaised across all the other scenes. Interestingly, one location, Food Wholesalers Ltd, had the second-highest number of brokerage roles, most frequently in liaison within the delivery scene, suggesting this location was a key place where actors from different scenes came together. However, when compared to the betweenness centrality calculation, neither David nor Food Wholesalers Ltd scored the highest.

The integrated script-network analysis enabled the identification of key points of deception (i.e., where the criminal enterprise tricked others, whether businesses or consumers, into transacting by mimicking legitimate processes). The enforcement authorities had not focused on these deception points, so the analysis enabled the regulator to pursue new lines of inquiry in their live investigations based on the vulnerabilities identified. To give one example of this, the regulator had initially focused on the endpoint where the illicit alcohol had been detected and the immediate distribution processes prior to consumption. However, the research here illuminated the key role of a small number of logistics businesses in Ireland that were regularly involved across multiple consignments or shipments, and they turned out to be key players in the enterprise. More specifically, the script-network analysis foregrounded the financial aspects of the criminal enterprise, in turn highlighting that two business actors had funded the operation. These actors covered costs of legitimate transnational haulage companies that were used to transport the products unknowingly. By 'following the money' to the benefactors, key actors who had been at the periphery became central to the investigation. Furthermore, the abuse and/or misuse of legitimate business in the cases reinforces the clear interdependencies between licit and illicit actors, markets, and networks.

However, the analysis also indicated that the network was efficient and resilient in that it was elastic and adaptive, able to reorganise around other distribution opportunities as some pathways were disrupted by the authorities and had developed a diverse array of delivery and distribution outlets that aided in spreading the risks. That said, the cases here represent known criminal activities, so perhaps their secrecy was lowered in the trade-off with efficiency and resilience. The 'unknown unknowns' may have been different.

Ego Networks and White-Collar Crimes

Given the paucity of large relational datasets for network analyses of white-collar and corporate crimes, the viability of whole-network analyses based on partial or non-existent data is undermined. Social network analysis is only as good as the relational data available. Additionally, the predilection for quantitative approaches to network analysis to generate statistical inferences about networks may lose sight of the rich, deep mechanisms that interconnect with an individual's network, and the decisions to engage in and not to prevent or take note of criminal behaviour. A further useful and perhaps more pragmatic approach may be to focus on understanding the ego-nets of individual white-collar offenders. Much of the previous discussion is concerned with whole-network analyses, rather than personal-network analyses, whereby the focus is on 'egos': that is, individual actors/agents and their ties to others or 'alters' (see Figure 3.6). The 'ego' is located at the centre of the network, and its position relative to their alters is analysed. The intention is not to construct an entire network or to connect the alters of one ego to another, but to understand the social environment of the individual ego (Borgatti et al., 2013: 28).

Data are collected from the individual ('ego') about the people ('alters') they are (or were) connected to, how and why they are connected to these people, their attributes, and the individual's perceptions of the ties among the alters (Borgatti et al., 2013: 262). This process can solely involve data from the ego (including perceptions of alters), utilising interviews or surveys, or be drawn from an already-analysed whole network from which alter data can be extracted. These relational data can form the basis of how we understand how (successful) crime commission is a function of the social ties the individual offender has with those in their immediate personal network, such as how ties and alters provide access to resources, information, collaboration, and so on (i.e., social capital). Alongside this, it can also be analysed how an individual offender's ties and alters influence their ways of thinking, feeling, and behaving, with particular focus on how offending behaviour may be learned from

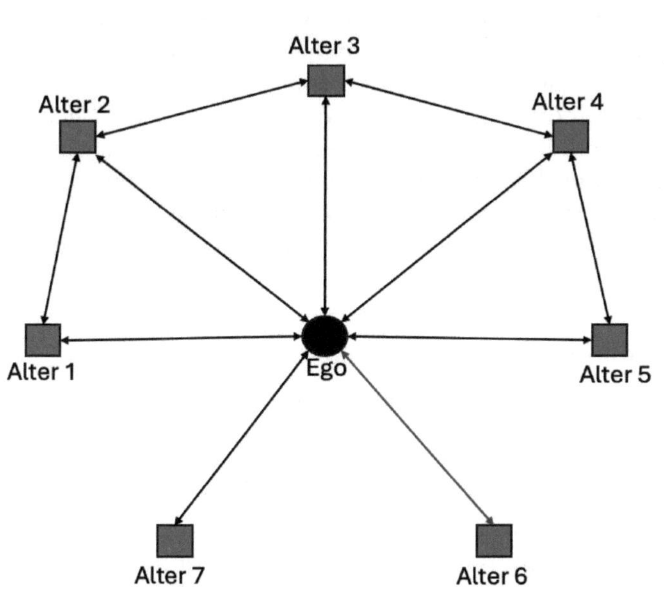

Figure 3.6 An Ego Network Visualisation

others (contagion). In addition, insight can also be gained into whether an individual ego's attributes relate to which alters they connect with; are there tendencies towards homophily: that is, seeking ties with actors who are similar (i.e., social homogeneity)? These various facets of ego networks can be analysed computationally to give insight into the relationships between the ego and the ego network.

To provide a more concrete example, we might interview a convicted white-collar offender who was involved in a major accounting fraud with a view to understanding the role of social and organisational resources in the fraud commission process. To begin with, we could ask the offender to list the names of all alters who provided, knowingly or not, information, knowledge, skills, access, and so on, that enabled the offender to carry out the fraud. Some 'enablers' may just be doing their licit job and not be aware of or notice anything criminal or suspicious. Offenders might also not identify these alters as active facilitators. In any case, where possible, a full list of alters would be beneficial. We could then ask the convicted offender to identify and explain their relationship to each of the alters (e.g. direct manager, co-employees in different departments) and the perceived strength of these relationships, their attributes (e.g. gender, age, position, trust, respectability, honesty, and so on), and the resource that was provided (e.g. information, funds, secrecy, use of computer, help collating data on the books, etc.), as well as any organisations in which these people work, if not in the same business. We can then ask about the relationships between the different alters. Analysis of these data can indicate whether offenders in accounting frauds were reliant on immediate co-workers, external actors, or actors with certain types of skills and knowledge, and whether or not those actors were believed by the ego – rightly or wrongly – to identify the criminality at the time of action. (This reflects a more subtle interpretation of the role of 'professional enablers'; see Levi, 2022.) Comparison with other ego networks of accounting fraud offenders can then be made to search for commonalities and differences in network composition and structure, but this, of course, depends on the willingness of offenders to talk, and their truthfulness and accuracy, given offenders may have an incentive to rationalise their actions post hoc, and paint their own actions in the best possible light.

Data and Sources

There is a paucity of data sources for social network analysis of white-collar and corporate crimes. In relation to criminal networks more generally, researchers have been reliant on surveillance data, interview data, experiential police data, and police crime reports, and more can be gained from combining these data (Malm and Bichler, 2011). For instance, Campana and Varese (2013) made use of wiretapped conversations generated as part of Italian police surveillance to understand ties within criminal networks, but the same data do not exist for white-collar and corporate crimes, where such surveillance techniques are rarely used outside or even within the US, particularly not at an early stage of the development of their relationships. (The European encrypted phone technology EncroChat, for example, was presumably not purchased by or marketed to corporate executives, few of whom would have routine relationships with major full-time crime entrepreneurs, so criminal collaborations analysed by its decoding and capture would only include classic 'organised crimes' and not well-organised white-collar crimes by people outside 'criminal circles'.) Similarly, Duijn and Sloot (2015) have argued in favour of utilising big data and big data analytics to understand organised crime network operation and adaptation, but, as discussed earlier, it is not clear where such data exists for white-collar and corporate crimes. They highlight law enforcement data, intelligence data more specifically, given its wider scope than targeted investigative data, and open-source data, including social media content. They also advocate for network analysis and script analysis. As Diviák (2020) notes, due to working with secondary data that is primarily intended for non-research purposes (investigation, prosecution, media coverage, etc.), different data sources may be biased in different ways (police predominantly focusing on information with a forensic impact on prosecutions of plausible targets or media focusing on public known figures or 'spicy' aspects). Being systematic, transparent, and methodologically sound in data collection and processing may help mitigate these biases and help us accumulate findings from different studies based on different sources.

Conclusion

Networks are an inherent component of the social world and, in relation to white-collar and corporate crimes, represent an important analytical dimension for understanding how offenders are connected to co-offenders, but also to other actors and nodes that are in some way related to the offending behaviour; a majority of white-collar and corporate crimes are conspiratorial in nature and organisation. In terms of those complicit and cooperating offenders, we also need to understand the extent and ease (or difficulty) to which willing criminals can identify and recruit co-offenders who are necessary or helpful for any given set of offences.

Social and dynamic network approaches enable us to identify the key players who occupy strategic (or vulnerable) positions within the network of the crime commission process, from where they oversee and control the various phases (scenes) and, in some cases, perform as interlocutors and brokers between different actors and resources. These actors may also exist within different sub-networks, creating a multiplex of various layers of network interaction. Network 'nodes' can represent various entities (people, organisations, resources, locations) involved in the scene, and the 'ties' between nodes represent the type of actions performed. Alongside this, as explored in Chapter 2, we can deconstruct the 'scripts' (i.e., scenes, actors, facets, permutations) of white-collar crimes and integrate these with the varying 'networks' (actors, roles, locations, products, and relations). This helps us understand what was done and what has to be done by whom in different 'scenes' in order to carry out the offences/behaviours. These 'scripts' and 'networks' can become part of lesson learning to help devise preventative and intervention measures more rigorously – that is, where to focus attention and the types of data required – as well as evaluate the impact of intervention on networks. In relation to organised crime activities, it has been evidenced that removing actors based on betweenness centrally is most efficient, followed by targeting the actors who possess the money (Bright et al., 2017), but whether this also applies to white-collar offending – both generally and for specific types – is not known.

White-collar and corporate crimes pose different questions for those seeking to understand criminal networks, as, unlike the organised crime groups that are predominant focus of social network analyses, where there is an obvious need for the network to remain secret and covert, white-collar crime networks are embedded in ostensible legitimacy as part of routine business and organisational environments. There are even cases in which the offending activities are not concealed. This includes aspects of the LIBOR manipulation and potentially other cases whereby internal interpretations of certain behaviours differ from those external to the organisation, such as where business actors perceive their offending as common business practice or even as lawful. These are crucial distinctions, particularly in relation to the tendencies of many white-collar offenders not to think they are actually doing anything wrong. There is a great need for empirical research into the networks of white-collar and corporate crimes, particular to aid an understanding of the relationships between networks and opportunity dynamics and required skills and knowledge and social/criminal networks at the elite end of society.

4 Finances

Introduction

A common and recurring theme across the varied behaviours analysed within the conceptual parameters of white-collar and corporate crimes is the centrality of finance and economic capital to the organisation of the activities. Of course, in terms of motivations, these are often crimes of finance, generating individual and/or organisational financial gains, either in the form of profit or savings, though gains may be less tangible (e.g., avoiding loss of face or social standing, but usually alongside financial gain). These finances need managing in some way, such as via varied methods of concealment or conversion, in order for the offenders to retain control and have access to usable assets in the legitimate economy. Similarly, in terms of the organisation of the behaviours, funds may be needed, directly or indirectly, to invest in, or cover, the operational or infrastructural costs of the commissioning of the white-collar crimes. For instance, in terms of resources, how are the funds for the crimes acquired and used without raising suspicion from peers or auditors, especially in a public company? In terms of costs, how do offenders arrange the opening of secret bank accounts or front companies in offshore locations to conceal the movement of illicit finances? This chapter engages with these important analytical questions to understand some of the material capacities of white-collar crime commission (see Chapter 6), and to present a framework for understanding the finances of white-collar and corporate crimes.

In terms of analysing how the finances of white-collar crimes are organised, unlike the outright pre-planned frauds that use businesses as a front for illegal schemes (e.g., VAT carousels, government COVID-19 frauds) or the illicit markets (e.g., the trade in illegal products and services) that are the normal focus of studies on illicit finance and money laundering, white-collar and corporate crimes are mostly committed by ostensibly legitimate businesses and organisations or professionals through the course of their occupations and occur in legitimate and legal markets. That is, legitimate occupational positions, organisational settings, and business practices/processes are key aspects of the opportunity structures of white-collar and corporate crimes (see Benson et al., 2024) and provide 'ready-made' markets, structures, and social networks

DOI: 10.4324/9781315100227-4

through which to conceal illicit behaviours. The financial aspects of white-collar and corporate crimes also reflect these otherwise legitimate business and organisational conditions; such crimes are 'parasitical' on legitimate business practices in which illicit behaviours can be conveniently concealed behind the daily routine behaviours of the offenders' legitimate occupations (Benson et al., 2024) and (in the eyes of third parties – bankers, legal professionals, and others – who may have anti-money laundering and financial sanctions obligations to exercise 'due diligence') in the forms of commercial organisation that mimic those of legitimate activities and constructions. Deconstructing such routines has a cost borne almost entirely by the third party.

With this in mind, we first analyse the *finances for* and the *finances from* white-collar crimes before exploring mechanisms and strategies for conversion, control, and concealment of any illicit finance. In doing so, we draw on the framework of Lord and Levi (2017) and their analysis of the financial aspects of transnational corporate corruption. That white-collar and corporate crimes require finance in some way is well known, but these financial aspects have not been sufficiently conceptualised. We address this gap by asking key empirical questions that need to be addressed to understand the financial components of white-collar and corporate crimes. For instance, what needs to be financed; how much finance is needed; and how are the finances generated, managed, and distributed? Similarly, what are the different forms of proceeds that emerge, how can offenders conceal the derivation of funds from these crimes while also retaining control over them, and how do they overcome particular obstacles and problems posed by controls (such as anti-money laundering)? This chapter addresses such core questions.

Furthermore, we foreground an analysis of the role of third-party facilitators and enablers (e.g., lawyers, bankers, accountants) who intentionally, incompetently, or unknowingly facilitate a range of white-collar and corporate crimes. While there is often an assumption that profits made through white-collar crime are absorbed as profit, we examine how such financial gain can also be reinvested back into criminal enterprise, a process more commonly associated with 'organised crime'. Indeed, this happens routinely when businesses on a 'slippery slope' towards collapse tell lies to stave off creditors and reinvest sales and sometimes employee pension funds to keep going. A focus on the money component of white-collar and corporate crimes not only helps us understand the organisation of these crimes, but also offers a plausible situational route to intervention. We again draw on our earlier empirical research into and expertise in white-collar and corporate crimes more generally to present an analytical and conceptual framework for investigating the organisation of such crimes.

The Finances *for* and *From* White-Collar and Corporate Crimes

Criminological theory, and, more specifically, crime script analysis, as we discussed in Chapter 3, provide a useful lens through which to analyse the financial aspects of white-collar and corporate crimes. They encourage us to think through the various operational and investment/infrastructural financial procedural requirements before, during, and after white-collar and corporate criminal activities. The financial components reflect the nature of the opportunity structures and corresponding scripts (Chapter 2), the actors involved as part of the criminal/social network (Chapter 3), and the capacities the individuals possess as part of their social relations within their organisations (Chapter 5). Thus, understanding the dynamics of opportunity and offending has implications for how the finances for and from these crimes must be organised, allowing us to focus on understanding the organisation of white-collar crime finances in terms of 'how would-be offenders confront problems of gaining finance, gaining access to crime opportunities, and retaining their freedom and crime proceeds' (Levi, 2009: 225).

For example, depending on the 'scripts' of particular white-collar crimes (see Chapter 2), the financial aspects will vary in terms of the context-specific, contingently necessary requirements of the commission process. For instance, generating or accessing finance or capital may be a necessary precursor to the crime, such as when traders or brokers engage in illegal front-running, as the buying or selling of shares requires financial capital. Alternatively, making use of finances for the activities of particular scenes in a white-collar crime script may represent one facet or pathway to successfully accomplishing the objectives, such as a cash payment versus promising future employment for a public official's child to induce the official with responsibilities for awarding contracts to give the contract to you. However, finances may also be contingently connected to white-collar crime commissioning, because if access to capital cannot be obtained, the front-running or the bribery may be hindered, changing the dynamics or even the capability of the intended white-collar crimes.

The upfront or trust capital of white-collar (and other) crimes varies. Not all white-collar crimes require the creation of finances in order to be carried out, but many will, and almost all will involve the generation of financial value. Finances needed for (and generated by) crimes are contingent on various antecedents that we explore next, including whether trusted others are key to facilitate the control, concealment, and/or conversion of the finances. With these varying aspects in mind, this section considers two sets of three analytical questions that relate to the finances *for* and *from* white-collar and corporate crimes:

The finances *for* white-collar crimes (inflows):

- What needs to be financed?
- How much finance is needed?
- How are the finances generated, managed, and distributed?

The finances *from* white-collar crimes (outflows):

- What are the different forms of proceeds that emerge?
- How can offenders conceal the derivation of funds from these crimes while also retaining control over them?

- How do they overcome particular obstacles and problems posed by controls (such as anti–money laundering and anti-bribery)?

It is important to think through finance issues in the context of the range of different white-collar and corporate crimes as well as the sort of perpetrators who are in some way involved. Some actors may operate alone and conceal their activities and intentions from their colleagues if necessary. In other cases, actors knowingly collaborate or are unknowingly or sometimes recklessly (i.e., see there is a risk and ignore it) incorporated into the criminal enterprise. However, in all cases, a defining feature is the pre-existing access to the legitimate offending environment and to legitimate business or organisational practices or mechanisms for generating and managing finances. But the range of actors involved will shape the dynamics of the financial aspects, whilst different actors and different opportunity structures will have different starting resources for the crimes, and this will likely vary over time and place. (It is rare and unlikely, for instance, that white-collar criminals will seek illicit sources to instigate their crimes when such resource can be obtained through legitimate means, even if the latter involves deception.) We should also distinguish personal illegal benefits, like embezzlement, from acts like bribery and price fixing that are for the benefit of the firm (unless detected) as well as perhaps for the individual(s) involved. This, of course, has implications for the control or concealment of the benefits generated.

The two sets of questions here encourage us to think through how these finance issues will be addressed. These questions will lead to a consideration of the likely financial inflows and outflows and correspond to what is needed for or generated from the direct and/or indirect operational, investment/infrastructural, and financial aspects of the crime commission process. Figure 4.1 visualises these financial aspects. *Inflows* refers to the transition of monies, if needed for the particular white-collar crime, intended to be used for particular financial costs associated with the activities. This might involve the diversion of existing and otherwise legally derived financial resource within a business or organisation. *Outflows* refers to the transition of financial value out of the white-collar crime for organisational or personal gains, or both, if needed, though sometimes the objective of the crime (e.g., with some anti-trust violations and continuing to trade whilst insolvent) is to maintain the organisation itself. This illicit value might be reinvested into further criminal activities or diverted to the funding of a 'criminal' lifestyle. For example, in cases of corporate foreign bribery, we see the concealment of existing company capital in the accounts behind opaque transactions such as moving funds for 'insurance', 'consultancy', or 'commissions', with value being generated in the form of contracts with foreign governments that, in turn, benefit the company and the employees involved. Or it might involve the creation of new finances internally or externally, obtained lawfully, but intended to be used to fund criminal activities. For example, the COVID-19 pandemic and associated economic crisis led to the creation of state-backed financial support schemes for existing businesses, such as the Bounce Back loan scheme in the UK, but some companies abused the system to obtain funds for unscrupulous purposes, such as the purchase of sports cars or to invest in fixed assets for personal gain, rather than business support.[1] Others created or purchased new companies and claimed for support to which they were not entitled. These were in addition to the large number of scams and corrupt contracts involving personal protection equipment (Levi, 2023). The rapid implementation of such schemes in times of financial, or other, crisis is often accompanied by light regulatory oversight and reduced transparency, in turn creating opportunities for such behaviours, as critical reports on COVID-19 support administration by the UK National Audit Office and the US General Accounting Office have indicated. But financial inflows are not always necessary for some white-collar crimes. For instance, corporate accounting frauds, such as that involving the German payment provider Wirecard, demonstrate how corporate frauds might, in fact, be based on the fabrication of non-existent financial stocks and flows with a view to inflating share prices and, in turn, generating illicit financial value (McCrum, 2022).[2] Methods often employed in white-collar crimes to control inflows and outflows generally involve deception, abuse of trust, and some form of concealment and conspiracy with others. Whilst using cash might offer the greatest anonymity to those involved, this is not pragmatically accessible within corporations where transactions are predominantly electronic with corresponding bookkeeping. The diversion of internal funds might be simplistic or complex, such as when utilising contrived financial arrangements with legal structures, so-called 'corporate vehicles', in multiple jurisdictions is key to how funds flow across borders.

Inflows are used to fund direct and/or indirect operational, investment/infrastructural, and other financial activities which, in turn, lead to outflows:

Operational costs: These relate to the finances required to enable the daily routine activities of the white-collar criminal enterprise that are central to the (continued) functioning of the crime. These costs are likely to be at the low-to-medium end of the cost spectrum, but more frequent, and relate to expenses and personnel (e.g., wages/payments for formal or informal services, such as the provision of data and information, or corrupt payments by newspapers to journalists and their sources or intermediaries for celebrity stories). We could also include in our analysis the financial cost of less

1 This Is Money (2020) 'Fraud fears over £31bn Rishi loans: Experts report some small business owners are using the 'emergency' cash to buy Ferraris', 13 July. https://www.thisismoney.co.uk/money/news/article-8518771/Fraud-fears-Rishi-loans-Emergency-cash-used-buy-Ferraris.html

2 FT (2020) 'Wirecard fights for survival as it admits scale of fraud', 22 June. https://www.ft.com/content/2581fda5-8c89-46b5-9acf-ba8a88d74d88

tangible materials, such as the use of company phones to organise a market manipulation conspiracy.

Investment/infrastructural: The inflows into investment and infrastructure relate to the funding of key locations and materials, such as buildings and facilities, or core service provisions (e.g., buildings, vehicles, and accommodation may be purchased to host and serve clients as part of illicit relations). These costs are likely to be at the medium-to-higher end of the cost spectrum but be less frequent.

Other financial activities: Other financial requirements might relate to standalone expenses that are neither ongoing nor investment in the enterprise, such as pay-offs and commissions in cases of bribery.

Necessity and Contingency in the Finances of White-Collar Crimes

In this financial 'model', we distinguish between the *necessary structures and relations* and the *contingent structures and relations* of the financial aspects of the white-collar crimes. Here we draw on the discussion in Chapter 2. There, we argued that, in terms of explanation, it is useful to distinguish between those relations, practices, and mechanisms that are *necessary* to white-collar crime commission and their *contingent* connections to the range of conditions that enable or restrict the crimes taking place. As the finances of white-collar crimes constitute social objects and relations that can have causal powers and liabilities (see Chapter 6), it logically follows that we can seek to analyse those financial aspects that are necessary or contingent to the white-collar crime commission process.

The *necessary structures and relations* reflect particular white-collar crime events and those processes, activities, and interactions that *must* occur for the specified white-collar crimes to take place after a conducive opportunity structure, generated as part of patterns of routine business or organisational activities, has been recognised, and the crime visualised. For instance, in Chapter 2 on scripts, we revisited the perspective of routine activities to consider the interaction and convergence of specific situations (e.g., a culture that institutionalises a tolerance of unethical risk taking), a target (e.g., the perceived simplicity of a particular white-collar crime), and the absence of capable guardians (e.g., a vulnerability in the processes of internal and/or external auditors) at particular times. These necessary aspects of the crime commission process will map onto particular operational, investment/infrastructural, and other financial requirements. Considering these dimensions, we might ask: In what ways do different necessary events or actions that constitute the sequence or procedures offenders must go through require funding? What needs financing before, during, and after the crimes? Which business practices or processes permit the financing of these dimensions and the concealment of the proceeds? Which capacities and skills are needed by which actors in the network to facilitate the crimes? Understanding these questions empirically builds a picture of the necessary financial aspects of any given white-collar

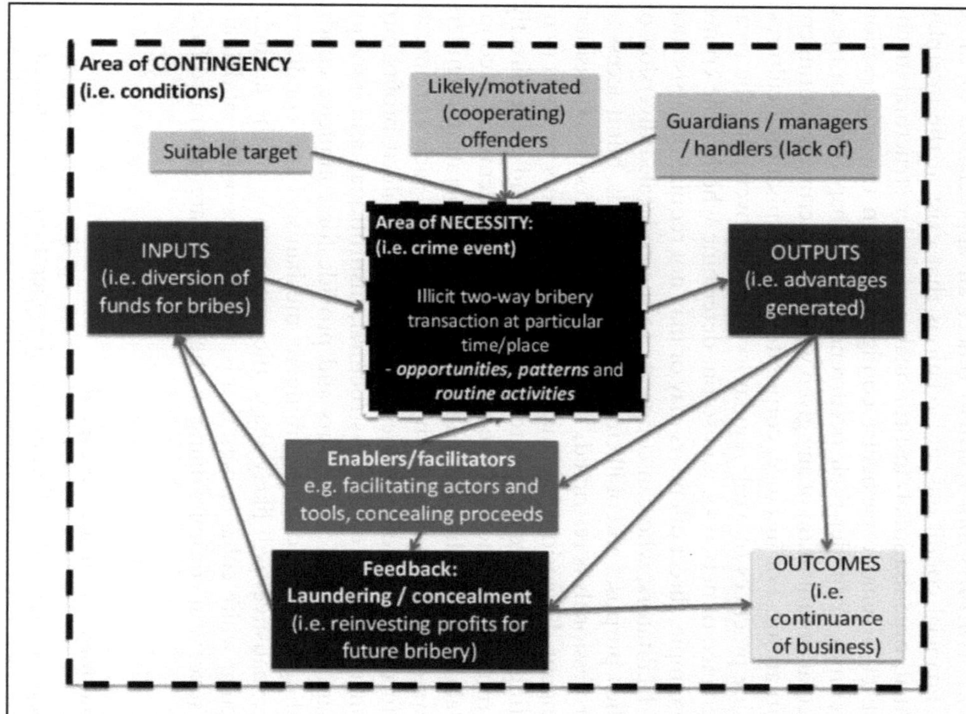

Figure 4.1 Necessary and Contingent Financial Structures and Relations[3]

3 Lord, N. and Levi, M. (2017) 'Organizing the finances for and the finances from transnational corporate bribery', *European Journal of Criminology*, 14(3), pp. 365–389. Copyright © 2017 by (Sage Publications). Reprinted by Permission of Sage Publications. Adapted to 'white-collar crime' scripts.

crime. For instance, whilst there may be certain financial fundamentals of the crime commission process, these necessary mechanisms also reflect individual, social, cultural, and material capacities (Chapter 6), including network relations (Chapter 3), that shape whether the crimes can be competently realised. Pre-existing knowledge, skills, and expertise in managing the inflows and outflows of finances for criminal purposes, for example, may be necessary components of the script.

The *contingent structures and relations* reflect an appreciation of those context-specific financial conditions and relations that exist at the interplay between individual, organisational/institutional, and wider structural mechanisms that restrict or enable particular configurations in the organisation of white-collar crimes or hinder their occurrence. (See Chapter 6.) In these terms, the particular organisation of any given white-collar crime is contingent on connected situations. For instance, corporate and organisational cultures, embedded routine practices of weak regulatory or other oversight, the creation and maintenance of networks, and so on, determine whether the crimes will occur. For example, direct offenders may or may not require the assistance of enablers and facilitators, who can cooperate in the concealed diversion of licit funds for illicit purposes and of illicit profits and proceeds, but if access to this group of professionals is restricted, the crimes may not occur. Considering these contingent dimensions, we might ask: Which actors or tools (wittingly or unwittingly) facilitate the white-collar crimes beyond those directly involved in the transaction, and how are such actors/tools identified as cooperators and collaborators by direct offenders? How do cooperating offenders conceal the flows of monies for or from illicit transactions, such as reinvesting profits for future white-collar crimes or incorporating illicit profits into the corporate finances? How do social-structural, institutional, and immediate contexts shape individual behaviours and provide for conducive conditions for offending? The following contingent mechanisms and conditions (the list is not exhaustive) will likely shape the organisation of the financial aspects of particular white-collar crimes: that is, the finances or capital that are needed for the successful commissioning of the crime, or are generated from the crimes:

- **Purpose and form of finances or capital**

The finances, as mentioned earlier, may be for operational, investment/infrastructural, or other financial purposes. The aims and actions include the continuation of the current and future criminal enterprise, but also the use of such funds for otherwise legitimate purchases (e.g., luxury goods and travel). These varying purposes will influence *how* the finances are created and diverted. Similarly, the form in which such financial assets are needed, such as for monetary (e.g., cash or invoiced payments to co-conspirators for real or fictitious services or electronic payments to Ponzi scheme investors), or non-monetary purposes (e.g., provision of tangible gifts, employment of relatives of the target[4] or targets themselves in corruption cases) will also shape the financial requirements and arrangements. Likewise, the nature of the crime is important: frauds will involve the voluntary transferring of wealth to offenders, embezzlement will involve the theft of lawful funds or assets from unknowing victims, while bribery will involve the giving of funds of legal and/or illegal origin for criminal intentions, or sometimes for the apparently licit intention of getting a contract they think they otherwise would not win.

One of the advantages enjoyed for financing by Ponzi schemes is that new investors provide the capital for repayment promises, but early actual repayments – which give the schemes their credibility – will have to be phased out (or the investors persuaded to re-invest their paper profits), or else the scheme organisers will not profit. Both Bernie Madoff and Allen Stanford (as well as Elizabeth Holmes in non-Ponzi scheme Theranos) used public involvement with and support by prominent people to give credibility to their large-scale enterprises, increasing the stability of investments by their victims, who were reassured by their presence. AI deepfakes can now be used, though they are useful more for short cons, as the person(s) faked may discover and complain, and advertising may be privately or publicly taken down, disrupting the scam or the AI-faked attack on the credibility of the person/business.

- **Nature of criminal/social network**

Does the white-collar crime involve individual actors, small groups within and/or outside a corporation, or more extensive networks? What are the significant ties that exists between cooperating actors, or those unwittingly involved or implicated? Which financial roles do these actors play? At which level of particular organisations are involved employees located (for example, 'ordinary employees', 'middle managers', and/or 'board executives')?

- **Nature of organisation**

How simple or complex are the human and/or financial structures used in the commissioning of the crime? Does it involve the use of corporate vehicles or offshore accounts; third-party professionals, intermediaries, and agents; and so on? How elaborate are the arrangements that are created for larger or smaller schemes, and who is involved in the creations of these, directly or indirectly?

4 In some Chinese corruption and building up influence cases, this was known as hiring 'princelings', often the children of party elites, but this approach was not restricted to China.

- **Level of pervasiveness**

  Is the white-collar crime pervasive within the organisation or occupational setting? Does it involve isolated, discrete incidents or systemic/ongoing states and conditions? How are finances kept secret from co-employees, if necessary?

- **Level of intent**

  Is the white-collar crime pre-planned well in advance, or is it more organic and responsive? (That is, is the white-collar crime, and therefore the required finances, part of a 'slippery slope' drift into crime or part of a more predetermined strategy?)

- **Size of organisation**

  Does the white-collar crime occur in small and medium enterprises, or larger organisations?

These contingent factors shape the finances that are needed or generated and, consequently, the particular ways in which any given white-collar crimes are organised. Concrete research, involving processes of abstraction and empirical observation, on the financial aspects of white-collar crimes can illuminate key causal mechanisms that come together with other aspects of the script in the commissioning or unfolding of white-collar crimes. It is not possible here to provide a comprehensive set of all possible realities within this very broad set of conditions. However, as part of analysing the financial aspects of any given white-collar crime, it is of benefit to identify all possible finances and actors involved before evaluating which aspects of the crimes are more costly than others and which are more frequent than others to gain insight in the necessary and contingent financial aspects of white-collar crimes. This can, in turn, inform an understanding of which finances are central to the white-collar crimes and offer an evidence-based route to intervention, along with informing explanatory accounts of the offending.

Case Example 1: Analysing the Finances of Transnational Corporate Bribery

Transnational corporate bribery is a white-collar and corporate crime that we have examined in great detail, in particular in terms of the regulation and control of these behaviours. (See Lord, 2014, 2015; Lord and Levi, 2015, 2017.) Referred to also as 'foreign', 'overseas', or 'international' bribery, it involves otherwise legitimate businesses that operate in markets outside their domestic setting and engage in corrupt transactions with public officials in those or other jurisdictions to win or maintain business contracts and interests. Transnational corporate bribery has emerged as a priority concern for nation-states, particularly as they are pressured to meet the legal and normative expectations and requirements of domestic and international anti-corruption communities, including intergovernmental organisations such as the OECD and UN, and their legal frameworks, and civil society organisations such as Transparency International. The accompanying scrutiny of legal implementations and monitoring of enforcement in individual countries ensure it remains of political concern domestically. (It is not suggested that only transnational bribery is of concern; countries can and do experience varying levels of domestic bribery: for example, in purchasing goods and services. However, less international pressure can be exerted on this.)

Transnational corporate bribery can be described as 'grand' – that is, where we see financially or materially substantial inducements made or offered, usually to senior political actors or their proxies, to win major procurement contracts – or 'petty', where we see small-scale payments, usually cash, used to facilitate or expedite particular processes or services that benefit a company, such as quick access for trucks through borders. In this chapter, we focus on the finances of the former, and the capital needed to cover varied inducements, such as monetary payments (commissions, kickbacks, etc.), valuable goods (lavish gifts, regular shopping expenditures, or other leisure activities), or less direct hospitalities (trips to exotic locations for seemingly lawful purposes). The money trail of these 'grand' transactions has received the most attention and scrutiny, but also represents an important strategic issue in the context of wider reform, such as is seen in attempts to make transparent the beneficial owners of corporate vehicles used for controlling illicit monies (e.g., the Corporate Transparency Act in the US or Companies House reform/the Economic Crime (Transparency and Enforcement) Act 2022 in the UK). A key defining feature in all these cases is the inherently illicit transaction (a specific event) or relationship (an ongoing state) between at least two willing or consenting active/passive actors that leads to an advantage in business for the corporation. (See Lord, 2014, for a more detailed analysis.) Transparency International (2021: website) suggests that grand corruption relates to offences against the UN Convention Against Corruption Articles 15–25 when

> committed as part of a scheme involving a high-level public official and comprising a significant misappropriation of public funds or resources, or severely restricting the exercise of the most basic human rights of a substantial part of the population or of a vulnerable group.

This would also include politically exposed persons.

At its most basic level of organisation, transnational bribery requires the creation or diversion of company funds or capital to fund the corrupt transaction(s). However, the scripts of these processes can vary depending on the contingent needs or conditions of the corrupt agreement, resulting in varying levels of organisational complexity, cooperating networks, pervasiveness, and need for concealment and conversion. For instance, the organisational requirements of creating 'slush funds' that are disguised in accounts attached to corporate vehicles formed as part of contrived financial structures in order to provide pay-offs to officials in other countries differ from the requirements for writing 'kickbacks', usually in the form of a value percentage of a contract, into agreements with corrupt officials. Although, in principle, such transactions could feasibly involve only two actors (briber and bribee), in practice, most cases involve multiple cooperating actors, within and outside the company, or social/professional networks of those actors core to the conspiracy; the networks shape the ways in which finances are generated and organised. In these terms, multiplexity may be a feature of such criminal networks, particularly in terms of pre-existing, established networks that are usually horizontally, rather than vertically structured, and such networks may vary in terms of their place on the ephemeral-to-longstanding axis, becoming more or less active over the duration of the bribery scheme. (See Chapter 3; Diviák and Lord, 2022.)

Deception, abuse of trust, and concealment/conspiracy are common techniques for white-collar offenders (Benson et al., 2024), and we see this with transnational corporate bribery and associated finances. For instance, unless the bribery is organised and pervasive across the whole corporation – that is, part of an internally transparent culture of corruption – offenders would need to hide their illicit activities and finances from uninvolved co-workers. For example, companies must keep detailed accounting records and potentially make them available to internal and external auditors, meaning competent offenders will aim to conceal their behaviour, and the risks posed to them depend on how active and competent the 'capable guardians' are. Concealing illicit transactions in larger corporations may be more straightforward due to the diffusion of activities and the volume of transactions (though internal and external auditing is sometimes stricter), but less so in smaller companies, making detection and subsequent individual accountability more likely, as senior managers and executives will be more closely connected to the bribery. That said, 'most bribes are paid by employees and agents, not top management' (Rose-Ackerman, 1999: 57).

When uninvolved colleagues become aware of the bribery, they may face obstacles to reporting, as 'walls of secrecy and silence' can emerge where cognitive dissonance, concerted ignorance, inaction in the face of knowing, or the fear of the consequences of disclosure of colleagues can create facilitative criminal conditions, particularly when the offenders are respected or central figures in the business. (See van de Bunt, 2010.) Those who do make disclosures, including compliance departments raising concern over such behaviours if they identify them, may also be neutralised by corporate interests and threats. Whether large whistle-blower rewards (most notably by the US SEC and tax authorities) can have much impact on this intra-corporate silence and stigma remains uncertain.

The Finances for *Corporate Bribery*

This section considers the first three questions outlined earlier:

- What needs to be financed?
- How much finance is needed?
- How are the processes inherent in this business organised to generate and distribute these finances in order for corporate bribery to take place?

When analysing the finances for bribery, legitimate corporations – or the employees acting on their behalf (for example, ordinary employees, middle managers, agents) – that enter into bribery arrangements must calculate the funds required for bribes, whether a one-off transaction or as part of an ongoing set of transactions, when opportunities arise through their business practices, and they must conceal these illicit practices from colleagues and/or routine detection mechanisms. Decisions to bribe are likely to be 'rational' (but bounded – that is, limited – by normative awareness, ignorance, imperfect information, or organisational cultures) calculations, because organisational economic interests guide the decision-making process of employees, although organisational cultures may promote redefined parameters of acceptable behaviours (for example, if neutralised in the light of competitor behaviour), or offenders may not be aware of legal requirements, even when operating in officially defined high-risk jurisdictions, if they bypass compliance officers who should be aware of these risks. (This latter scenario undermines models of rational choice theories, even when it contains an element of wilful blindness – 'if you don't ask, you won't find out what is not allowed'.) Furthermore, in terms of the level of pervasiveness, corporate bribery rarely involves an isolated, discrete incident but rather is a series of discrete incidents or is more systemic, reflecting an ongoing state or condition, or a series of illicit transactions. This determines how the finances will need to be generated by the bribing firm and individuals involved, and how it will need to be accounted for in the business. This is not an issue for bribery cases only, but also with other types of white-collar crime. For instance, when news organisations pay staff and/or outsiders for hacking into celebrities' media, this may need to be justified for accounting purposes, creating offences of false accounting.

In terms of the actual monies involved, it is clear that the finances needed for grand bribery are substantial. For example, Airbus SE is a major aerospace company registered in the Netherlands but with multinational operations, and is the world's largest aircraft manufacturer, as well as a major producer of civil and military aerospace products. In January 2020, Airbus SE negotiated a global settlement with US, UK, and French authorities[5] to bring to a conclusion to

5 In the US, Airbus SE entered into a DPA with the Department of Justice (DoJ) and a consent agreement with the Department of State. In France, the functional equivalent of a DPA is the

alleged bribery, and failures to prevent bribery, in multiple countries, including Malaysia, Sri Lanka, Taiwan, Indonesia, and Ghana. The non-trial agreements required Airbus SE to pay approximately €3.6 billion (including just over €2 billion to the French authorities, almost €526 million to the US authorities, and €991 million to the UK authorities). The case involved multiple counts of bribery. To quote one example from the UK Serious Fraud Office's DPA with respect to the conduct in Malaysia, the statement of facts indicated that:

> Between October 2013 and January 2015 EADS[6] France SAS, later Airbus Group SAS, paid US$50 million as sponsorship for a sports team ('Sports team'). The Sports team was jointly owned by AirAsia Executive 1 and AirAsia Executive 2 but was legally unrelated to AirAsia and AirAsia X. Airbus employees also offered an additional US$55 million. This offer was not finalised and no payment was made.[7]

This represents just one of many counts across the three jurisdictions but illustrates the substantial level of the funds required for the bribery (US$105 million). In terms of the UK DPA, almost €586 million was disgorged from Airbus SE in reflection of the profits made in the counts brought in the UK, indicating the substantial capital or material benefit derived from the bribery. There are many other cases, such as Rolls Royce in the UK, Siemens in Germany, Elf Aquitaine in France, Telia in Sweden and the Netherlands, Odebrecht in Brazil, and Och-Ziff in the US. The bribes involved in these cases are a variable, but sometimes modest sub-set of the harm done to the victims. Both the bribe takers and the bribe givers seek a 'satisficing' rather than a maximum benefit, but the collateral damage from bribery and other corporate crimes is often far greater than the direct profits to the individual, networked, and corporate perpetrators.

In terms of common methods of organisation across these cases, we can decipher the following:

- Falsification or obfuscation of accounting records to conceal irregular payments – constitutes an ***abuse of trust and concealment.***
- Improper payments/inducements made via 'middlemen', intermediaries, or agents in corresponding countries. These payments cover costs/commissions of the agent/intermediary plus subsequent bribes, often determined as a percentage of the contract gained or product sales – ***conspiracy.***
- Monies transferred via corporate vehicles and complex financial structures such as offshore accounts – ***deception, diversion, and concealment.***

Convention Judiciaire d'Intérêt Public (Judicial Public Interest Agreement), which Airbus SE entered into with the Parquet National Financier (PNF).

6 European Aeronautic Defence and Space Company France.

7 Airbus SE-SFO DPA statement of facts, p. 12.

The purposes of a corporate bribe can vary, and the forms of bribes have been variously conceptualised and categorised, and this has implications for the type of finances required and how they are generated. For example, distinctions have been made between bribes that are 'according to rule' and bribes that are 'against the rule'. (See Oldenburg, 1987.) The distinction here refers to whether or not the underlying purpose of the bribe is to ensure the commission and/or omission of an act that a public official would otherwise undertake as part of their routine daily activities. In most grand bribery cases targeted by enforcement authorities, public officials receiving or demanding bribes would be acting 'against the rule': that is, breaching their occupational duties, such as notifying a particular company of the details of competitor bids during the tendering process for public procurement contracts, or awarding a contract to a company that is less suited to state/public needs than another in exchange for a bribe (that is, the official is abusing the trust inherent in the occupational role). Whilst many cases may also involve 'according to rule' bribery, for instance when a border official expedites the movement of lorries through checkpoints on receipt of a pay-off (that is, allowing legitimate lorries through borders is part of the official's occupational role) or the accelerating of an application process for the granting of a permit or licence. As Rose-Ackerman (1999: 15) notes, '[s]ince time is money, firms and individuals will pay to avoid delay. In many countries a telephone, a passport, or a driver's licence cannot be obtained expeditiously without a pay-off'. However, such 'petty' bribes seldom retain the focus of enforcement authorities looking into transnational corporate bribery, who pursue the 'big fish' or may not have a remit to pursue facilitating payments which are not always criminalised (as they are not in the US under the FCPA 1977).

The particular forms of the bribes themselves can vary. For example, some are of a monetary or money-equivalent nature, and others are not. An OECD (2007) paper analysed known cases of bribery in public procurement and demonstrated that a range of tangible benefits may be given, including gifts, travel, entertainment, payment of domestic expenses, works in private homes, computers, jewels or expensive watches, free shares in companies, and sexual services. The paper established that money, either in cash or electronic form via commissions and fees, is often desirable as it is 'rapid, simple and practical' and brings immediate value (OECD, 2007: 47). Though anti–money laundering and (for example, in Latin America) anti-corruption efforts have been developing since then, these points remain valid. As the report indicates,

> Money may be given in hand; but money is most frequently transferred to the official's account or an account designated by the official (e.g. a third party beneficiary). The account may be located in a foreign bank, perhaps in an offshore centre. Bribers may also give the bribee or a third party free disposal of a credit card on a company's account or offer free shares in a company. Finally, a case was presented where the bribe was organised via a loan that was never reimbursed. The types of arrangement

> in these last two examples are considered particularly difficult to detect and investigate.
>
> (OECD, 2007: 47)

Thus, cash bribes may be taken from large commission fees paid to the third party may be regular payments to encourage officials to turn a blind eye to illegal activities (drugs/people/mineral smuggling, etc.) or may be standalone, one-off payments for a specific act or omission. The purpose of the pay-off may sometimes go beyond the inducing of or a faster decision about a specific act or omission and intend to acquire the official for an extended period of time. (An exclusive focus on individual transactions would be a mistake since bribes can be part of a cumulative process, and it may be hard for individuals who once 'fall' to get out of future transactions since they may be susceptible to blackmail.) Synonyms of 'pay-off' include kickback, grease money, and baksheesh.[8] Commissions usually take the form of a percentage of the money received for a given transaction or a sum to the responsible agent or intermediary. Cash or valuable considerations such as businesses, real estate, or securities may involve written contracts that appear to be lawful. For instance, in the case of Sarclad Ltd in the UK, a company that designs and manufactures technology for the metal industry, selling products internationally, bribes were paid systematically via a network of intermediary agents working in foreign countries. Sarclad entered into agreements with these agents, providing remuneration through commission as a percentage of the value of the contracts subsequently won for the company.

We can distinguish between the direct and indirect costs of bribery. Direct costs include the amount required for the bribe itself, whether cash or other monetary value (for example, shopping trips, hospitalities). Cash poses particular questions about how offenders are able to conceal from or deceive colleagues when withdrawing cash from corporate accounts, or involve them as conspirators, even if they are simply following instructions. However, in the current legal environment of anti–money laundering, potential theft allegations, and the UK Bribery Act, it is hard to see how accounts staff can easily go along with this undeceived, even if they are disincentivised by the fear of dismissal or non-promotion to ask questions of their senior executives. Nonetheless, in such cases, offshore accounts and shell firms can obscure the transfer of monies cross-jurisdictionally in order to protect beneficial owners of particular accounts but also enable corporations and offenders to move money electronically, hidden as ambiguous (and creative) accounting/financial transactions (for example, 'services', 'commissions') before cash is withdrawn in less regulated systems and directed to foreign public officials. Indirect costs include the company resources required, such as the investment of time by

8 'Baksheesh' refers to a small amount of money or a gift that can be given as a tip or a bribe to persuade someone to do something favourable for the giver that is common in parts of Asia, Africa, and the Middle East.

employees away from wholly legitimate business activities or the use of company equipment and technologies. Time and material resources are required for the bribery: planning, commission, post-crime risk management, concealment of profits, and so on, all require resourcing. Other indirect costs may be actual regulatory fines and criminal penalties, plus supervision costs, but these accrue only if and when action is taken. (Regulators, prosecutors, and judges can also sometimes be bribed.)

It is not possible to estimate the figures involved in all direct and especially indirect costs. Indirect costs do not really have to be paid specifically, and to the extent that the bribes are for the firm to get business, they are balanced against the benefits. However, understanding the wider finances involved in bribery is important for when we begin to consider how to prevent bribery from taking place. In both cases, bribes that originate with particular corporations must be accounted for, even if they are distributed via third parties and obscure accounting practices, and some records must exist, given the finances generated from pre-existing income from legitimate means (at least in the primary/initial bribery transaction). Financing crime is inhibited by the risks both of losing the investment and of introducing criminal liability to those who otherwise would not face the risk of prosecution (Levi, 2015: 3).

The Finances From *Corporate Bribery*

This section addresses a further three questions outlined earlier:

- What are the different forms of proceeds that emerge out of the bribery?
- How do offenders conceal the derivation of funds from these crimes while also retaining control over them?
- How do they overcome particular obstacles and problems posed by controls (such as anti–money laundering)?

Except in cases of extortion by the bribee (easiest when the bribe payer has many fixed assets in the bribee's jurisdiction), the finances generated by the bribery for the briber are at least equal to, but likely even greater than, the finances required for the bribery; otherwise, the illicit transaction has no economic rationality. The finances from transnational corporate bribery at the 'grand' level most frequently include direct and tangible advantages such as the awarding of a business contract or the granting of a particular permit for business operations. The value of such tangible outputs can be determined through assessing, for instance, the value of the contract obtained (formal disgorgement as part of enforcement actions takes this objective approach) or the potential business generated through access to a particular market or area, although the latter scenario presents greater valuation obstacles than the former.

Although such advantages are direct, in some cases, it can be difficult to ascertain their financial value, particularly when assessing the value of gains from low-level 'petty' corruption or 'facilitation payments', but in all cases, some form of monetary advantage is obtained. Facilitation payments in reality increase business operating costs, because payments may be unexpected and inconsistent, although it is likely risk assessments undertaken by corporations would identify such possibilities. In the aggregate, these 'bribes' can be costly, but, in contrast to the financial gain at the high end, they remain worthwhile 'expenses' because profits from contracts in the millions substantially outweigh facilitation payments in the hundreds or thousands.

Tangible advantages may also be more indirect, such as the creation of fees, dividends, and revenues provided by subsidiaries that were directly involved in the bribery. For instance, in the UK case of Standard Bank, which entered into a DPA after being indicted for 'failing to prevent bribery', the bribery involved payments diverted to a local Tanzania company by the name of Enterprise Growth Market Advisors (EGMA) that, in turn, benefited several government officials in Tanzania. The corrupt payments were generated through inflating the required fee from an initial 1.4% of gross proceeds of funds raised by Standard Bank (and its sister company) as part of private placement proposal on behalf of the government of Tanzania to 2.4%, with the extra 1% constituting the corrupt payment.[9]

Corporate offenders do not always specifically 'launder' the finances generated from bribery in the commonly understood sense of the concept (that is, referring to the need for criminal proceeds to be legitimised or integrated into the established financial system). Advantages and profits are automatically returned as part of an otherwise legitimate business transaction that could have occurred with or without the bribery. If the bribery itself remains hidden, there is no action. Rather, the difficulty is ensuring that funds handed over to third parties or targets actually are used for the goals intended by the briber. If the goals intended are not met, the briber has little opportunity for recourse because they can hardly notify formal authorities to seek compensation. The key issue is for offenders to keep the bribery concealed and to retain control of these monies. (See Levi, 2015: 10.) Little attention has been paid to the risks of being complained about by losing bidders for contracts, for example, but there also remains a risk from internal corporate whistle-blowers, from auditors, and from bankers and others making suspicious activity reports, which may (or may not) be followed up by criminal investigators, usually in the briber's or a third party jurisdiction like the US, since the financial investigators in the jurisdiction of the contract may be under the political control of the bribee. Managing such risks may itself incur further costs should colleagues or other 'regulators' need paying off.

Methods of concealment are shaped by how pervasive and organised the corporate bribery is. We might consider offenders' position in hierarchical organisational corporate structures such as whether the bribery involves

9 https://www.sfo.gov.uk/cases/standard-bank-plc/

'ordinary employees', 'middle managers', and/or senior board-level employees and executives. This would shape the available opportunities for concealment of the practices and cooperation that would be required. For example, if illicit profits were directed via the use of corporate vehicles, then this would likely require senior collusion and notable organisational support/ignorance, and it can be expected that offenders' behaviour in such cases would require a certain level of pre-planning to ensure that profits and gains can be concealed. To conceal the profits, some form of collusion and/or cooperation with external actors such as accountants and lawyers may be required to facilitate these processes, though informational shielding and distortion may reduce the risks from them. As Levi (2015: 10) notes,

> this involves trust in a particular person or persons – perhaps a member of one's close or extended family or ethnic/religious group – or trust in an institution, such as a bank or a money service business (MSB) or a lawyer who may be a trustee of a corporate entity, to an extent sufficient to defeat whatever level of scrutiny will actually be applied.

Trust is central across the process of the illicit transaction: offenders may abuse the trust given to them by employers or shareholders (unless they are 'amoral' and have no conception of such abuses) but must also trust others themselves to ensure the bribery is sufficiently concealed and profits usefully diverted and controlled. Rose-Ackerman (1999: 98) notes, 'the ability to establish trust based on close personal relationships helps reduce the risks of disclosure . . . [and] . . . provides a guarantee of performance when payment and quid pro quo are separated in time'.

Those on the demand side of the transaction or relationship may need to conceal the origin of the funds if they wish to use them within legitimate financial structures (rather than simply spending the money or sinking it into less surveilled assets). A Financial Action Task Force (FATF) (2011) report created a 'typology' on laundering the proceeds of grand corruption (more of a categorisation based on anecdotal evidence than an empirically/theoretically informed set of 'types') and identified the following central mechanisms that can be used to facilitate this process: corporate vehicles and trusts, gatekeepers (that is, facilitators and enablers), domestic financial institutions, offshore/foreign jurisdictions, nominees, and cash. There are clear commonalities in the modus operandi of control and concealment by both briber and bribee. However, these high-level mechanisms cast only an abstract light on the mechanisms.

Whereas the focus here is primarily on the supply side (that is, companies that generate and pay bribes), attention must also be given to the structures used by those on the demand side to launder the proceeds of their corruption and hide or conceal assets obtained with these funds. More specifically, there has been a shift towards analysing flows of illicit finance via corporate vehicles and the obstacles to establishing who the beneficial owners of these vehicles and their assets are. For instance, the Fourth EU Anti-Money Laundering Directive (2015) defines beneficial ownership as 'any natural person(s) who ultimately owns or controls the customer and/or the natural person(s) on whose behalf a transaction or activity is being conducted'. A 'beneficial owner' is 'a natural person – that is, a real, live human being, not another company or trust – who directly or indirectly exercises substantial control over the company or receives substantial economic benefits from the company' (Global Witness, 2013: 3). Key features, therefore, are the control exercised and the benefit derived (van der Does de Willebois et al., 2011: 3). A detailed analysis of 213 grand corruption cases between 1980 and 2010 identified that over 70 percent (150) involved the use of at least one corporate vehicle that concealed, at least in part, beneficial ownership. In total, 817 corporate vehicles were used in those 150 cases; the US was the jurisdiction with the highest number of registered corporate vehicles, followed by the UK and its Crown Dependencies and Overseas Territories. (See Van der Does de Willebois et al., 2011.) Such vehicles also enable the concealment or management of lawful assets and finances towards the funding of criminal activities, or clean funds for dirty ends (Zabyelina, 2015). Later global scandals, such as the Panama and Paradise papers, have shone a light into the dark world of illicit finance and the construction of global, multi-jurisdictional financial arrangements that increase confidentiality (or secrecy in 'tax havens') for the beneficial owners of these legal structures and their associated assets. There is now evidence that the use of opaque and anomalous company ownership structures and arrangements corresponds with an increased tendency for such companies and their beneficial owners to be involved in illicit activities (Jofre et al., 2021). Relatedly, those who do create opaque company ownerships structures to manage their illicit finances prefer to make use of stable and peaceful jurisdictions and avoid jurisdictions with high levels of corruption, implying a rational approach to making use of the systems of reputable countries with high levels of secrecy or confidentiality (Aziani et al., 2022).

Lord et al. (2019) demonstrate this misappropriation of otherwise legal markets and constructs, such as corporate vehicles, as facilitators of crime. Their research reinforces, as with much white-collar, corporate, and organised crime scholarship, the ambiguities that exist in legitimate spheres, the blurred interfaces between the licit and illicit, and the social harms that can arise from otherwise lawful financial structures and arrangements. For instance, corporate vehicles, despite being lawful entities, enable their users to create an illusion of legitimacy through the abuse of otherwise lawful business arrangements and provide effective anonymity for the owners of illicit assets and insulation from enforcement, particularly when organised across jurisdictions with favourable features, and there is a necessity for third-party professionals to facilitate their misuse (Lord et al., 2018, 2019). A significant amount of trust must be placed in these third-party facilitators to ensure wealth and assets are managed accordingly. In these terms, corporate vehicles provide opportunities for managing illicit finances that individuals alone cannot access, but which require some element of third-party collaboration and facilitation.

The professional intermediaries facilitating corporate vehicle misuse are company formation agents (CFAs), trust and company service providers (TCSPs), and other agents who set up and manage corporate vehicles on behalf of others. These are usually legitimate service providers, such as accountants, lawyers, notaries, or specialists in company formation. Little is known about the motivations of those professionals who assist criminal enterprise in this way, but some form of collusion or assistance from them – whether witting or unwitting (or wilfully blind) – is usually required. There may also be an element of incompetence; research by Findley et al. (2022) involved impersonation of known individuals who had been sanctioned following the Russian invasion of Ukraine to assess how formation agents interact in those circumstances, and, in some cases, they were able to obtain company services. Furthermore, a stratified market exists for professional intermediaries that can service the management of illicit finances, and this consists of (Lord et al., 2019) actors and providers (differentiated in terms of their clientele, access, advertising, and available products/services), commodities and products (of varying assigned values determined by the features and specifications of the vehicles offered), and services (including a range of different types of service over time with varying levels/extents of service, duration, and nature). The structure of and changes in these markets and the actors, products and services are shaped and driven by *supply* (of different products and services across different jurisdictions), *demand* (by actual and potential clients of varying types and with different intentions/purposes in mind), *competition* (between and within jurisdictions and between different formation agents operating in varying segments of the market, secrecy wars), and *regulation* (presence and competence of capable guardians, legal asymmetries, and lacunae that shift supply/demand/competition dynamics).

A further related issue here is that financial institutions such as banks are 'far too willing to do business with anonymous companies' (Global Witness, 2013: 7), and here we might also include other legitimate professionals and organisations such as legal, accountancy, and related fiduciary firms. Criminal accountability is being shifted towards such 'facilitators' and 'enablers' of criminal behaviour by criminalising even the unwitting awareness of their facilitations (for example, lack of due diligence) and increasing potential sanctions, but the role of such facilitators remains under-researched, and there is a lack of valid, systematic data and sources on the phenomenon. (See Middleton and Levi, 2015, for an analysis of the roles of lawyers in facilitating organised crime, and Campbell, 2015, for detailed analysis of s. 45 of the act.) For example, in the UK, cases that led to convictions of professionals for facilitating money laundering rarely involved corporate vehicles (Benson, 2020), implying many high-level money laundering cases are going unprosecuted. It is clear that the misuse of corporate vehicles is a serious issue, impacting the functioning of financial systems and market integrity, and generating social harms across society.

In view of these laundering techniques, we might also consider the problems and obstacles that offenders must confront in order to be successful, and these include the 'nature of the detection, reporting and the investigative regime that is in place' (Levi, 2015: 10). For example,

> [T]he identification of 'suspiciousness' by professionals and others with a legal responsibility to combat money laundering is often a judgment that the people and/or transactions are 'out of place' for the sort of account they have and the people they purport to be.
>
> (Levi, 2015: 10)

In the case of licensed professionals, these vary considerably by jurisdiction and remain hotly contested (Levi, 2022). However, as discussed earlier, a key feature of such offending behaviour is the appearance of both the respectability of the offenders and the legitimacy of the business practices involved; these generate both cultural and technical obstacles to detection.

Case Example 2: Analysing the Finances of Embezzlement

Our second example considers a fraud and embezzlement scheme. In March 2023, Kevin Chiu, a former business relationship manager at a bank headquartered in Manhattan, was arrested and charged in the US on four separate counts – fraud, embezzlement, money laundering, and aggravated identity theft – relating to the alleged theft of over $2 million from his mostly elderly clients' accounts over several years.[10] Clients were selected who were unlikely to scrutinise their accounts, and – on a far smaller scale than Madoff – he was able to generate fake accounts to show them. As with many white-collar crimes, whilst the fundamental offending relates to theft, we see poly-criminality, in that the theft required fraud and ID theft as part of the modus operandi, and the stolen funds were subsequently laundered (that is, their nature was disguised): in this case, to invest in stock trading, which was unsuccessful. The sealed complaint provides rich details about the nature and organisation of the embezzlement, and gives us insight into how the before, during, and after financial requirements.[11] In June 2023, Chiu pleaded not guilty,[12] but after negotiations, he changed his plea to guilty on one charge and, in March 2024, was sentenced to four years in prison with three years'

10 https://www.justice.gov/usao-sdny/pr/former-bank-employee-charged-million-dollar-fraud-and-embezzlement-scheme

11 https://www.justice.gov/usao-sdny/press-release/file/1570631/download

12 https://www.financial-planning.com/news/ex-jpmorgan-private-banker-fighting-fbi-embezzlement-charges

supervised release, and agreed to repay $1.6 million compensation to JPMorgan Chase, which presumably had reimbursed the account-holder victims.[13] We analyse the case details next.

The Finances for *and* From *Embezzlement*

The core aspect of Chiu's crime was theft from the client accounts at the bank where he worked. To enable this theft, it was necessary to create a scheme to divert funds owned by or under the custody or control of the bank. Inevitably, these crimes involved the movement of the proceeds Chiu created, in turn constituting money laundering (para. 3) as well as using without authorisation the personal financial information of the clients he defrauded, a form of identity theft (para. 4).

To embezzle funds from a place of work, finances are not usually required to prepare and/or undertake the criminal activities. Some preparatory finances may be required, however, to create tools to facilitate the theft, such as costs associated with setting up accounts in different banks, creating corporate or other vehicles through which the assets may be transferred, or paying off or rewarding (trusted) third-parties who may handle the funds on the embezzler's behalf. Such mechanisms would need to be created in advance of the theft to ensure conduits are in place to receive the monies and to do so rapidly and reliably. However, sometimes few if any advance funds will be needed as existing facilities can be used. For instance, Chiu embezzled funds from six accounts owned by five clients at the bank where he worked. He repeatedly transferred funds from these accounts to a 'brokerage account' in his mother's name held at another financial institution. In the case of one victim, a 74-year-old woman, Chiu exploited her request not to receive mailed copies of her accounts from the bank but for Chiu to provide these in person when she visited the bank, allowing him the opportunity to falsify the documents, and also request signature on blank transaction forms for future misuse. He also set up an email account for the client and used it to email himself false transaction requests.

In another case, in which the victim was a limited liability corporation, Chiu fraudulently transferred funds from the account into the brokerage account, but then sought to cover this gap in funds by transferring funds from the first victim's account into the limited liability company's account. To cover up this first cover-up, he then transferred funds from a third victim, a male individual, and fourth victim, a business, to the first victim's account. Chiu also embezzled funds from a fifth victim, a 74-year-old woman, to the brokerage account and to victim 4's account to conceal the theft. In other words, Chiu transferred funds multiple times between one embezzled account to another

13 United States v. Chiu, S.D.N.Y., No. 1:23-cr-00262, 3/15/24; https://news.bloomberglaw.com/litigation/ex-jpmorgan-chase-banker-gets-48-month-sentence-for-client-theft.

embezzled account in order to conceal that theft had taken place, as he sought to replenish the funds that had been moved by falsifying signatures or otherwise defrauding the bank and clients.

In terms of the finances *from* the embezzlement, Chiu used his brokerage account to purchase shares in Tesla along with other short-term stock trading. Chiu apparently lost most of the money he traded on the markets (one reason fewer assets are recovered than are defrauded). He also transferred funds from the brokerage account to a second bank account he controlled (as indicated by the associated email address and IP address location) and a third account in his name. The transactions took place one or two days after the initial embezzled funds were transferred via the payment system Zelle. Chiu also arranged for funds from the second bank account to be used as a loan to a girlfriend. The funds were then immediately deposited back into the second bank account and back to the brokerage account. Other funds were also withdrawn as cash from the second bank account, transferred to a Venmo account (a mobile application that allows friends to split bills. etc.) or made to an American Express account in Chiu's and his girlfriend's names. If the trading had been profitable, the funds might have been repaid, and no one would have realised that a fraud had taken place. However, the defendant overestimated his trading skills and/or luck.

Conclusion

This chapter has sought to raise questions about the financial aspects of white-collar and corporate crimes as part of the organisational dynamics of the crimes. As with many white-collar crimes, the finances required for and generated from the activities often remain hidden or concealed behind or within the routine business practices that constitute the offenders' occupational duties or organisational environments, and this creates issues for routine detection measures. To illuminate these dynamics further, we analysed the finances for and from transnational corporate bribery, highlighting particular features, methods, and mechanisms that need to come together for the crimes to take place, as well as the finances of a case of embezzlement and fraud.

While this chapter offers theoretical and conceptual insights into the organisation of the finances of white-collar crimes, transnational corporate bribery and embezzlement specifically, there is a clear need for empirical inquiry to enhance the evidence base to allow for more evidence-based interventions and subsequent evaluation of good practice. The cases analysed here are not representative of all cases of bribery or embezzlement; in fact, whilst there may be necessary common mechanisms between these and other analogous cases, we expect there will be variations based on the everyday contingencies of life, as different contexts lead to different organisational aspects. The organisational perspective allows us to think about which mechanisms and relations are necessary and common, and which are not. Analysing the finances of white-collar crimes can be approached in a systematic way: for instance, by drawing on a script analysis to identify the finances required and the actors involved in every case, including the financial necessities and contingencies, then thinking through the value and incidence of such financial activities, mechanisms, and processes. This, in turn, can offer useful insights, not only for building explanatory accounts, but also for informing policy interventions geared towards 'following the money'.

5 Geographies

Introduction

This chapter analyses the 'beyond-national' organisational dynamics of white-collar and corporate crimes. We build on Lord et al.'s (2020) framework for considering white-collar crimes 'beyond the nation-state' to deconstruct the *inter*national, *multi*national, *trans*national, *global* and *non-/de-territorial* aspects of white-collar and corporate crimes to encourage scholars to pay close attention to the ways in which seemingly domestic only, or clearly global, white-collar crimes may have significant beyond-national organisational components and mechanisms, that may be key to how these crimes are accomplished or hindered. Scholars of white-collar crime often recognise the significance of the global, and of the globalisation of these crimes, but the associated beyond-national dynamics have not been extensively conceptualised or interrogated empirically. The terms Global North and Global South are useful for making broad focal distinctions but themselves are over-broad, neglecting considerable national variation in each category. In our view, these aspects should represent a key analytical issue for research seeking to understand and explain the differing configurations, interrelations, and organisational dynamics of those white-collar crimes that variously transcend jurisdictional boundaries, and these dynamics directly connect to the scripts, networks, finances, capacities, and structures discussed in this book.

The chapter is structured as follows. Following Lord et al. (2020), we first discuss the emergence of white-collar crimes that transcend jurisdictional boundaries alongside the concept, and supposed processes of globalisation, and what this means for white-collar offending and control. Second, we consider what is meant by 'beyond-national': that is, the domestic, international, multinational, transnational, global, supranational, and non-territorial/digital relations and how we might apply these concepts to understand different organisational elements of white-collar crimes. Third, we discuss how temporality (i.e., change over time), interdependency (i.e., interrelations), and gestalt (i.e., configurations and 'scripts') are important analytical issues for studies of beyond-national white-collar crimes. Fourth, we present an in-depth analysis of the Wirecard case (alongside other relevant cases) to illustrate the

DOI: 10.4324/9781315100227-5

significance of considering the geographical or territorial scope of white-collar crimes and their control. Our core contribution in this chapter is to encourage scholars in this field to consider the social relations and dynamics of white-collar crimes (as discussed throughout this book) that shape or drive how and why they are organised beyond the individual nation-state. As demonstrated by Lord et al. (2020), this includes investigating the conditional relationships between white-collar crimes, business activities, and purported processes of globalisation.

Globalisation and White-Collar and Corporate Crimes

When we think of the seminal work of Edwin Sutherland (1983), and his empirical analysis of the 70 largest US corporations and their legal violations, the tendency is to assume or focus on the *domestic* organisation or generative context of the varied activities, such as unfair trading practices, corruption, and so on, that he came across. Although supply chains have become more international over time in industrial and technological products, many of the cases Sutherland analysed may well have been organised beyond the US and generated through globalised business and capital, but whether or not he thought much about it, this is not an issue interrogated by Sutherland in his research. This US focus was a feature of major studies of white-collar crime in the decades following Sutherland's work (e.g., Clinard and Yeager, 1980; Weisburd et al., 1991; Clinard et al., 2019). As Lord et al. (2020) note, whilst white-collar crime scholarship has expanded globally since the turn of the 21st century, with major contributions from Europe and beyond, there nonetheless remains a tendency for empirical research that foregrounds national or local level analysis on the nature, extent, and scope of white-collar and corporate crimes that does not sufficiently foreground the organisational dimensions of these behaviours beyond individual nation-states. (See also Lord et al., 2021, on research traditions in corruption research in Europe.) To some extent, this is not surprising: most prosecutors and regulators focus on domestic harms and businesses, though jurisdiction may be international, and this is the dataset that most of us have available to work with.

This (original) tendency in scholarship to focus on the local and national levels remains important and necessary, but white-collar crimes *are* increasingly global phenomena, with some of the most significant cases transcending national boundaries (Friedrichs, 2007: 163). On that latter point, we can draw attention to many recent cases that reinforce the organisation of white-collar crimes across boundaries. For instance, corporate corruption cases, including Airbus, Odebrecht, Rolls Royce, Siemens, Telia, and so on, demonstrate how companies export criminal behaviours to other, usually low-income countries to further their interests. Cases of the corporate facilitation of money laundering and failures to prevent this, such as HSBC, ING, Danske Bank, and so on, illuminate how financial institutions make use of cross-jurisdictional financial structures and systems to arrange, facilitate, or fail to prevent the conversion and concealment of criminal and illicit finances. Accounting frauds, such as Wirecard, demonstrate how companies can externalise and minimise the risks associated with their crimes to other jurisdictions, exploiting cross-jurisdictional regulatory mismatches and gaps in market oversight. Such cases that transcend geographical and jurisdictional boundaries reinforce how opportunities are generated through processes of globalisation, alongside emerging patterns of routine business activities characterised by greater interconnectedness and interdependencies. As Zagaris (2015: 2) notes in relation to the environment that gives rise to international economic crimes (of a white-collar nature), '[c]ontemporary transnational criminals take advantage of globalization, trade liberalization, and emerging technologies to commit a diverse range of crimes and to move money, goods, services and people instantaneously for purposes of pure economic gain, political violence, or both'. Consequently, the (at times ambiguous) concept of globalisation has been discussed in relation to those white-collar and corporate crimes that involve a global or beyond-national dimension. (See Passas, 1999, 2001; Passas and Goodwin, 2004; Friedrichs, 2007; Dicken, 2014; Rothe and Friedrichs, 2015.)

In some ways, globalisation has enabled white-collar and corporate crimes to elude detection and successful enforcement intervention, even deterring many interventions whose likely success is estimated to be low. Van Wingerde and Lord (2020) discuss three key aspects of globalised economies that have shaped the elusiveness of white-collar crimes at the beyond-national level. First, a greater interconnectedness of ideas, information, capital, people, goods, and services has emerged and continues to emerge globally. Information and knowledge are more readily accessible, products and services can be more widely consumed, and people from different societies and communities have more possibilities to connect. However, such processes have also generated increased opportunities for illicit activities to be organised across borders and harmful products to be traded, and, in turn, a potentially greater population of offenders, victims, and targets. As Grabosky (2009: 132) notes, white-collar and corporate criminals are able to make the most of 'criminogenic asymmetries' (Passas, 1999): that is, mismatches and gaps that emerge between the structural, legal, political, economic, and cultural conditions of different jurisdictions. These asymmetries permit not only the organisation of criminal and illicit activities beyond individual nation-states, but also varied unethical and harmful activities that may be legal elsewhere (Passas, 2005; Passas and Goodwin, 2004), though the extra-territorial nature of some laws in some jurisdictions now enables greater enforcement scope. For instance, white-collar 'crimes' can usefully be organised in grey areas when legal definitions differ across countries, meaning enforcement responses cannot always be effective as we see with corporations engaging in regulatory arbitrage by shifting operations to more lax regulatory systems. An example of this would be corporations with multinational operations undertaking manufacturing in foreign countries where labour and environmental laws may be less developed, allowing the corporation to engage in harmful activities that would likely be deemed illegal in their home country. Or companies may export their pollution to other countries as we saw in the case of Probo Koala, a carrier ship owned by Dutch-based company Trafigura, which dumped hazardous waste in the Ivory Coast, and, as van Wingerde (2015) analysed, was able to do so due to the limits of environmental law in globalised economies and the obstacles to regulating large, powerful multinational corporations. Thus, the differences and similarities between nation-states are key to how white-collar crimes might be organised across or between jurisdictional boundaries. Note, however, that these 'inefficiencies' in transnational controls also apply to counterfeit medicines and other products that harm corporate interests and may also harm consumers.

The second issue relates to the mobilities of non-tangible, non-physical things such as digital markets, products, and services. For instance, technological innovations have changed the dynamics of crime scripts and social/criminal networks as white-collar and corporate crimes (and other cyber-enabled and cyber-dependent crimes that are not in scope here) can be organised in new ways and/or in other jurisdictions without a need to be there physically. There is an issue of scale and entry costs of crime since some of these capacities were always present in the history of organisational crimes. This creates organisational variation in the spatial connections between offenders, victims, and offending locations. It also enables offending actors, at a cognitive level, to neutralise their behaviours and choices more easily, as the harms generated and victims created are elsewhere ('out of sight, out of mind'). At a practical level, remote technologies create enforcement obstacles: for instance, as extra layers of mutual legal assistance in forensic investigations emerge that make it more difficult to obtain evidence from overseas jurisdictions, even if those jurisdictions are not actively hostile. Relatedly, modern technologies are the foundations and contexts of much business activity in which we see digital markets and economies structuring economic relations with the aid of algorithms and machines that have semi-autonomous capacities. In these terms, the relationship between the social and the technical, and the tensions between them are emergent realities of white-collar crime offending. For example, in October 2022, celebrity Kim Kardashian settled charges from the Securities and Exchange Commission (SEC) 'for touting on social media a crypto asset security offered and sold by EthereumMax without disclosing the payment she received for the promotion'.[1] Kardashian agreed to pay US$1.26 million in penalties, disgorgement, and interest, and to cooperate with the SEC's ongoing investigation. The fundamentals of this case are nothing new, in that well-known people have historically been used to promote and make more credible investment 'opportunities'. However, the digital infrastructure enabled the company EthereumMax, via Kardashian, as an 'influencer', to reach vast numbers of people across the globe instantaneously (in a way that was not possible pre–Web 2.0 and that disrupts earlier methods) and encourage

1 https://www.sec.gov/news/press-release/2022-183

investment into volatile and poorly/unregulated crypto markets (a digitally dependent phenomenon). The legal violation in this case was the failure of Kardashian to publicly disclose she was being paid to endorse the product, thus not promoting the product in an unbiased way. We do not know whether or not her disclosure would have led to less investment in the product, but this was not a necessary part of the violation and was not part of the administrative case.

Finally, purported processes of globalisation have been accompanied by key independencies between people, markets, and industries, ensuring that activities in one place impact other places. The global financial crisis of 2007–2008 showed how global financial markets are inherently interdependent, as are the actors, entities, organisations, professionals, contracts, and policies that constitute these economies. (Though perhaps because their banks were slower to use collateralised derivatives, Australia and Canada were less affected than were the UK and the US.) To some extent, interdependency creates flexibility for business operations, but it can generate gaps in ethics and accountability as decision-making is diffuse, in turn shifting accountability away from where it to ought to be held.

The key issue is that, in a globalised economy, rich analytical insights can be gained by foregrounding the beyond-state organisational dynamics of white-collar and corporate crimes, even where these are seemingly tangential – the most local of white-collar crimes are in some ways interconnected with, or embedded in, structures and systems that transcend boundaries, including digital infrastructures such as the financial system, especially in relation to the movement or concealment of illicit finances or savings via front companies across countries with confidentiality provisions. In these terms, processes of financial and physical supply chain globalisation create opportunity structures for white-collar crimes across jurisdictional boundaries, potentially altering the scripts of these crimes from their historical domestic organisation; how they are organised can vary depending on what is necessary for the activities under different circumstances and conditions in order to accomplish them successfully. Some white-collar crimes have only been made possible through globalisation, and little is known about why some opportunities are realised when others are not.

However, we should not assume that globalisation and globalised economies inevitably lead to white-collar crimes being organised beyond individual nation-states, particularly when such crimes can be carried out domestically without needing to introduce a beyond-national dimension. As Levi (2008: xxxiv) notes,

> [P]art of the lesson here [from long-firm frauds in the United Kingdom in the 1960s and 1970s] is that globalization of crime is not automatic but is part of the conditional relationship between crime, controls and opportunities that reflects the general patterns of business activities.

These relationships shape the organisation, distribution, and concentration of white-collar offending across jurisdictional boundaries. Globalisation is one explanatory mechanism that contributes to how some white-collar crimes have beyond-state aspects, usually alongside the developments in business operations (Levi, 2008). Of course, undertaking research that incorporates the beyond-national dynamics of white-collar crimes, especially when doing so comparatively, presents not just empirical, but also intellectual challenges. Embedding oneself in more than one culture to fully understand the relevance of different dynamics is beset with pragmatic and conceptual obstacles (see Nelken, 2010); hence, the need for cross-cultural collaborations and multiple embedded case-study analyses.

Conceptualising the 'Beyond-State' Aspects of White-Collar Crimes

It remains common for scholars to focus on white-collar crimes within the jurisdictional boundaries of particular sovereign states reflecting the governing power that these states have over their territories, and, by definition, over the crimes that occur within these boundaries. (Extra-jurisdictional reach is a feature, however, of certain domestic legal frameworks for responding to particular white-collar crimes, such as the US and the UK in relation to international bribery.) Of course, considering boundary changes over time in relation to white-collar crime opportunities and implications might also be valuable, particularly in regions where there has been notable transition in recent decades, as differentials can emerge or disappear. However, given the relatively static nature of state boundaries, how might we better conceptualise the different ways that white-collar crimes may transcend such boundaries? As Lord et al. (2020) argue, we often see terms such as *inter*national, *trans*national, *multi*national, *global*, *supra*national, and *digital* used to describe the organisation of crimes across or between borders, but these concepts have not been systematically deconstructed. For the authors, this raises question such as whether these different concepts have different meanings, or are synonyms for the same phenomena. Whether attempting to clarify these vocabularies is merely a semantic endeavour or has implications for research, policy, and regulatory/enforcement strategies and operations. Whether these concepts reflect varying organisational dynamics of white-collar crimes or not. In this section, we build on the ideas of Lord et al. (2020) to unpick these questions further.

Table 5.1 (adapted from Lord et al., 2020) outlines some key analytical questions that inform the geographical context of such white-collar crimes, the likely characteristics and referents that relate to each, and the implications for regulation and control. The intention here is to provide some indicative, rather than exhaustive, questions that researchers ought to consider when analysing white-collar crimes. For instance, why might any given case of corporate fraud make use of other jurisdictions? Are the criminal activities coordinated from one jurisdiction or collaborative across many? Why do some jurisdictions offer value to those organising white-collar crimes, is this value restricted to merely nominal activities, or is there 'real business' going on? Is it significant that there is a movement of resource across borders? Such questions are important for how we explain the scripts, including the necessary and contingent structures and mechanisms, of white-collar offending. Even disregarding the 'known unknown' and 'unknown unknown' cases that make these crimes contested spaces, valid data on the extent or scale of white-collar crimes that occur across these varying levels are not readily available, whether focusing on domestic only cases or those with beyond-national complexity. In these terms, whilst we cannot infer about proportions of white-collar crimes across these levels of analysis, it is our view that insights can be gained into the organisational dynamics of varied beyond-state white-collar crimes, starting with analyses of known cases and scandals, and building our understanding further. An appreciation of how white-collar and corporate crimes are rarely limited to national boundaries but are frequently multi-jurisdictional within and beyond particular nation-states or regions, and interconnected with varying global systems should be of interest to white-collar crime scholars.

Whilst we separate out different scopes of inquiry, these are not exclusive, and there may be overlap as part of different white-collar and corporate crimes. The particularities of each individual case will determine the most relevant level of inquiry, though it is likely that most white-collar crimes involve digital and/or internet-connected systems, not least because almost all money movement is digital. For some analyses, it may be enough to simply state that some white-collar crimes extend in scope beyond the domestic level, enabling scholars to proceed to focus on the phenomenon that interests them, whether motivations, situations, or underlying causes. In these terms, whether such crimes are labelled international, multinational, or with some other term makes little difference, as they are all variations of crime beyond the nation-state. However, at a more incisive analytical level, these different concepts can have different meanings, or point to different questions that inform variations in how these crimes are organised. For instance, a notable empirical question to pose is how we can better understand variations in offending within and across different jurisdictions and the factors that drive this, including why it might be necessary to organise white-collar crimes across borders. Alongside this, it is beneficial to investigate the distribution and concentration of different white-collar crime types across jurisdictions to better understand why some white-collar crimes are organised as they are and whether key similarities or differences exist in the organisational dynamics over time. The dimensions in Table 5.1 provides a framework for structuring such analysis: that is, for interrogating and questioning varying beyond nation-state configurations of white-collar offending. As Lord et al. (2020) suggest, by delineating the geographical connections of places, people, and ideas, and by considering the corresponding concentration and distribution of white-collar crimes within and across jurisdictions, we are better placed to develop more plausible explanatory accounts and to inform regulation and control.

Table 5.1 Key Issues Relating to the Geographical Scope of White-Collar Crimes and Their Control

Scope of Inquiry	*Likely Characteristics/Referents*	*Key Analytical Questions*	*Implications for Regulation and Control*
Domestic	Domestic white-collar crimes are inherently connected to a single nation-state and are organised within individual sovereign boundaries. (Any beyond-state aspects, such as flows of money, are contingent and not necessary to the organisation of the activities.)	• Is the white-collar crime entirely generated within one nation-state? • Can the white-collar crime be ***sufficiently*** organised by utilising resources in only one jurisdiction?	Domestic authorities limited by (extra-) jurisdictional boundaries responsible for regulating the activities and able to do so without external assistance.
International	International white-collar crimes predominantly pertain to a single nation-state, as the behaviours are coordinated in one jurisdiction, but they draw on resources in other jurisdictions, implying interaction between those nation-states. (In international white-collar crimes, it is necessary to involve resources from another nation-state that are not accessible in the home state, but the choice of other states is contingent on the organisational requirements and/or the knowledge of the organiser(s)).	• Is the white-collar crime generated within one nation-state but have a necessary ***reliance*** on resources from other nation-states? • Is coordination of the crime undertaken entirely by actors in one jurisdiction? • Why is another jurisdiction necessary for the organisation of the white-collar crime?	***Inter***national dimension introduces limitations of sovereign states to respond to crimes that require resources from elsewhere. Mutual legal assistance or data-sharing provisions are needed to fully investigate and regulate the activities.
Multinational	Multinational white-collar crimes involve activities in at least two jurisdictions coordinated from a 'home' country. These crimes are organised and adapted in terms of the local contexts and markets, but the crimes in the primary nation-state are less ephemeral.	• Is the white-collar crime generated within one nation-state but externally perpetrated with ***coordination*** of activities in other nation-states a key feature of the activities? • Why are the criminal activities orchestrated to take place in other jurisdictions, and which conditions drive this?	As with ***inter***national crimes, ***multi***national crimes imply further complexities for regulatory authorities where the evidence in the 'home' country is insufficient for prosecutorial action. The spatial separation, or externalising of victims and actions from the 'home' country, reduce prioritisation, particularly in political-economic climates where will or resources are absent.

(*Continued*)

Table 5.1 (Continued)

Scope of Inquiry	*Likely Characteristics/Referents*	*Key Analytical Questions*	*Implications for Regulation and Control*
Transnational	Transnational white-collar crimes are more complexly organised, in that crimes occur in at least two jurisdictions with coordinated decision-making located in each jurisdiction involved. (These crimes also involve a significant cross-border component and, by definition, no sole coordination by actors in any given nation-state.)	• Is some aspect of ***collusion*** and ***collaboration*** across nation-states necessary or evident in the white-collar crime? • Do actors with core decision-making responsibilities exist in at least two jurisdictions? • Is there a flow of product, finances, or other matériel across borders? • Why does the crime require decision-making responsibilities in different nation-states?	Multiplicity in organisational aspects implies the need for coordinated, multi-state, or regional coordination of regulatory activities. Some more 'active' or dominant domestic authorities are likely to drive the enforcement response, variously incentivising authorities elsewhere to participate.
Global	Global white-collar crimes are those that involve activities in multiple regions and continents but with a more decentralised coordination of activities in each region and country, whereby the principles of operation in each location relate to a centralised core rationale.	• Are the white-collar crimes ***decentralised*** in terms of the criminal activities but organised in line with ***centralised*** principles that shape their organisation across diverse regions? • Do the means and methods of crime commission vary across jurisdictions, and why might this be the case?	At the global enforcement level, formal joint investigation teams may be established, particularly where the harms are substantial. Global settlements are becoming more common, as case ownership is shared across jurisdictions. In some cases, bilateral and multilateral treaties or agreements may be established.
Supranational	Supranational white-collar crimes incorporate illicit activities undertaken by organisations or actors who are part of bodies or unions that transcend the interests of any individual nation-state and operate above the nation-state.	• Do the motivations for committing the white-collar crimes ***transcend*** any individual actor or group of actors, including states themselves, in the pursuit of ideological agendas that exist above nation-states?	Regulatory activities significantly shaped by conventions and legal frameworks generated by supranational and intergovernmental institutions, with models of functional equivalence permitted.

(*Continued*)

Table 5.1 (Continued)

Scope of Inquiry	*Likely Characteristics/Referents*	*Key Analytical Questions*	*Implications for Regulation and Control*
Non-territorial/ digital	Non-territorial white-collar crimes refer to those that predominantly exist or are purely dependent on (internet-connected) cyber and digital systems, rather than 'traditional' white-collar crimes executed through opportunities provided by the digital space (i.e., cyber dependent, rather than cyber enabled or cyber assisted).	• In which ways have information and communication technologies generated opportunities for (new types of) white-collar crimes in *de-territorialised* spaces? • Are there significant connections to physical locations, and what are these interconnections between the digital and non-digital?	Digital contexts obscure locations of offenders, victims, and regulators, making it difficult to establish whether there is a beyond-national component, and, if so, from where the activities are being coordinated. This, in turn, obscures and makes uncertain the regulatory response.

Source: Adapted from Lord et al., 2020[2]

2 Adapted from Lord, N., Zeng., Y. and Jordanoska, A. (2022) 'White-collar crimes beyond the Nation-State', in E. Erez and P. Ibarra (eds) *The Oxford Encyclopedia of International Criminology*, Oxford: Oxford University Press, pp. 1361–1385. Copyright of Oxford University Publishing. Reproduced with permission of the Licensor through PLSclear.

As indicated in Table 5.1, at the domestic level, it might be stated that white-collar crimes are both internally generated in the nation-state and self-sufficient in terms of the access to what is needed for the crimes. For example, the *cum-ex* (and *cum-cum*) scandal in Germany (but also in other European jurisdictions) involved an aggressive form of dividend arbitrage between 2001 and 2012 that led to around €150 billion in costs for European taxpayers.[3] In the case of Germany, the behaviours were organised to exploit tax law (changed in 2012) that allowed multiple parties to reimburse the same tax dividend. In essence, the scheme involved at least three investors, A, B, C, one of whom owned shares in company X and, in turn, received a dividend payment from the company before being reimbursed for the tax taken and selling the remaining shares to a second investor, who, in turn, sold them to a third investor, with that third investor also able to be reimbursed for the tax collected – in other words, multiple tax reimbursements were made possible even though the tax had been collected only once by the tax authority. (See Figure 5.1.) Thus, the scheme could be organised sufficiently in one jurisdiction utilising resources in that jurisdiction only, though there were variations of the scheme with an *inter*national element, also as, for instance, traders in London were able to contrive so-called 'manufactured overseas dividends' (MODs) to offset liabilities.[4] The Cologne prosecutor's office alone has had 120 investigations pending against at least 1,700 defendants, including the former senior tax partner of Freshfields Bruckhaus Deringer in Germany, who has been sentenced to 3.5 years' imprisonment; the firm advised about 25 financial institutions on such deals and, by 2024, had paid €60 million to avoid criminal prosecution and settle damages linked to his work.[5]

3 European Parliament (n.d.) The Cum-ex files – information document. https://www.europarl.europa.eu/cmsdata/158435/2018-11-26%20-%20Information%20paper%20on%20Cum-ex%20-%20Cum-cum.pdf (Accessed: 9 September 2024).

4 BBC (2021) 'Tax cheat schemes costs governments billions', 21 October, available at: https://www.bbc.co.uk/news/business-58984813 (Accessed: 16 March 2023).

5 Financial Times (2024) Ex-Freshfields lawyer convicted over tax fraud received €2mn severance pay, available at: https://www.ft.com/content/28fc06cb-b9db-4af4-a854-297c3ba5b4e4 (Accessed: 14 February 2024).

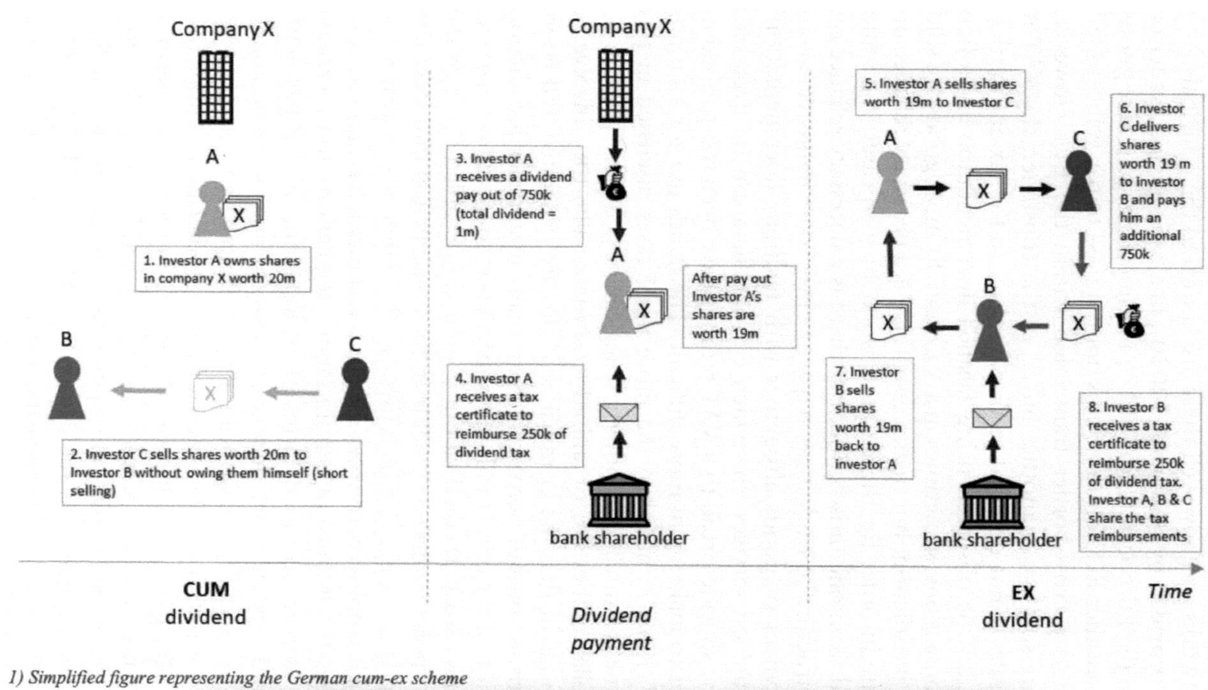

Figure 5.1 A Simplified Visualisation of the German Cum-Ex Scheme

Source: European Parliament (nd)[6]

6 European Parliament (n.d.) 'The Cum-Ex files – information document', available at: https://www.europarl.europa.eu/cmsdata/158435/2018-11-26%20-%20Information%20paper%20on%20Cum-ex%20-%20Cum-cum.pdf (Accessed 16 March 2023).

When white-collar crimes are organised *inter*nationally, it is likely they predominantly pertain to criminal activities coordinated within one jurisdiction but rely on another for resources, such as when requiring access to certain goods or materials, or to minimise enforcement risks. These may also be products of existing networks and how well these are known to the principals.

In the example provided by Lord et al. (2020), in a basic missing trader or acquisition fraud in the European Union (EU), a business may purchase goods from a supplier in another EU country but is not required to pay value-added tax (VAT), as this is a cross-border transaction within the EU. However, when the goods are sold on to another buyer, or the consumer, the VAT it charges on those sales is not declared to or passed on to the tax authorities. This arrangement can be obscured using falsified documentation and often involves further transactions, sometimes in a 'carousel' form, as goods are sold on to another EU jurisdiction, but in any case, there is a necessary reliance on another nation-state in order for the fraud to work. In such cases, the fraud could be organised from one jurisdiction, but there is a necessary reliance on the regional infrastructure to exploit tax requirements. Some fraudsters avoid the physical movement of goods altogether with fictitious documentation, including VAT fraud on services, for which customs data can be bypassed. Such frauds became so widespread that VAT refunds have been reorganised in some EU countries to make them more difficult. The frauds use corporations as instruments of crime, rather than the more usual cases discussed in this book in which crime is a sideline to otherwise legitimate activity.

When white-collar crimes are organised *multi*nationally, they involve at least two jurisdictions in that the criminal activities are generated and coordinated in one jurisdiction but perpetrated externally in another jurisdiction with the organisation of the crimes tailored to particular contexts and markets. For example, Davies (2021) studied labour exploitation enabled through the European Union's 'posted workers' scheme in the construction industry. The phenomenon of 'posted workers', which involves the temporary migration of workers sent by their employers to work on projects abroad, has allowed construction companies to circumvent certain labour regulations and increased exposure of these workers to varied forms of exploitation, such as payments below local standards, unfair salary deductions, and/or poor working conditions. In essence, corporations have been able to exploit regulatory frameworks to enable poor practice and non-compliance in other jurisdictions that they would not be able to do in their host jurisdiction. In these terms, harmful (and criminal) activities may be orchestrated in these ways to make the most of the availability of a large population of potential victims (e.g., low-skilled, low-pay workers) and capitalise on regulatory lacunae in the EU legal infrastructure. These contingent conditions shape how and why white-collar crimes are organised in certain jurisdictions but not others.

With *trans*national white-collar crimes, the organisation of the criminal activities is usually more complex, with collusion between actors with decision-making responsibilities spread across at least two jurisdictions. In contrast to international or multinational crimes, transnational white-collar crimes involve a notable cross-border component and, by definition, no sole coordination by actors in any given nation-state. Notable examples of such crimes provided by Lord et al. (2020) include major market manipulation cases, such as the London Interbank Offered Rate (LIBOR) and Euro Interbank Offered Rate (EURIBOR) scandals that involved a conspiracy of traders and submitters in multiple jurisdictions in the same corporations but also between corporations. In such cases, the implicated actors were able to decide what was needed to rig these market rates at any given time and work together across jurisdictions, such as the United Kingdom and the United States, with information, data, ideas, and finance flowing across borders via digital spaces. That said, the purported illegality of these schemes is now being increasingly scrutinised, with past convictions being quashed and criminalised behaviours now being deemed to have been within the rules, or at least not explicitly against the rules in the US and Germany. Verity's (2023) journalistic investigation into the case has drawn attention to an alleged high-end conspiracy between political and banking elites from six countries to influence the LIBOR setting, and a subsequent cover-up of state involvement that was not disclosed to governmental inquiries or in the criminal court to juries; this failure of disclosure – a common issue not restricted to white-collar crimes – in turn may have resulted in miscarriages of justice.[7] The coordination of rate manipulation at this cross-national level for the greater economic good (in the aftermath of the global financial crisis) perhaps also brings a *supra*national aspect to this case, but at the 'crime commissioning' level, the interactions of traders across borders (whether illegal or not, and whether engineered by those traders or by their business and political seniors) provide insights into the dynamics of organisation. Such transnational organisation was similarly seen in the foreign currency exchange manipulation, or Forex (FX) scandal, which was organised via digital communications across multiple financial institutions and jurisdictions. In such cases, criminal opportunities are recognised in different jurisdictions, and the realisation of these in practice is instigated by local actors with relevant expertise and knowledge of their markets: hence, the need for coordination and decision-making in different places. There is also the flow of information and ideas across borders to facilitate, making the manipulations possible.

In terms of *global* white-collar crimes, it might be that white-collar crimes and associated activities are organised in multiple regions and continents, with activities organised in a decentralised way according to legal and cultural contexts in each jurisdiction involved but driven by centralised or core principles in relation to the underlying rationale of the crime. For instance, consider the case of the missing 'cryptoqueen', Dr Ruja Ignatova, who launched a new

7 https://www.cityam.com/david-davis-calls-for-review-of-authorities-role-in-libor-probes-in-light-of-new-evidence/

cryptocurrency, OneCoin, on the back of Bitcoin's success, promising to make investors millions (Bartlett, 2022). The OneCoin revolution quickly became global, with people investing monies into the cryptocurrency platform from hundreds of countries. Ignatova toured the globe, 'selling' the product in presentations and talks, assisted by local influencers who persuasively marketed the product and encouraged people to invest, following a multi-level marketing (MLM) structure and network to do so. Yet OneCoin was a fraud from the start, essentially a pyramid scheme, with no robust blockchain to support the cryptocurrency, and by the end of 2017, billions of dollars, as well as Ignatova (whose whereabouts remain unknown at the time of writing in 2024), had disappeared, leaving serious financial harm for investors around the world. At the Department of Justice's (2022) press release on the case, following the guilty plea of OneCoin co-founder Karl Sebastian Greenwood, stated:

> OneCoin operated as a MLM network through which members received commissions for recruiting others to purchase cryptocurrency packages. This MLM structure influenced rapid growth of the OneCoin member network. Indeed, according to OneCoin's promotional materials, over three million people invested in fraudulent cryptocurrency packages. OneCoin records show that, between the fourth quarter of 2014 and the fourth quarter of 2016 alone, OneCoin generated €4.037 billion in sales revenue and earned 'profits' of €2.735 billion.
>
> (US Department of Justice, 2022)

Thus, we saw the fraud organised in a decentralised manner across multiple jurisdictions, involving multiple actors in each of these locations, whilst a more centralised objective endured: that of deceiving investors to generate criminal profits. Such practices are more widespread in high-end money laundering cases – others are quite local and banal – in which advantage is taken of disparities in law or – more common now that compliance with FATF formal rules is more widespread – enforcement practice. The analysis of 'signatures for sale' by Neilson and Sharman (2022) illustrates the ongoing abuses of the corporate form, notwithstanding global anti–money laundering reforms. Given the limited resources available for white-collar and corporate crime enforcement, conduct that increases the effort for law enforcement and regulators makes criminal justice action more difficult. The methods are similar but with contextually specific variations.

With *supra*national white-collar crimes, illicit activities are undertaken, or enabled, by those organisations, institutions, or actors that are part of bodies or unions that transcend the interests of any individual nation-state, operating above the level of the nation-state, and often for more ideological motivations. Lord et al. (2020) cite the example of Friedrichs (2007), who has argued that international financial institutions such as the World Trade Organisation, the International Monetary Fund, and the World Bank may be complicit, or at least criminally negligent, in serious crimes against those who live in developing countries. (Though since these international organisations are not criminally liable, we take this as metaphor rather than literally.) Friedrichs (2007) suggests that while the World Bank does not intend to do harm, its mode of operation is criminogenic, with those involved hiding behind a veil of secrecy and being insufficiently accountable. As a further example of this, Gladkova (2021) studied the role of the EU as an enabler of food production harms. She analysed the impacts of EU food policy and regulations on meat farming in Northern Ireland, arguing that the EU's regulated market model creates asymmetries, biased interests, and the conditions for food harms. Consequently, processes such as the encouraged industrialisation of meat production, the use of subsidy mechanisms that serve the interests of larger farming operations, the pursuit of capital accumulation in line with the common market's alignment with capitalist systems of production, and so on, generate criminogenic potential, even if this is not intended. Indeed, the gross and net iatrogenic impacts of many control policies are important objects of analysis, whether or not controls meet what Grabosky (1995) termed 'counter-productive regulation'. Supranational white-collar crimes are not as explicitly linked geographically to particular locations as the other categories in Table 5.1, but they are connected to institutions that have particular political, legal, or ideological intentions, though these, in turn, are often connected to certain regions or groups of nation-states.

In the 21st century, we have seen rapid technological progress, and this has influenced the dynamics of white-collar and corporate crime offending in that corresponding behaviours can partially or predominantly take place within cyber and digital systems. Digital ecosystems comprising varied social, technical, and socio-technical relations and systems underpin and enable most, if not all, white-collar and corporate financial crimes, directly or indirectly, as part of corresponding before, during, and/or after processes, influencing how different white-collar and corporate crimes are organised and configured (scripts and networks) under different conditions, redefining the interdependencies and interconnections of digital and non-digital offending dynamics. Of course, even in those cases with a significant cyber/digital component, there are varied connections to physical locations or territorial regions as there is human involvement (unless, at some point, we see generative artificial intelligence acting independently in non-compliant ways, such as with online trading, but even then, harms and victimisation will affect human actors directly or indirectly). In these *de-territorialised* spaces, we see how new and emerging information and communications technologies generate varied opportunities for white-collar crimes that do not have significant connections to physical locations. Notable examples include high-frequency trading in financial markets that permit traders to utilise entirely automated processes to manipulate global financial markets (so-called 'flash trading') (Lewis, 2015; see also Györy (2019). In such cases, there is clearly some physical connection to the human actors involved and their physical locations, but the behaviours and activities occur in digital spaces that permeate the entire globe.

This conceptualisation aims to prompt inquiries about the organisation of white-collar crimes across borders and over time, rather than offering a comprehensive empirical or theoretical framework for their analysis. It seeks to understand the factors that necessitate such organisation, including the involvement of various actors and the reasons behind it. Clarifying these terms goes beyond semantics and has significant implications for building theories (e.g., what is the impact on criminological explanations when offending is across different cultures and legal regimes?), shaping policy responses (e.g., how do geopolitical contexts influence the legality and response to certain behaviours?), and developing enforcement strategies (e.g., what can authorities do in one jurisdiction alone without assistance or coordination in other jurisdictions that facilitated or were a step in the location of the crimes or in the transmission of the proceeds thereof?). Furthermore, this perspective encourages white-collar crime researchers to consider the necessary and contingent aspects of these crimes beyond individual countries, to analyse the conditions driving the criminal enterprise, and to explore the connections between the organisation of white-collar crimes and the patterns of routine business activities in a globalised context. This approach can provide insights into how the organisational dynamics of white-collar crimes differ based on the jurisdictions involved and the reasons for these differences.

Finally, Lord et al. (2020) point to three key analytical dynamics – gestalt (i.e., configurations and 'scripts'), interdependency (i.e., interrelations), and temporality (i.e., change over time) – to further examine these beyond-national dimensions. For example, white-collar crimes that operate on a beyond-national scale, as opposed to those that are mainly domestic, tend to differ in the 'scripts' that actors and their networks follow to conduct and organise their illegal activities, including financial arrangements (Chapter 4) and the emergence or availability of opportunities (Chapters 2 and 3). How are criminal networks formed, structured, and sustained in these scenarios, particularly when there is geographical separation between the offenders? As per routine activities theories, we can expect the convergence of the elements of crimes across multiple jurisdictions to become more intricate. In such instances, the specific situations, targets, and lack of capable guardians need further thought. How do patterns of white-collar crime at the beyond-national level compare to domestic ones? Do routine activities and corresponding social relations differ across various jurisdictions? How can context, including cultural diversity, be integrated into explanations? How does the nature of industries influence the distribution of offending at domestic versus beyond-national levels? For instance, financial markets, which are globally oriented and heavily influenced by digital innovation, provide a ripe environment for transnational and global white-collar crimes. The increased global interconnectedness of ideas, information, capital, people, goods, and services shapes the organisation and dynamics of white-collar crimes. These are significant empirical questions, as understanding these factors and conditions can contribute to theory development.

Interdependency is an intrinsic aspect of today's social world, particularly evident in white-collar crimes with beyond-national dimensions. White-collar offenders and their crimes in one jurisdiction are interconnected with others through collaboration, cooperation, and collusion. This interdependency is also visible in the use of multi-jurisdictional financial arrangements and digital systems. The impacts of these crimes can ripple globally, as demonstrated by the 2008 global financial crisis and even, in a more modest way, by international Ponzi investment schemes. There is both convergence and divergence in the behaviour and practices of institutions, organisations, and elite individuals, as ideas, information, and methods transcend borders, with actors learning from each other. Common patterns can be observed in the flow of illicit finances through culturally and socially diverse countries. Tensions also arise between different nation-states and between nation-states and supranational organisations like the EU and the Financial Action Task Force, as laws, policies, and norms regarding elite deviance vary or sometimes converge. These interdependencies are accelerating and intensifying, and the reliance on collaboration among people, markets, and industries has grown alongside globalisation.

How white-collar crimes unfold and develop over time in relation to the extent to which they involve different jurisdictions or regions at different stages of the offending is an important analytical question. Do white-collar crimes with a ***multi***national[8] dimension begin as ***inter***national[9] crimes? Or are ***trans***national[10] white-collar crimes more ephemeral in nature, as actors come together to collaborate fleetingly before focusing on crimes at the ***domestic***[11] level? These are empirical questions that can inform how we understand the ***beyond-national*** nature of white-collar crimes. But we should be aware that 'time' can be conceptualised in different ways, such as more subjective accounts of individual perceptions of how long things take, or as a means to organise social behaviours. In terms of understanding the organisation of white-collar crimes at the ***beyond-national*** level, it is beneficial to analyse time in an objective sense in order to observe empirically how events take place over specified periods and why. Additionally, understanding 'duration' (start-end), 'tendency' (direction of prevailing movements over time), 'sequences' (an ordered list of events), 'timing' (an examination of the spacing of events in time), and 'path dependence' (how past arrangements and historical legacies structure individual and collective behaviour) is relevant. Finally, as discussed in the context of globalisation, the growing mobility of digital markets, products, and services over time provides new avenues for organising illicit activities.

8 Criminal activities in at least two jurisdictions but coordinated from a 'home' country.

9 Criminal activities that mainly pertain to a single nation-state, as the behaviours are coordinated within one jurisdiction, but they draw on resources in other jurisdictions.

10 Criminal activities occur in at least two jurisdictions with coordinated decision-making located in each jurisdiction involved.

11 Criminal activities that are inherently connected to a single nation-state and are organised within individual sovereign boundaries.

Examining these changes at various points in time can enhance theories of white-collar crime offending. For instance, as opportunities for white-collar and corporate crimes emerge, they may only be realisable for a certain period of time. For example, in cases of insider dealing, obtaining knowledge about future trades may only be valuable for a period of time before that knowledge becomes public, at which point its value is reduced. Or, with cases of crypto investment scams, the urgency associated with initial public offerings of new cryptocurrencies may only last for a short period of time as the 'herd' aims to invest quickly ahead of the rest of the market before (victim) investors realise all is not what it seems. The relationship between opportunities and the time before they are no longer available is interesting to consider from a research perspective. Relatedly, new technologies may speed up the crime commission process, giving less objective time for interventions by third parties and law enforcement/regulation before such crimes are completed, although they may still be dealt with in slower time if the businesses involved survive. Understanding the speed at which white-collar or corporate crimes need to be, or are, organised poses significant questions for how we explain the crime commission process and the pressures on controllers.

The Wirecard Fraud

In this section we present an in-depth analysis of the Wirecard case to illustrate the significance of considering the geographical or territorial scope of white-collar crimes and their control. At the time of writing, three former executives of the now-collapsed German online payment company, Wirecard, are on trial in Munich, charged with fraud, embezzlement, and accounting and market manipulation.[12] Markus Braun (former CEO of Wirecard), Oliver Bellenhaus (former head of Wirecard's Dubai subsidiary) and Stephan von Erffa (former head of accounting) face up to 15 years in jail. Braun and von Erffa deny wrongdoing, while Bellenhaus has admitted his role and is acting as the prosecution's chief witness, and in February 2024, he was released from jail.[13] In a related civil action in September 2024, Braun and two other former executives, Alexander von Knoop (former chief financial officer) and Susanne Steidl (former chief product officer), were ordered to pay €140 million plus interest in damages to the defunct payment group's administrator over violations of professional duties.[14] Another key protagonist, Wirecard's former COO Jan Marsalek, fled Germany, and his location remains unknown. Russia is suspected, as he was allegedly recruited by Russian intelligence (the GRU) in 2014,[15] but he is now on Europol's most wanted list, 'strongly suspected

12 https://www.ft.com/content/a61d0dae-7faa-4233-87bc-78d22b7fcb86
13 https://www.ft.com/content/b1a4dea7-7375-43d5-b8c9-b54c4293b562
14 https://www.ft.com/content/cb71080a-b9d9-4ac5-aa27-c676c025d9b3
15 https://www.ft.com/content/f15610a0-e94d-4672-bc73-f2e5e364f2d1

of having committed commercial gang fraud, the particularly serious case of embezzlement and other property and economic offences'.[16] Wirecard collapsed in 2020 after the company admitted that €1.9 billion in cash and half its revenue did not exist. Wirecard started off as payment processor for online adult content and gambling sites, before buying out a small bank and other payment processors, becoming a key go-between for businesses to access global financial systems, and, in turn, expanding its market share and revenues. At its peak, the company's value reached €24 billion in 2018. The scandal came to light following the relentless investigating and reporting by the UK's *Financial Times* newspaper, led by journalist Dan McCrum. McCrum (2019) published a story stating:

> Internal company spreadsheets, along with related correspondence between senior members of Wirecard's finance team, appear to indicate a concerted effort to fraudulently inflate sales and profits at Wirecard businesses in Dubai and Ireland, as well as to potentially mislead EY, Wirecard's tier-one auditor.[17]

In essence, as McCrum (2022) explains in his book *Money Men*, Wirecard employees fabricated documents about outsourced payment processing operations in Asia that did not exist in order to fraudulently inflate the company's revenue, to give the impression that internal targets were being met and growth was being achieved. Further, client details and financial relationships were forged to circumvent scrutiny and audits. For instance, there were two banks in the Philippines that were said to be holding the funds but had never been Wirecard clients. Wirecard sought to discredit McCrum and the FT investigators, even alleging market manipulation for profit to encourage a criminal investigation into them. There were also audit failures from EY, which was reluctant to challenge Wirecard executives in public when misleading statements were being made.[18] The much-criticised regulators BaFin saw Wirecard as a German champion and saw the FT as conducting a mistaken campaign against the firm. It was only when the revelations in the *Financial Times* led to KPMG being brought in later in 2019 to forensically investigate that the fraud was confirmed.

The 'beyond national' organisation of the Wirecard fraud was necessary for Wirecard to sustain the enterprise over many years. For instance, whilst the criminal activities were predominantly coordinated by a few key protagonists from Germany and Wirecard's headquarters in Munich, there was a reliance

16 https://eumostwanted.eu/cs/node/946

17 McCrum (2019) 'Wirecard's suspect accounting practices revealed', *Financial Times*, 15 October, available at: https://www.ft.com/content/19c6be2a-ee67-11e9-bfa4-b25f11f42901

18 Storbeck (2021) 'EY and Wirecard: Anatomy of a flawed audit', 26 October, available at: https://www.ft.com/content/bcadbdcb-5cd7-487e-afdd-1e926831e9b7

on fabricated and fictitious financial relations and transactions with actors and third parties in other jurisdictions, such as in the UAE, Singapore, and the Philippines. Had the Wirecard employees sought to fabricate or forge financial relations with (fictitious) Germany-based companies and third parties, the fraud would have been more difficult to sustain, with scrutiny more likely to detect misconduct. The international dimension enabled enforcement and auditing risks to be reduced, as money flows were obscured within plausible financial structures that could be managed by Wirecard. For instance, even when EY auditors went to Asia to scrutinise the payments processes, they were given prepaid debit cards by Wirecard, enabling Wirecard employees to track and manipulate data from these transactions that would subsequently be shared with EY. Similarly, fictitious transactions to real companies in other jurisdictions allowed Wirecard to fabricate commission payments of €1 billion from three companies – Al Alam (Dubai), Senjo (Singapore), and PayEasy (Manila) – to the banks in the Philippines at the centre of the scandal. The KPMG special audit quickly identified this financial hole.

In the case of Singapore, another key player, Edo Kurniawan (former vice president of controlling and finance of Wirecard Asia Holdings and later subject of an Interpol Red Notice, having absconded),[19] whilst also being key to the 'charming' of EY auditors visiting the region (McCrum, 2022: 154), encouraged employees there – two of whom were jailed in 2023 for breach of trust – to 'cook the books'. As McCrum (2022: 155) explains:

> What Kurniawan sketched out was a practice known as 'round tripping'. A lump of money would leave the bank Wirecard owned in Germany destined for the subsidiary in Hong Kong which was applying for the payments licence [to issue prepaid cards]. But it would stay there only momentarily; just long enough to satisfy regulators that the business was well funded. Next the cash would depart to sit briefly in the books of an external 'partner', from where it would travel back to Wirecard in India. In each country the individual legs of the trip would look to local auditors like legitimate business. In Hong Kong the partner was a supplier being paid, while in India it was a valued Wirecard customer. In reality, the money would move in a circle.

These artificial money flows across jurisdictional boundaries – also found in other large corporate scandals such as the Abraaj Group (Clark and Louch, 2023) – exploited gaps in cross-national auditing, enabling the enterprise to be maintained. (See Brivati, 2022, for a more empathetic perspective on Abraaj.) Multiple jurisdictions were involved with particular schemes organised in different contexts, with either coordination from within Germany or

19 https://www.police.gov.sg/media-room/news/20220907_issuance_of_interpol_red_notice_against_edo_kurniawan_in_connection_to_wirecard_inv

perpetration of the activities elsewhere. The choice of which other jurisdictions to make use of was contingent on how and why the frauds was organised in certain ways in some places but differently elsewhere.

In terms of the 'gestalt', or configurations and scripts of the Wirecard case, a more in-depth analysis would explore how the actors and networks involved were established, arranged, and maintained over time. This would require a deep historical analysis of the company and employee histories, seeking to understand which structures and mechanisms created a need to engage in fraud (e.g., losing revenue as certain countries, such as the US, banned online gambling early in Wirecard's emergence) and, in turn, how the opportunities for fraud were recognised and the required behaviours determined. The interconnectedness of different markets (e.g., gambling) and how these influenced the organisational dynamics of the Wirecard fraud need further scrutiny to understand the conditions and circumstances that generated the decision to engage in fraud. It is not certain at present the degree to which espionage and more secret connections affected these decisions. The interdependencies of the Wirecard case are also key. For instance, the behaviours in Germany, the UAE, Singapore, and the Philippines are internally connected and inter-reliant, and these dynamics are enabled through digital infrastructures (e.g., online money flows). How the Wirecard case unfolded and developed over time and how it incorporated other jurisdictions and actors in the enterprise are important analytical questions that inform how we explain the 'how' and the scale of these corporate crimes.

Conclusion

This chapter, following the framework set out by Lord et al. (2020), has sought to encourage scholars of white-collar and corporate crime to consider the analytical benefits of focusing on the 'beyond-national' aspects of the crimes they examine. By thinking through the *inter*national, *multi*national, *trans*national, *supra*-national, or *global* aspects of the crimes and/or corporations under study, even if these are predominantly national in nature, we can further unpack the features and components of these important 'beyond-national' dynamics. This can be done alongside the rich empirical, conceptual, and theoretical insights we see in the field into the dynamics and conditions of white-collar and corporate crimes that occur largely within individual jurisdictions.

In the chapter, we considered purported processes of globalisation, and how these influence opportunity structures for white-collar and corporate crimes, as well as the scripts, networks, and other organisational dynamics of these behaviours. Whilst globalisation has affected these dynamics, just because new opportunities or methods materialise does not necessarily mean white-collar crime offending will change, particularly if actors can continue to organise their behaviours as they always have done successfully and profitably. Thus, the globalisation of crime may not automatically occur alongside the globalisation of business, as white-collar crimes are shaped by the 'conditional relationship between crime, controls and opportunities that reflects the general patterns of business activities' (Levi, 2008: xxxiv). Similarly, how emerging processes of de-globalisation (e.g., as nation-states withdraw interactions with other regions following political change, such as Brexit in the UK) affect white-collar crimes must also be studied. Also, as we discussed earlier, even the most seemingly local occurrences of white-collar crimes can incorporate other jurisdictions by virtue of digital and cyber systems.

White-collar crime offending is complex, and varied factors and conditions influence motivations to offend, based around potential offenders' risk perceptions as well as realities (which can change over time), and the networking, capacities, and capabilities of offenders. As researchers, we encounter many obstacles to investigating the beyond-national aspects of white-collar crimes, particularly where we would ideally visit other jurisdictions to undertake data collection. Language barriers, funding and other resources, determining appropriate methodologies, recruiting appropriate research participants, and even identifying academic collaborators can be difficult. Where it can be done, great intellectual gains can be made. New lines of inquiry for comparative multi-jurisdictional research might involve time-series analyses (see Braithwaite, 2016), deliberative accounts of informed expertise across varied cultures (see Lord et al., 2021), or multi-site embedded case studies (see Maesschalck, 2021); these approaches offer ways of exploring variations across jurisdictions and pursuing the construct validity of similarities and differences. We might also look to access new forms of 'big data' at the domestic and global level, such as financial transactions, company ownership, trade relations, and so on, as these can offer a route to mapping key aspects of white-collar crime organisation beyond individual nation-states. It is clear, as Lord et al. (2020) argue, that better understanding of the varying characteristics and features, as well as the differing configurations, interrelations, and organisational dynamics of those white-collar crimes that in some way transcend jurisdictional boundaries, including their distribution and concentration across space, is significant for white-collar crime theory and research.

6 Capacities

Introduction

This chapter analyses the capacities for the commission, or unfolding, of white-collar and corporate crimes. That is, there are human, social, material, and cultural capacities that create the pre-conditions for white-collar offending – we consider these as mechanisms of white-collar and corporate crime commissioning. These capacities interact with and inform the opportunity structures, 'scripts' (Chapter 2), and networks (Chapter 3) of white-collar and corporate crimes and enable different offending behaviours under different circumstances to flourish or fade. We deconstruct these capacities, which may or may not be observable to/observed by researchers, to demonstrate the multi-faceted and socially complex structures and mechanisms that underpin white-collar and corporate crime commission; this is because varying capacities facilitate or restrict the accomplishment of white-collar crimes. Understanding the observable and unobservable multi-dimensional antecedents of offending is key for developing explanatory accounts of white-collar crimes.

We then focus more specifically on the individual offenders and their observable capacities. An often under-researched and under-theorised area of criminal behaviour generally, and white-collar and corporate crimes more specifically, is how we understand the skills, knowledge, and expertise required of individual offenders to undertake what can be complexly organised behaviours. White-collar crimes often require a certain level of 'know-how' and/or professional licences in order to be accomplished, but the different kinds of expertise, knowledge, and skills required for different white-collar offences have not been conceptualised and often not even researched explicitly. The skill sets, expertise, and knowledge of different actors can enable or can restrict offending, and this has implications for the need to collaborate with others (if would-be offenders have the chance to do so) or to refuse opportunities. It can even stimulate or close off perceptions that such crimes – whether or not defined as such – are plausible. In these terms, we develop a framework for understanding variations in expertise, skills, and knowledge and how these variations can stimulate, permit, or constrict offending behaviours when opportunities arise.

DOI: 10.4324/9781315100227-6

A Capacities Framework for White-Collar and Corporate Crimes

In 2015, Volkswagen admitted that 11 million cars in its group (Volkswagen, Audi, and Porsche) had been fitted with so-called 'defeat devices' designed to intentionally cheat emissions tests in the US. In 2017, the company pleaded guilty to associated crimes and received criminal and civil financial penalties totalling $4.3 billion, whilst six executives were also indicted as part of the criminal conspiracy.[1] Some were also separately charged in Germany for a range of offences. (The VW group has spent more than €30 billion in legal fees and pay-outs to customers, including a $15 billion settlement in the US and a £193 million settlement in England and Wales.[2]) The fraud trial[3] in Germany of the former VW chief executive Martin Winterkorn has been delayed for years because of his ill health,[4] but a German court ruled in December 2023 that he must stand trial on market manipulation charges.[5] The trial finally started in September 2024.[6] The following quote from Jack Ewing's rich analysis of the Volkswagen case study neatly distils the key aspects of the scandal that together enabled the fraud to take place:

> The [statement of facts] described the technical impasse in 2006 that led Volkswagen managers to resort to a defeat device. It told of how higher-ups overruled engineers who objected to the illegal software. The statement explained how the defeat device was refined over the years to make it more effective. It recounted how Volkswagen executives concocted an elaborate cover-up when regulators became suspicious, and how they destroyed evidence once they realized they would be exposed. The statement of facts made it clear that a broad criminal conspiracy was at work. The people involved were high-ranking executives, compliance managers, engineers, quality control experts, software specialists, and in-house lawyers. Volkswagen was portrayed as a place where the people in charge were all too willing to resort to illegal behavior to fulfil the company's ambitions.
>
> (Ewing, 2017: 333–334)

In order to become competitive in the US car market, whilst also promoting a narrative that the company's diesel technology was clean and environmentally

1 DoJ Indictment: https://www.justice.gov/opa/press-release/file/924401/download. See also the 2018 Netflix documentary, Hard NOx.

2 https://www.theguardian.com/business/2016/jul/26/volkswagen-emissions-scandal

3 https://www.theguardian.com/business/2019/apr/15/former-head-of-volkswagen-could-face-10-years-in-prison

4 https://www.theguardian.com/business/2022/may/25/volkswagen-settles-uk-dieselgate-claims-with-193m-payout#:~:text=It%20has%20become%20one%20of,because%20of%20his%20ill%20health

5 https://www.dw.com/en/vws-dieselgate-ex-ceo-market-manipulation-trial-to-resume/a-67846143#:~:text=Former%20Volkswagen%20(VW)%20chief%20executive,but%20has%20now%20been%20revived

6 https://www.bbc.co.uk/news/articles/cn5r9rgg6yno

friendly, a complex web of actors, departments, behaviours, and technologies came together over time and place, driven by high ambition and a culture of success at all costs, to defraud individuals, the market, regulators, and competitors. The desire to beat Toyota to become the world's number one manufacturer was also a factor. Whilst in 2024, Toyota remains the world's biggest car manufacturer in terms of sales, Toyota itself is implicated in various scandals, including irregularities in certification tests for diesel engines and forged results in relation to safety tests by Daihatsu (owned by Toyota).[7] Other German and non-German companies also deployed emissions-cheating devices. How illegal schemes diffuse throughout an industry or across industries – and which, if any, resist becoming involved in such schemes, especially if they have the techniques to do so – is an interesting empirical research question.

This is one of many cases of white-collar and corporate crime that involve an interplay between the behaviours and motivations of individuals within organisational cultures that can create goals unlikely to be achieved by lawful responses, particularly when regulations are considered by involved actors as overly burdensome. (Though as 'outsiders', it is difficult to appreciate how such actors perceive attempts to reduce emissions that are harmful to public health: we have to make a judgment call about the extent to which academics or documentary makers working in retrospect can adequately reflect the perspectives of insiders *as they existed at the time of the offending*, which, in this case – unlike most forms of crime for gain – took place over an extended period.) Not all white-collar and corporate crime cases are as complex as the Volkswagen case, but in terms of better understanding how these cases come about – that is, understanding crime commission – we need to recognise the interplay of individual capacities and their potential for criminal behaviours, how these are embedded in unobservable structures and relations that exist within particular organisations and society more generally, and the mechanisms and conditions that activate, or enable, such crimes to flourish or fade. Our framework of crime capacities allows us to consider the multi-faceted nature of how and why white-collar crimes actually take place.

We use the term 'capacities' to refer to the variety of mechanisms that determine the ability of an individual to visualise and realise a white-collar crime opportunity, and enable or restrict the commission, or unfolding, of white-collar crimes. Individual white-collar and corporate offenders possess variable capabilities of action that are often embedded in social relations (but are also influenced by biological/psychological factors) that, under certain conditions, shape the outcomes of their attempts to engage in crime. Whether or not these individuals encounter, recognise, and realise a white-collar crime opportunity when it presents itself is also determined by their capacities for the crimes. Figure 6.1 visualises the key dimensions that constitute the dynamics of white-collar crime capacities.

7 https://edition.cnn.com/2024/01/30/business/japan-toyota-world-top-selling-automaker-2023-intl-hnk/index.html#:~:text=Despite%20the%20good%20news%20for,old%20problem%20with%20exploding%20airbags

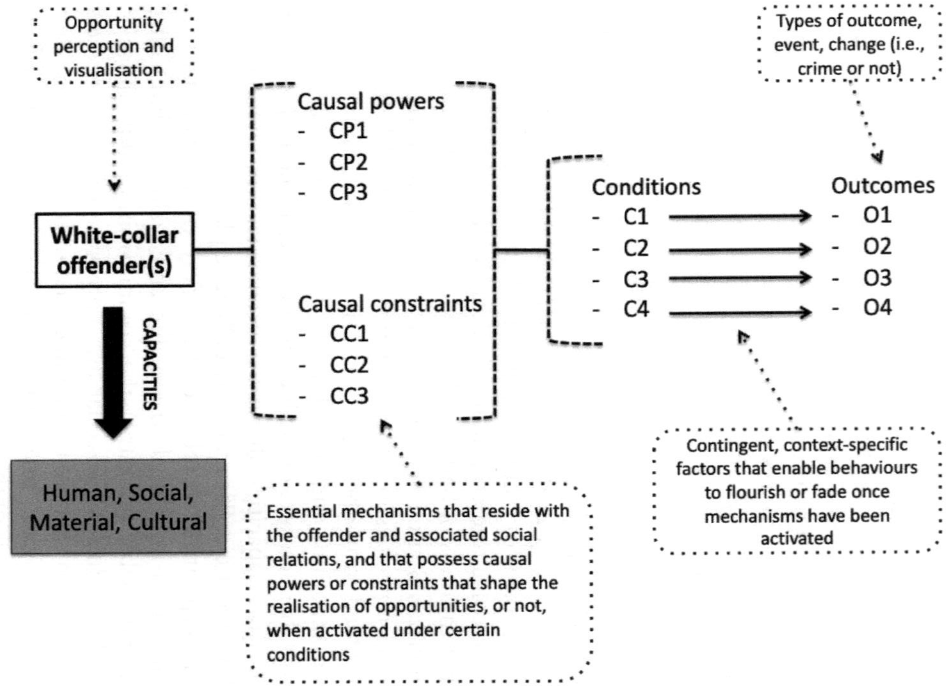

Figure 6.1 A Capacities Framework for White-Collar and Corporate Crimes[8]

8 Adapted from: *Method in Social Science: A Realist Approach*. Revised 2nd edition by A. Sayer, Copyright (Routledge @ 2010), p. 109. Reproduced by permission of Taylor & Francis Group.

Thinking through these multiple dimensions provides a logical framework for interrogating the varied factors that must come together, and how and why they do, for white-collar crimes to take place. The complexity of open systems and the social world means it is unlikely that formal, comprehensive accounts can be developed as we are unable to access full and valid data on all such structures, powers, constraints, conditions, and outcomes. That is, some structures or capacities may be unobservable through empirical research, yet these are nonetheless real drivers of actual events that we experience and can empirically observe. For example, the ego and financial self-reward associated with individualism under conditions of venture capitalism may be a mechanism that contributes to an individual's involvement in financial crime, but these influences are difficult to directly observe empirically when it comes to looking at specific instances of fraud. In these terms, our objective as researchers of white-collar crimes to make connections between the (i) 'real' underlying generative structures and mechanisms (identified through processes of abstraction to isolate potential causes in thought, based on prior theoretical knowledge or insights) that come together to enable (ii) 'actual' white-collar crimes to occur (i.e., crimes committed) that can, in turn, be (iii) observed 'empirically' in particular contexts.[9] In these terms, such realist accounts of the social world, and the commissioning of white-collar crimes, recognise that realities are stratified and emergent, consider integrated agency-structure accounts, and foreground multi-dimensional causal tendencies. (See Sayer, 2010; Gorski, 2013.)

To provide a more concrete insight, we can see that the 'scripts' discussed in Chapter 2 aim to capture the particular mechanisms that come together to produce different ways of carrying out white-collar crimes, or fail to do so. As we saw in the case of market manipulation in relation to the LIBOR rigging, four essential scenes were identified: (i) calculated positioning and identification of co-collaborators, (ii) recruitment of collaborators, (iii) (ephemeral) manipulation, and (iv) recompense and solicitation. The coming together of these necessary 'mechanisms' was, in turn, contingent on various context-specific conditions, such as the knowledge and skill sets of traders working in this domain, their abilities to communicate requirements to co-opted co-offenders, the cultural expectations of the institutional environment, and so on. Implicit in this mode of thinking, analysing, and theorising is the centrality of thought experiments and processes of

9 On a comparative note, the mainstream research tradition of positivism tends to search for causality within the domain of the 'actual', whilst interpretivism denies that the domain of the 'real' exists. Consequently, the former leads to superficial analysis of observable events only, insufficiently engaging with the 'real' unobservable structures that generate these; the latter may reflect a narrow perspective of the world, as approaches in this tradition foreground discursive practices and lived experiences, but do not always go beyond this to consider the causal powers of social structures that exist independently of human consciousness. (Even more problematically, such perspectives may move towards relativism, in turn undermining an assessment of which theories or concepts are more plausible in any given context.)

abstraction to identify these mechanisms by considering various frames of reference (e.g., varied policy, social scientific, practice orientations) to think about the underlying social structures that generated the identified mechanisms. For instance, in the case of the market manipulation, we might ask ourselves what must be true in order for this particular crime event to be made possible. By asking this question, we can see that an underlying paradox in regulatory and organisational actors acting as both 'capable guardians' and 'facilitators of misconduct' was at play, reflecting wider trends in regulation. Similarly, processes of financialisation and accelerated finance capitalism created difficult-to-observe structures that shape how traders interpret their workplaces. For instance, it is now argued that the process of financialisation that occurred in the decades prior to the global financial crisis of 2007–2008, leading to the expansion of financial markets and products globally, created conditions such as financial and social inequality alongside deregulation that were conducive to an array of financial malpractices and frauds (e.g., sub-prime mortgages). Financialisation refers to 'the organizational and political–legal arrangements that facilitate making profits and increasing value for companies and their shareholders through financial transactions' (Prechel, 2016: 294), but the effects of such arrangements are not always directly observable.

We can expand this example of market manipulation further in reference to Figure 6.1. For instance, if our object of study is the market manipulator as white-collar offender, then we can argue that these actors have structures: that is, internally related factors that constitute the person and influence their (non-)actions, such as their knowledge and expertise of rigging possibilities, their propensity for unethical behaviour, and their role in the workplace or societal position. We refer here to these structures as 'capacities' to capture their generative potential. These capacities of offenders shape the causal powers they possess, such as an ability to obtain non-public information (causal power 1), or share this information with other actors external to their own organisation (CP2). Similarly, they may possess what are termed causal constraints, such as inadequate funds to reimburse recruited co-offenders in a timely manner. They may also lack the discipline to pay them (e.g., because they prefer spending on having a good time or because of personality issues) (causal constraint 1), ignorance of how to conceal the manipulation from compliance teams or external auditors (CC2), the presence of particularly competent and/or honest compliance teams (as with independent forensic accounting team Second Sight in the post office[10] fraud review, though senior management at the post office sidelined them precisely because they were both honest and competent) (CC3), or a lack of access to other people to undertake required activities for them (CC4). Under specific conditions, such as the

10 For an overview of the post office scandal, see https://www.bbc.co.uk/news/business-56718036.

manipulator being put under more pervasive managerial oversight (condition 1), or the information not being acted on by other market actors as implicitly required (C2), different outcomes will occur, such as substantial profit generated through manipulation (outcome 1), little profit generated as the market did not move accordingly (O2), or a decision not to utilise non-public market information (O3). As different conditions produce different outcomes, they can be said to be contingent on causal powers, rather than fixed.

In examining white-collar crimes in this way, we can see how such offending is a product of multi-faceted social relations where specific white-collar offences are shaped by various mechanisms and factors as they come together in particular places and at particular points in time. This is what has been referred to as a 'concrete' concept of causation as opposed to successionist accounts, whereby *x* is said to cause *y* as this relationship may be repeatedly observed. In these terms, 'a causal claim is not about a regularity between separate things or events but about what an object is like and what it can do and only derivatively what it *will* do in any particular situation' (Sayer, 2010: 105, emphasis in original). Correspondingly, causal potential is always present but is only activated under particular conditions.

To illustrate this in even more concrete terms, Figure 6.2 reflects back on the Volkswagen case to demonstrate these causal dynamics. If we start with the individual conspirators involved, we see that they possess a range of capacities that make the fraud possible. Some of these capacities are internally generated, representing a part of the individual; others are externally shaped, embedded in particular social relations (e.g., division of labour). The individual offenders implicated in the fraudulent conspiracy possess particular knowledge, skills, and expertise and varying personalities, relational positions, and so on, that determine how they visualise the potential ways for realising the emissions fraud, or 'scripts'. The opportunity and visualisation of the emissions fraud first came about in 2006 as VW sought to enter the US car market based on a strategic narrative of 'clean diesel' ahead of stricter environmental regulations (in relation to nitrogen oxides specifically) coming into force in 2007. The project was referred to internally at VW as the US'07 project. However, it soon became apparent to engineers at that time that VW did not possess the required engine technology to meet US emissions standards. It is at this point that a more 'creative' script was needed if VW was to facilitate the expansion into the US. But whilst an opportunity arose, how this would be undertaken and endure over time reflected the capacities of those individuals involved. A range of employees at different levels of the organisation were implicated over the timeline of the fraud, from departmental engineers and technologists, tasked with developing software to circumvent US emissions standards, through departmental managers and also senior executives sitting on the VW management board who reported directly to the CEO, Martin Winterkorn. Whether Winterkorn was aware of, or actively involved in, the cover-up of the fraud remains unclear and legally undetermined in mid-2024, with conflicting

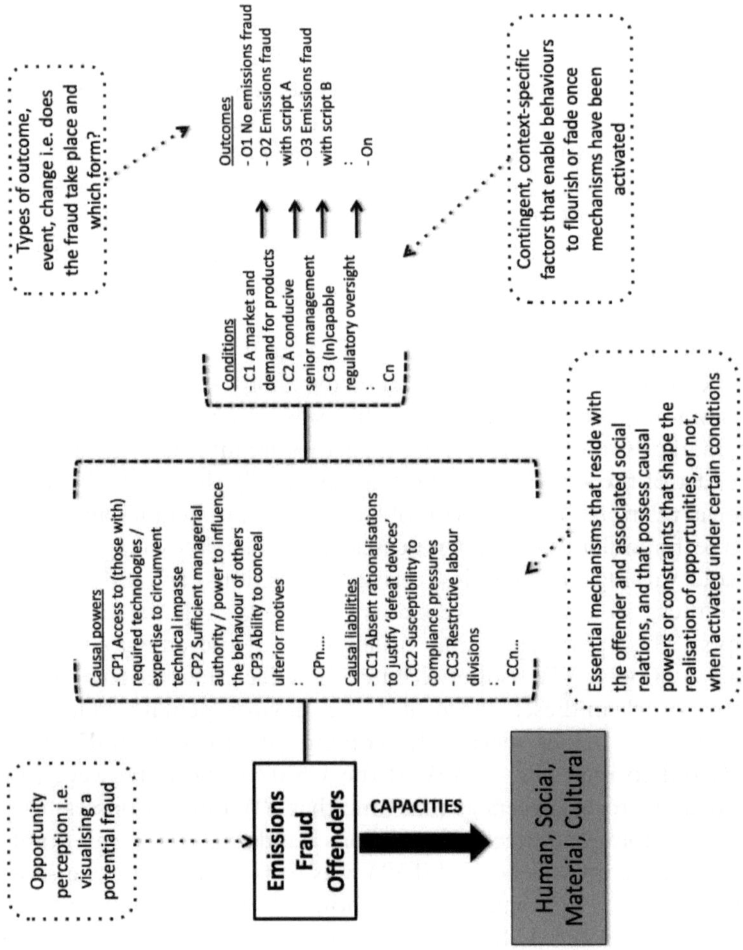

Figure 6.2 A Capacities Model for Emissions Frauds

statements being made publicly by VW, Winterkorn, and suspended/indicted former employees.[11]

In terms of crime capacities, it is first useful to examine the key aspects of the case as based on the Department of Justice indictment of Volkswagen and the corresponding statement of facts. This was also largely informed by the guilty plea of James Robert Liang, an engineer who worked at Volkswagen between 1983 and 2008, including on the defeat device at the centre of the case. Liang provided an insider account of the internal organisational dynamics, decision-making, external deception, and dishonesty.[12] In 2006, two key supervisors at VW, Jens Hadler (head of engine development, 2007–2011) and Richard Dorenkamp (head of engine development after-treatment department, 2003–2013), directed employees to design and implement the defeat device to recognise when the engines were being tested on dynamometers and perform in a compliant mode ('dyno mode') before reverting back to a mode with substantially reduced effectiveness of the emissions control. Dorenkamp specifically authorised engineers to use the defeat device 'despite concerns expressed by certain VW AG employees about the propriety of designing and activating the defeat device software' (Department of Justice, 2017: 15–16).

Various technical issues arose with the project, leading to disagreements over the direction of the approach in 2007 during a meeting presided over by Hadler who, 'despite knowing that only the use of the defeat device software would enable VW diesel vehicles to pass U.S. emissions tests' (Department of Justice, 2017: 16), authorised Dorenkamp to proceed. This was the starting point of a more widespread use of defeat devices in various car brands and model years from 2009 to 2016 that went on to include intentional cover-ups and regular concealment from the US regulatory authorities and consumers. For instance, in 2012, some of the diesel vehicles encountered hardware issues that VW engineers believed were a result of increased stress placed on the exhaust system from being driven in dyno mode. This was explained to two other senior supervisors, Heinz-Jakob Neusser (head of engine development, 2011–2013) and Bernd Gottweis (quality management and product safety 2007–2014), who both encouraged further concealment and went on

11 Handelsblatt (2017) 'Suspended manager sues VW over bonus', available at: https://www.handelsblatt.com/today/companies/heinz-jakob-neusser-suspended-manager-sues-vw-over-bonus/23568200.html?ticket=ST-3748194-LMc74CB57HhFp6ckRyfp-ap6 (Accessed 15 June 2020).

12 At the time of writing, Liang is one of only two VW employees to have pleaded guilty to having a role in the emissions conspiracy. Indictment available here: https://www.justice.gov/opa/file/890761/download. The other is Oliver Schmidt who was released early in 2021 after being transferred to Germany from the US, where he was sentenced to seven years' imprisonment: https://www.justice.gov/opa/pr/volkswagen-senior-manager-sentenced-84-months-prison-role-conspiracy-cheat-us-emissions-tests. The first executive to be convicted in the scandal was Rupert Stadler, former CEO of VW subsidiary Audi, who received a suspended prison sentence and a fine in June 2023. He was convicted of fraud after admitting to his involvement in the emissions cheating scheme.

to perfect the cheating software by enabling a steering wheel angle recognition feature to enable it to know when it was being tested on the dynamometer.

In 2014, the West Virginia University's Center for Alternative Fuels, Engines, and Emissions published the results of a study commissioned by the International Council on Clean Transportation (ICCT) indicating discrepancies in emissions produced when under road conditions in comparison to testing on the dynamometer. However, rather than admit to the violation, Neusser and Gottweis, along with two other senior employees, Oliver Schmidt (general manager in charge of the environment and engineering office, 2012–2015) and Jürgen Peter (VW quality management and product safety group and liaison between VW and the regulatory agencies in 2015), continued to conceal the defeat device, but the regulators were now aware of the potential violation. On 3 September 2015, VW confessed to regulators, and, according to VW, CEO Winterkorn was informed of the defeat device the following day. How high up the scandal went in the organisation remains uncertain, but as Ewing (2017: 334) suggested, '[a]though no current or former members of the management board were named as suspects, Neusser and Gottweis, among others, report directly to Winterkorn. The emissions cheating reached to the management board's doorstep'. Giving evidence in 2024 in a €9 billion investor class action civil lawsuit, Winterkorn testified he didn't know the device was implemented and later, when the US authorities were probing the issue, he didn't know they would react in such a harsh manner that required immediate information of the markets. He assumed VW would promptly produce a legally and technically flawless solution to dispel the concerns. That's what his engineers told him, he said. 'Had everything been explained to me correctly, I wouldn't have hesitated to take the right steps', he said. 'I would have traveled to the USA myself to negotiate with the authorities'.[13] Therefore, he had no reason to believe he was misleading investors or 'the market'.

The Volkswagen case demonstrates the multi-faceted causal and contextual factors that come together at particular moments in time and in particular geo-historical locations, and how the emissions fraud came about due to the coming together of diverse factors and mechanisms that, in turn, were generated by deeper structures. Given its complexity, the VW case may be an exceptional event even among corporate crimes, but our argument here does not depend on its being generalisable to other such cases. However, by focusing on concrete crime types, their scripts and mechanisms, their contexts and conditions, and the structures and capacities that generate them, it is possible to think in terms of generalising to other related forms of white-collar and corporate crimes to see whether similar mechanisms are present, whilst achieving insight into specificity. This represents a concrete conception of causation.

13 https://www.bloomberg.com/news/articles/2024-02-14/ex-vw-ceo-winterkorn-faces-scrutiny-over-role-in-diesel-scandal

Capacities and White-Collar Crimes: Human, Social, Material, and Cultural

When we write of the capacities of white-collar offending, we are referring to those essential mechanisms that reside with the offender and associated social relations in which they are embedded: that is, the psycho-social internally and externally existing and interacting relations. These capacities, or mechanisms, possess causal powers or constraints that, when activated under conducive conditions, shape whether individuals or groups seek to realise particular opportunities for white-collar crimes, and whether they are accomplishing their goals or not. The ability of white-collar and corporate offenders to act on opportunities for their crimes is shaped by varied capacities that determine individual competences, access to opportunities and networks, and conducive environments. Thus, 'a causal claim is not about a regularity between separate things or events but about what an object is like and what it can do and only derivatively what it *will* do in any particular situation' (Sayer, 2010: 105).

Figure 6.3 presents the different types of capacity relevant for white-collar crimes: human, social, material, and cultural. Of course, there is overlap between these, and the mechanisms we discussed are not exhaustive, but indicative of the factors that shape white-collar crime events. We explore these in further detail next.

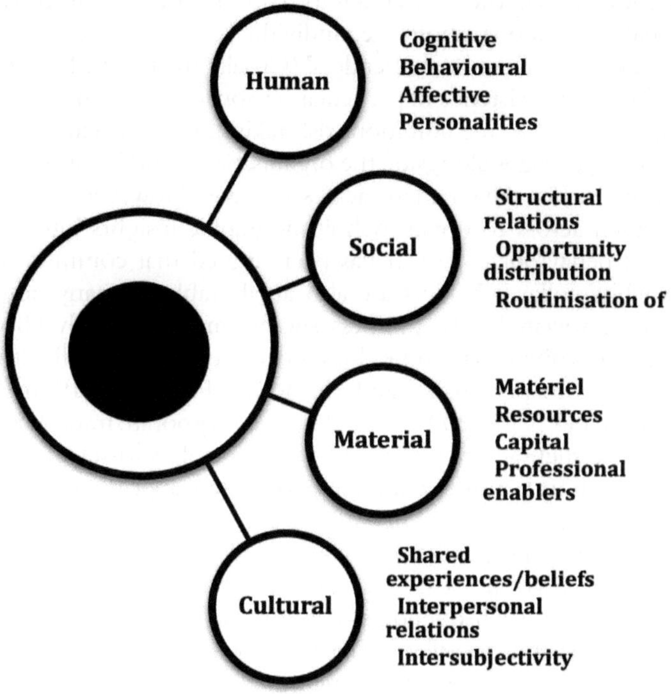

Figure 6.3 White-Collar Crime Capacities

Human Capacities

Human capacities and mechanisms refer to the *cognitive* (how actors think), *behavioural* (how actors behave), and *affective* (how actors feel) dimensions that shape whether any given individual can see and then realise a crime or profit-generating opportunity. These include those subjective perceptions of objective opportunities: That is, visualising how an opportunity could be realised and the potential risks and gains, and possessing the knowledge and 'craft' of how this would be done. It includes those skill sets and behaviours that individuals possess and whether these are sufficient for the crime. If not, others with relevant expertise, qualifications, and skills may need to be recruited. It also includes whether actors feel confident in their abilities to engage with an opportunity, which, in turn, reflects their individual personalities. These human capacities reside within individual offenders but are necessarily embedded in geo-historical social relations, such as educational experiences, social networks, access to extra-curricular learning, and so on. In these terms, we consider it important to recognise an individual's embeddedness in the social and material worlds and how these interact with their psychological constitution.

Early criminology was preoccupied with identifying the differences between 'criminals' and 'the rest of us', but the white-collar offender fell outside this (over-simplistic) analysis, as such elites did not appear within the convicted population. In these terms, 'the restricted information about [white-collar] offenders means that less is known about their individual characteristics or personalities than is the case for conventional offenders' (Croall, 2001: 80). It might be beneficial to examine the existence of particular personality traits and characteristics, such as impulsivity, extreme ambition, risk taking, egocentricity, or narcissism ('the dark triad'), perhaps alongside the organisational and institutional cultures and structures within which these actors operate. However, accessing these difficult-to-reach actors to obtain rich ethnographic insights into motivations and drivers of behaviour is rare. It has been argued that common traits identified with white-collar offenders are also attributable to many non-criminals and are often associated with business success more generally (Box, 1983). That said, 'some white collar crime does indeed seem to be difficult to explain without reference to personality and character' (Friedrichs, 1996: 218). For instance, Babiak and Hare (2007) have described corporate fraudsters as 'snakes in suits', arguing such actors represent an identifiable sub-set of psychopaths, with later research indicating 'white-collar offenders appear to exhibit selected personality traits that are consistent with the construct of psychopathy' (Benson and Manchak, 2012: no page number). Relatedly, Soltes (2016) analysed the motivations (or at least the post-hoc rationalisations) of white-collar offenders, considering also how such offenders draw on their intuition and gut feelings to inform their decisions to offend. This reinforces the interaction between the cognitive, affective, and behavioural dimensions of offending.

It remains unclear if there are personality differences between white-collar offenders and others in similar institutional settings (or who have the ambition and skills to manoeuvre themselves into such settings), or if white-collar offending is more a consequence of differential socialisation into particular (sub)cultures (see Shover and Hochstetler, 2006; Benson et al., 2024). As we've argued elsewhere,

> The latter 'fraud is normal' (at least in particular occupational settings) view over-predicts the actual incidence of fraud among those with opportunities to commit it, whereas the 'fraudsters are psychopaths' view under-estimates the prevalence of deception in the general population by focusing on high-frequency career fraudsters. Both models have difficulty in accounting for change in general levels of fraud between societies, over time and – for individuals – over the life course.
>
> (Levi and Lord, 2023: 484)

Age also shapes the cognitive, behavioural, and affective responses of individual would-be offenders, and might also determine which types of white-collar crime are actually achievable. For instance, more mature offenders (e.g., over 50) are less likely than younger ones to possess the skill set or expertise required to carry our white-collar offences that are dependent on, or enabled by, complex digital technologies. Relatedly, they may face obstacles if looking to recruit and trust younger people with whom to conspire and collaborate to accomplish the criminal script. As these younger offenders age, different scenarios may play out in terms of the use of technologies in white-collar crimes, as they will have grown up thinking in those terms, though further technological innovation might continue the age-technology dynamics we see today. In our view, life course and criminal career scholarship ought to expand to incorporate those actors with a later onset of crime, since opportunities for white-collar crimes tend to come as individuals progress in career terms, gaining access to new offending environments previously not encountered. There are notable data available on who convicted white-collar offenders are (e.g., predominantly male, white, generally older than non-white-collar offenders, middle-class) (see Soothill et al., 2013; van Onna et al., 2014; Benson et al., 2021), on the age at which they start and how frequently they offend (van Onna et al., 2014; van Onna, 2020), and whether they are specialists or generalists in their offending (Soothill et al., 2013). However, further insight is needed into how white-collar offence types change over time as conditions (e.g., post-conviction) begin to restrain or constrict previously accessible opportunities, especially those that need regulatory or professional approval. This is one area in which the categories of white-collar and organised crime (and, for that matter, cybercrime) begin to overlap and cause difficulties for overly rigid criminological thinking.

According to Piquero and Benson (2004: 161), trajectories of so-called punctuated situationally dependent offending draw attention to involvement in offending occurring at different (later) point in the life course, when different opportunity structures materialise, and actors from different (compared to those involved in conventional crime) sectors of the social structure tend to get involved. In other words, the opportunity to offend may become available to the individual only after he or she has obtained a certain occupational position, and the motivation to commit crimes for which they already have opportunities may be activated only if the individual experiences some crisis in his or her personal or occupational life. These offenders may then have longer criminal careers (Piquero and Weisburd, 2009), in some cases into their 70s, as Levi found with bankruptcy fraud offenders in the UK (Levi, 2008). More recently, studies of the life course or criminal careers of corporations have emerged, aiming to understand patterns of offending and risk factors over time in relation to *corporate* recidivists (Blokland et al., 2021), updating earlier understandings from Sutherland and Clinard and applying them for the first time to Europe.

Whilst there may be little evidence to support associations between white-collar offenders and their psychological constitution, variations in personalities are inevitably key factors in decision-making and part of a fuller explanatory account of white-collar offending. For instance, those with more entrepreneurial dispositions or abilities may seek out opportunities to defraud or to be corrupt, whereas others with propensities for crime require the serendipitous interaction of conducive situational factors to be able to see and act on the criminal opportunity. In these terms, Weisburd and Waring (2001) have usefully distinguished between occasional 'crime as an aberration' offenders, intermittent 'opportunity seekers', and chronic 'stereotypical criminals', but, as Piquero and Weisburd (2010) have noted, a focus on the propensity to commit crime is valuable only for analysing chronic stereotypical offenders.

The Craft of the White-Collar Offender

In addition to, and relating to, personalities, important individual factors include the craft of the offender. That is, the competent and confident application of necessary expertise (i.e., skills and knowledge developed through learning and experience) that shapes an offender's ability to visualise and carry out crimes of varying organisational complexity whilst avoiding detection, conviction, and proceeds of crime confiscation/theft by other offenders. For instance, derived from opportunity theories and routine activities models, there is often an assumption that for crimes to take place, there must be a motivated offender, an opportunity, and a lack of capable guardianship. However, while these are necessary conditions for all transgressions, they alone are not sufficient for crimes to actually take place. For instance, however strong their motivation, if offenders do not possess relevant expertise or skills, the crime may not take place (or at least not with 'adequate' much less optimal proficiency). Understanding how the human capacities of individual actors shape interactions with criminal opportunities in particular situations is important to our framework.

Levi (2008: ch. 3) analysed the 'craft' of the so-called long-firm fraudster: that is, business actors who carried out bankruptcy frauds by obtaining credit from lenders and avoiding repayment by failing to keep their businesses solvent. Levi divided 'craft' into two categories: the obtaining of goods on credit, and the avoidance of conviction and imprisonment. (We might today add 'preserving unspent proceeds from others', whether law enforcement or other criminal predators, as an additional element.) He argued further that those fraudsters able to succeed in both areas were 'top-class fraudsters', whilst those who succeeded in the former but not the latter were 'middle-range fraudsters', and those who failed at both were 'incompetent fraudsters'. The implication here is that we inevitably know little about those top-class fraudsters who are able to remain hidden from law enforcement unless our research methods gain access to this community of actors. Central to success in obtaining goods on credit was a confidence-inspiring front; thus, personality or psychological traits may limit or facilitate certain white-collar crimes. Levi (2008), in his analysis of long-firm fraudsters, identified how the ability to withstand tests of cool and character distinguished classes of such fraudsters, that they saw this as a major aspect of their status system and a cause of satisfaction. In these terms, we see that the craft of the white-collar offender reflects the competent and confident application of necessary skills and knowledge to produce a desired outcome or change. Of course, chance events (good or bad luck) can lead to exposure or escape from intervention, as can the level of investigative resource available and motivated to combat the type of fraud or the perceived (by law enforcement) dangerousness of the actor.

The craft of the white-collar offender not only concerns their confidence and character, but also requires a certain level of expertise, consisting of specific skills and knowledge that have use in particular contexts. For instance, which skill sets do would-be offenders require in order to carry out different types of white-collar crimes? Referring back to the VW emissions fraud, the authors of this book, for instance, might be able to recognise the potential for the development of a defeat device to circumvent regulations and understand how it might be done, but (disregarding the fact that we have no access to the opportunity structure) we do not have the skills and knowledge to carry it out, so we would need to recruit others to fill these gaps, and this would require us to work out a way of doing that. This is the distinction between having what has been referred to as 'interactional expertise' (that is, sufficient expertise to interact with emissions fraudsters and analyse their behaviours) and 'contributory expertise' (that is, sufficient expertise to contribute to the actual field of analysis). (See Collins and Evans, 2007.) Whilst Collins and Evans (2002) analysed expertise and experience in the context of science studies and the production of knowledge in different scientific fields, we can also apply this useful distinction to criminal offending. In other words, contributory expertise refers to those actors who have the ability to actually do certain illicit things in certain contexts (such as design and develop defeat software), rather than just understand how those things are done at a more general level. Skills and knowledge in particular domains or fields are situated, but potentially portable. In addition, the skills and knowledge that individuals possess also shape their judgments about any given course of action or non-action.

Expertise for white-collar-crime offending raises questions around the sort of knowledge that is required to make decisions about courses of (non-) action, about which actors need to possess this knowledge, and about how such knowledge is shared within and across networks to enable it to contribute to crime commission. The indicted offenders in the VW emissions scandal possessed such contributory expertise. For instance, the head of VW engine development at the time of the development of the defeat device was Jens Hadler. Hadler possessed a doctorate in engineering, indicating the requisite expertise to understand the character of the 'problem' that was encountered, and how it could be overcome, but, as departmental head, he also possessed the authority, together with other senior supervisors, to direct the activities of his engineers to design, create, and implement defeat devices without feeling the immorality of doing so, or recognising the illegality and/or immorality and overcoming scruples about this via 'techniques of neutralisation'. One such engineer was James Liang, the first individual convicted in the case, who was a longstanding employee at VW. Liang had expertise and experience in software engineering and was involved in the design of diesel engines and, in turn, was part of the group of conspirators who developed and updated the defeat software. These actors possess skills and knowledge, or contributory expertise directly relevant to the emissions scandal, making their capacities situationally relevant. Without re-training and gaining experience elsewhere, for instance, they would be limited in their capacities to carry out other white-collar offences such as embezzlement or accounting fraud, which require different types of contributory expertise. The rise of cyber skills means that less training and practice may be needed for innovative corporate ventures than with the VW case. Likewise, in the case of Theranos, the combination of an attractive idea (cheap and easy blood diagnostics) and attractive 'unconventional' life stories from key entrepreneur and Stanford University drop-out Elizabeth Holmes, the 'defeat device' had less scrutiny than did diesel emissions before raising millions from wealthy entrepreneurs (Carreyrou, 2023). However, VW did not require external funding for 'diesel-gate', whilst Holmes's defeat device was mainly used to send blood to conventional centres for analysis without telling either the tested or the testers what they were doing (at an unsustainable transactional loss). The Theranos story, fascinating as it is, is far less organisationally complex, was entirely US based, and involved a charismatic 'fake it till you make it' start-up bureaucracy rather than a global corporation like VW that, at the end of the 2022 financial year, had over 675,805 employees, with a vast iconic reputation to lose and whose car sales held up well, notwithstanding this highly publicised scandal which was kept in the news for years by civil and criminal trials and (like Theranos) popular documentaries. A key question is whether the knowledge and skills required for white-collar offending are somehow different to more widely shared knowledge and skills (tacit) and/or how they vary by different types of white-collar crimes. The skills to sell pump and dump stocks are generic, so the actual area of trading that they represent is irrelevant. The skill lies in being able to 'tell the tale' in such a way that an 'acceptable' number of victims part with their funds. Other components of the fraud, for example the distribution of the funds and opening or acquiring of a sufficient number of bank accounts for 'money muling' to help launder the funds, may not be possessed by the tale tellers. This is a radically different set of skills from the VW, Theranos, and LIBOR offenders.

Social Capacities

The capacities for white-collar crimes are embedded not only *in* individuals, but also often in social relations. These social relations can be enduring in nature, reflecting long-standing structures in society, or more ephemeral, reflecting short-lived connections. They are shaped by the routine activities of business and organisations, and also relate to the distribution of opportunities for white-collar crimes, whether or not those 'objective' opportunities are realised in practice. In Chapter 2 on 'scripts', we also considered opportunities; their structures, concentration, and distribution; and how they are products of routinised patterns of social activities. Such factors are relevant as part of a discussion of social capacities, but rather than reproduce similar insights here, we encourage readers to revisit Chapter 2. Instead, we now focus on social structures and how they produce contingently necessary 'scripts' or mechanisms and social relations that together shape white-collar offending realities.

Structures and Relations

To understand white-collar crimes and their organisation, it is necessary to consider the antecedents of the white-collar crime commission process. That is, thinking about particular manifestations of white-collar crimes that overlay onto context-specific opportunity structures arising through social patterns of routine activities and determine which scripts will be realised and which networks will emerge gives insight into the actual white-collar crime events that occur. This includes the underlying structures that generate mechanisms that have the power to cause or restrict any given manifestation of a white-collar crime. These deeper but 'real' structures that shape causal mechanisms may not be observable and require us to first identify them in thought, illuminated and informed by prior empirical research into white-collar and corporate crimes.

To provide a more concrete example, in the case of the VW emissions fraud, the causal powers of middle- and senior-level managers, such as Richard Dorenkamp and Jens Hadler, two of the key protagonists, are not reducible to their individual characteristics or managerial positions alone, but are also a product of varied pre-existing and independent structures. For example, we could identify the following structures (S):

S1: the interdependent relationships of Dorenkamp and Hadler with their subordinates and superiors, reflecting the divisions of labour ingrained in modern business.

S2: the interaction of Dorenkamp and Hadler with company goals, assumptions, and values and, in turn, the integration of organisational and individual belief systems.

S3: the competitive pressures that exist for their and VW's business in the market, such as obstacles to entering already competitive markets, in this case the US, where other US manufacturers dominate, and are perceived to have an unfair local advantage.

These are just a few examples of structures that exist independent of individual industry actors, but that contribute to the emergence of particular mechanisms that influence offending, in this case the emissions fraud. (See Chapter 7 also.) We can see that the geo-historical context at the time of the VW case consisted of an enterprise culture within which the pursuit of individual and business advantages was, and continues to be, encouraged in line with free-market principles and other political-economic processes such as de- or re-regulation. Such conditions have (re)produced social inequalities and incentivised high-risk business cultures, whilst simultaneously receiving governmental and political support, such as through the creation of limited liability companies to reduce the personal consequences of failure. The actors at the centre of the VW scandal sought to align individual and organisational gain, whilst pursuing an increased share of the market. Unlike Wirecard, however, these 'national champions' did and continue to produce real goods which worked, rather than financial engineering which turned out to be largely fictitious.

Such structures can vary in their nature and intensity. For instance, employment relations may be more ephemeral and subject to change than market competition, which is a more enduring concern for businesses. But it is only in particular situations and under certain conditions that causal powers will be activated, or causal liabilities suffered. In other words, the engineers directed by Dorenkamp and Hadler to develop a defeat device always had the potential or power to create such software, whether they needed to or not, but this potential was only activated when their subordinate position to their seniors was used to encourage it and as external market conditions changed and created the pressure for the fraud, amongst other contingent conditions. The opportunity was always there, but the context and conditions changed. Had these individual engineers not been part of a subordinate working relationship, they may not have been inclined to knowingly engage in fraud; they may well have interpreted the cheating as part of their duty to the business and its employees and customers, since 'the cars' were otherwise 'good' and – perhaps – the emission rules were created by environmental obsessives and were not 'truly' legitimate. It is therefore the social relation as well as the human capacity that enabled the fraud. In our view, an analysis of these cultural, political, and economic conditions under which white-collar and corporate crimes occur ought to feed directly into the structural analysis in our organisational framework.

Material Capacities

'Material capacities' refers to the 'tools' of the crime. That is, which matériel, resources, precursors, equipment, data, and/or capital are needed for any given white-collar crime? We cannot separate individuals, and their human and social capacities, from the physical and electronic tools they need to undertake white-collar crimes. Doing so would create an artificial distinction when an ability to obtain or use particular resources can be central to crime commission, or how the crimes unfold. (See also Chapter 2 on 'scripts'.) For example, for a corporation to bribe a foreign politician to win or maintain a business contract in their jurisdiction, funds need to be identified that can be used for the bribe, whether cash or some other tangible incentive. But how are these funds generated and concealed from co-workers (including internal audit and compliance), external auditors, or regulatory authorities? They may therefore need to establish shell companies, identify local agents, and fabricate or misprice transactions for goods or services to conceal the bribery. To conceptualise this further, and following on from the previous discussion, different white-collar and corporate crimes will require different materials, some physical and tangible (e.g., defeat device software), others electronic or socially constructed (e.g., online capital or legal structures). The dynamics between the required material capacities and the human and social capacities are significant in that certain materials may have widespread use in varied white-collar crime types (e.g., a limited liability company can be used in tax evasion or foreign bribery), which creates possibilities for specialising or diversifying criminal activities, or repeating crimes. In many cases, obtaining appropriate materials will require assistance from others, either as collaborators or so-called professional enablers, such as accountants, lawyers, or other actors who can provide services for the commission of white-collar crimes. In other cases, offenders can make use of existing materials in their workplaces but conceal the misuse of these for deviant behaviours.

Taking the example of the VW emissions fraud, what material capacities were required to realise the crimes? How might a car manufacturer, such as VW, obtain or develop and install software and hardware to facilitate cheating on emissions tests? For instance, software needed to be generated to instruct the cars' computers how to respond under certain conditions; thus, corresponding data and operating programmes were embedded in the hardware (i.e., the computers in each car) and interacted with the cars' operating systems. This was referred to by those involved as the 'acoustic function', 'switch logic', 'cycle beating', or 'emissions-tight mode'. The computer systems would have been in place irrespective of the emissions fraud; it was the software that was key to how the crime unfolded. But the components and technology for the software were sourced from another major German company, Bosch, which was also implicated in the scandal. Bosch paid a $327.5 million fine in the US in 2019 for its facilitative role in the crime commission process,[14] whilst Bosch provided the lines of code for the software; the company maintained that it was the car manufacturers that were responsible for calibrating and integrating the software into vehicle systems. But this reaffirms the need for professional enabling by others, whether wittingly or unwittingly (and by whom within the corporations) as to the *criminal* purposes.

Capital, in the form of investment in engineering and technology personnel, was needed. Again, this would represent usual business investment, but the resource was indirectly being used for deviant purposes. Similarly, the costs of the corresponding materials, such as computing power, would also have been part of the design and manufacturing process. Data on emissions testing procedures would also have needed to be obtained and understood (e.g., to recognise that steering wheel angle can be an indicator of being tested, as the steering wheel is not being turned when the car is in operation). Understanding these processes would have informed the development of the defeat software. Finally, in terms of precursors, an intriguing aspect of this case (and one reason the fraud was so extensive) relates to the business model of VW that involved shared parts and software across different VW brands (e.g., Porsche, Audi, etc.). Whilst this enabled efficiency and cost reductions in manufacturing as Porsche cars had some of the exact same parts as VW cars, it meant that once the emissions scandal broke, a much wider net of cars and brands of different market prestige was implicated in the fraud.

Cultural Capacities

'Cultural capacities' refers to the existence of shared experiences, social conventions, and interpersonal relations in different offending contexts and environments and how actors differentially socialise in particular (sub)cultures. For instance, if collaboration is needed, there must be other actors who share the primary offender's perception of the opportunity and who are willing and able to offend with them, or who perhaps can be controlled by and relied on by the offender. They may need to bully compliance officers if they cannot conceal their illicit purposes. Thus, inter-subjective beliefs and experiences may dictate whether an opportunity can be realised or not. If actors do not or are expected not to tolerate certain ways of behaving, this can create obstacles to the offending or its continuation over time.

In the VW case, as Ewing (2017: 154) notes, '[w]ritten or unwritten rules of behavior that would have constrained the Volkswagen engineers were weak or non-existent. As Volkswagen later admitted, there was a tolerance

14 FT (2019) 'Bosch reaches $328m settlement in VW emissions scandal', 1 February, available at: https://www.ft.com/content/964a2f72-e898-11e6-967b-c88452263daf; for a later German and Eurojust raid on Kia and Hyundai in 2022, see https://cleantechnica.com/2022/07/04/another-diesel-cheating-scandal-this-time-its-hyundai-kia/

for breaking the rules and a lack of checks and balances'. Ewing further identifies that a culture had been constructed whereby unethical behaviour was tolerated; key approval, decision-making responsibilities, and software development overlapped; and compliance actors did not possess requisite technical expertise to understand the nature of the emissions software and also lacked an understanding of potential regulatory penalties. There was no whistle-blower system in place, meaning concerned employees had nowhere to report (even if they had been so inclined), and where senior executives (and union leaders) were often embroiled in other scandals (e.g., prostitution) that, in turn, communicated a message of 'acceptable immorality' (Ewing, 2017: 154). In these terms, various cultural capacities were at play, activating the causal potential of individual employees, as behaving unethically was accepted in the sub-cultures within the business, and even prioritised, with employees' associations likely to be more frequent, more intense, and for longer duration, introducing conditions that form part of a multi-faceted account of such crimes. This culture was a legacy of senior leadership over many decades. To this, we would add that even if compliance officers had known about potential penalties, these would have seemed highly theoretical to them, since they had not seen them imposed. They might also have needed to be aware of the different probabilities of both detection and formal intervention in the US compared with Germany. If they had been aware and had raised the issues, what would have been done about the complaints?

White-collar offending, then, is often explained in relation to (i) the rational choices that those with opportunities make in pursuit of personal (and/or organisational) gain as the lure of offending, together with a lack of restraint and oversight, and perhaps changing circumstances, becomes more tempting (see Shover and Hochstetler, 2006); (ii) how such individuals might rationalise or 'neutralise' their offending behaviour (e.g., 'everyone is at it', 'I was protecting the business'); and (iii) the lack of attachments that such individuals have to society (e.g., perceiving there to be no direct victims, in contrast to most 'conventional' crimes). However, individual-level explanations do not sufficiently account for the influence of organisational cultures or wider political-economic/cultural structures and can 'underestimate the pressures within society and organizational structures which impel those individuals to commit illegal acts' (Schrager and Short, 1978: 410).

The micro-, meso-, and macro-level influences on white-collar crime (see Vaughan, 2007) can be analysed through the lens of the organisation and organisational cultures. The organisation provides the means, setting, rationale, and opportunity for corporate deviance (Punch, 1996, 2011). Some organisations may exhibit pathological characteristics (e.g., a diffusion of responsibility, an absence of clear operating procedures, low internal compliance, or destructive social dynamics), but such associations and internal linkages are difficult to test empirically, especially if one aims to test how common they are in non-offending/undetected offending analogous organisations. Except where a trail of emails and internal phone recordings make them manifest – as in recent banking rate–fixing scandals – it can be difficult to prove beyond a reasonable doubt that senior staff had active knowledge of misconduct. Such difficulties in attributing liability are quite unlike those in areas of crime for gain, for which we have merely to link the actor to the act (though proof of knowing involvement in 'organised crime' can also be difficult). This raises issues for our construct of the 'crime commissioning process' discussed earlier: some frauds and other corporate crimes may be planned/commissioned from the start, but others emerge (or fail to emerge) in the dynamics of business activities. Abstract analysis of 'crime commissioning' may still require specification of the conditions for its emergence, but it may not be planned in the way that, say, Ponzi schemes or 'long-firm (bankruptcy) frauds' (Levi, 2008) are planned.

The attitudes of senior managers have long been recognised as important (Clinard and Yeager, 1980) as the 'tone from the top' shapes how behaviours are (re)defined as acceptable or not. But rather than having a cohesive and singular 'corporate culture', there may also be sub-cultures in organisational and institutional settings that can be in tension, with the key being to understand how and why the priorities of certain cultures, groups, or departments are considered more important than others. For instance, the professional ethics of lawyers or accountants may give way to commercial pressures to advise how far companies (including those associated with foreign 'oligarchs') can get away with certain activities, as they try to hit their own personal commercial targets set by the firm. The organisational mindset is further reinforced through processes of organisational selection and socialisation while 'walls of secrecy and silence' may also emerge as colleagues, through cognitive dissonance, concerted ignorance, or an absence of interest in or fear of disclosing the truth, do not blow the whistle on deviance in the workplace (van de Bunt, 2010).

Practices, processes, and collective decisions to benefit the corporation become more than simply the sum of individual actions (Fisse and Braithwaite, 1993; Punch, 1996). In such settings, the morality, voice, and internal restraints of 'good' individuals may be suspended and become lost in the 'groupthink' of the organisation, a context reinforced by the potential for the depersonalisation of one's actions and the cognitive dissonance of colleagues. Rationality becomes bounded with amoral calculations for the benefit of the business taking priority (Kagan and Scholz, 1984). Thus, the structure, culture, and personality/identity of business are key variables that help us explain why some companies and managers turn to deviant solutions/practices (Punch, 1996). The same logic can be applied to Russian and other drug cheating in the Olympics and World Championships, although there, national disciplinary measures against dissenters would be severe indeed, and sometimes fatal (Paoli and Donati, 2014; Rodchenkov, 2020).

Understanding white-collar and corporate crimes requires us to analyse the situations, processes, contexts, and structures that pressure, drive, generate, or 'make rational' decisions to engage with an opportunity for crime. There is some overlap here with viewing white-collar and corporate crimes as 'situated action' (Suchman, 1987). This has long been recognised in the area of organisational crime (see Vaughan, 1996, 1998, 2007), and reinforces that '[a] fundamental sociological understanding is that interaction takes place in socially organized settings. Rather than isolating action from its circumstances, the task of scholars is to uncover the relationship between the individual act and the social context' (Vaughan, 1998: 31). In these terms, we must consider how specific situations, including the material and social circumstances and conditions, shape offending behaviour.

Conclusion

Focusing on the capacities and mechanisms of white-collar and corporate crimes is more than an analysis of individuals, situations, and contexts; it's also an analysis of the relationship between the objects of study – in this case, white-collar crimes and offenders – and the relations, mechanisms, and conditions related to their occurrence. Questions of capacity imply empirical analysis of complex sets of social relations and dynamics. Analysing the interactions and substantial (necessary and contingent) relations within and between (i) remote distal causes (e.g., the contingent geo-historical antecedents of white-collar crimes, including colonial legacies), (ii) situational opportunities and proximal factors (e.g., particular settings and routine activities of those involved, including the 'scripts' of the crime commission process), and (iii) (pre-existing) networks of offender cooperation and collusion (e.g., the substantial social relations of connection between different causal groups) is needed for a truly comprehensive understanding of these behaviours.

In our view, contextualised theories of rational choice, and the dynamics between choice, organisation, opportunity, and context (Benson et al., 2016), are most promising in explaining white-collar and corporate crimes (in a non-deterministic way). Such theories 'build from a rational actor framework that shows how offending decisions are affected by instrumental and normative considerations. Such theories can take into account micro-, meso-, and macro-level influences and have important policy implications' (Simpson, 2013: 325; see also Vaughan, 2007). This involves identifying how motivated (and cooperating) offenders *necessarily* interact with suitable targets and criminal opportunities in the absence of capable guardians in particular settings and how these interactions and settings are shaped by wider social-structural antecedents and contexts. But offenders need to have skills and confidence as well as motivation, targets, and conducive situations and conditions.

7 Researching Organisation

Introduction

Research into white-collar and corporate crimes can be particularly challenging, especially when we aim to speak with or observe 'offenders', directly or indirectly, as this may require accessing corporate and other organisational subsystems for empirical research, making it difficult to analyse the natural environments and settings of offending behaviours and therefore to understand and/or adequately measure the motivations of those implicated. This applies also to studying public and private organisations that aim to control white-collar and corporate crimes.

In this final chapter, we present a vision for undertaking social scientific research and building theory on the organisation of white-collar and corporate crimes. *Inter alia,* we discuss the identification of the 'building blocks' of white-collar crimes: that is, those structures that generate the mechanisms and relations of white-collar crime commissioning or the unfolding of the crimes over time. We explore different types of research strategy, making a case for concrete research that synthesises processes of abstraction and empirical investigation, and consider how intensive and extensive research methodologies and strategies that offer different accounts of the social world can be used – independently, mixed, or combined – to collect and analyse data on the key factors and issues outlined in the book. We examine current and potential data sources that can inform our understanding of the key ideas addressed in the previous chapters. In doing so, this chapter proposes a programme of further research in the area of white-collar and corporate crimes to advance the area empirically, conceptually, and theoretically.

Identifying the Building Blocks of White-Collar Crimes

As discussed in Chapter 6, there are some social structures that are not directly observable by us as social scientists, but which generate the coming together of particular mechanisms that possess the causal powers (and/or causal constraints) of the commissioning, or unfolding, of white-collar and corporate crimes. A key process in identifying these structures is abstraction:

DOI: 10.4324/9781315100227-7

that is, first isolating in thought what may or may not constitute these structures. This might involve interrogating previous empirical and theoretical literature with a view to developing propositions likely to shape the scripts of white-collar crimes, or it might involve thought experiments to isolate which structures are worth investigating. Structures are defined as 'sets of internally related objects or practices' (Sayer, 2010: 92). Structures can exist out there independent of our thoughts about them, and by identifying the structure of social objects or practices, we can then think about what their existence presupposes.

Figure 7.1 depicts social structure in relation to the corporate bribery of foreign public officials. (Structures will vary when focusing on private-to-private or commercial bribery, or when focusing on domestic bribery only.) In terms of the coming together of the necessary relations of bribery, we know that at least two actors are required: a person who pays or offers a bribe, and a person who accepts or requests a bribe. (In this example, 'bribee' also includes extorters of bribes.) These two actors are further connected through the necessary practice or relation of an illicit transaction, whereby the inducement is transferred or exchanged to the other for a particular benefit. In the case of transnational corporate bribery, the briber in this illicit transaction is necessarily part of a private company, and they undertake their duties on the company's behalf. The briber may be a direct employee of the company, or an individual broker (which may also be a legal entity) operating on behalf of the private company. In this example, we could also distinguish between publicly listed private companies, which have particular disclosure and audit obligations, and privately held companies, like venture/vulture funds, which have fewer obligations, though they are still, in theory, liable under civil and criminal law. This is an important distinction. Similarly, the bribee is necessarily part of a public organisation: their particular position enables them to provide the benefit sought. The existence of an illicit transaction that connects the private and public sectors also presupposes the existence of *international* commerce and a market, in turn creating a further layer of necessity in this particular structure. In these terms, structures constitute both large social objects, such as financial markets, but also small social objects, such as particular individuals and their shared conceptual understanding of business and associated illegalities. We can reduce this even further by recognising that non-social objects, such as the particular neurological or psychological constitution of an individual, form part of these structures. Together, all these objects form a structure that generates bribery opportunities and commissioning, though we recognise that the terms 'structure' and 'commissioning' may carry an etymological baggage that sounds preconceived rather than a dynamic, unfolding process as sometimes happens.

These structures are theoretically changeable but, in practice, are enduring and stubborn. The people or organisations that occupy particular positions within the structure, such as the briber, who might be in sales or other

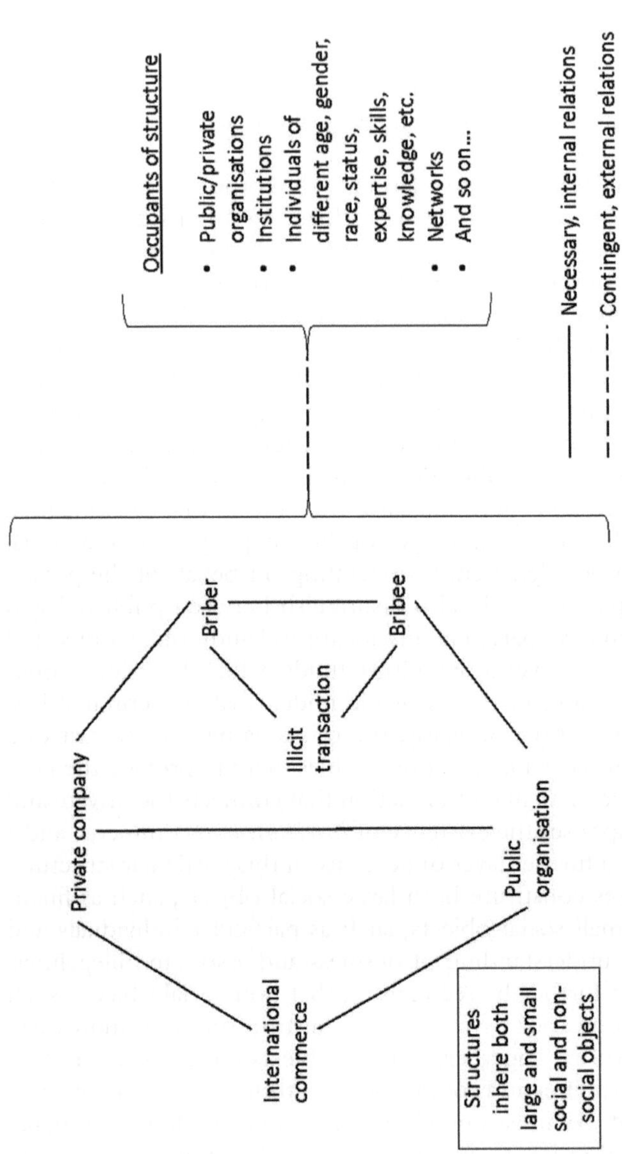

Figure 7.1 Thinking About Transnational Public Bribery Structures

relevant roles, or the public organisation that procures particular goods and services, and awards contracts, do not possess the same attributes or characteristics of the position itself. For instance, whilst a sales manager might have common attributes across varied business types, the people who occupy these roles are only contingently connected in that they may be of varying age, gender, race, status, and so on. In these terms, replacing one person in a high-bribery-risk position with another person may not resolve the potential for bribery, as the structure continues to generate opportunities, so the individual is only partially a driver of corrupt opportunities. That said, change does sometimes happen, meaning such structures may, under different conditions, not generate bribery opportunities. In other words, whether opportunities are objectively there or not, and whether individuals subjectively recognise them or not, can vary depending on the conditions that are present. This may not be predictable in advance and certainly is not deterministic.

This line of argument is particularly relevant in cases of corporate and organisational crime. It is not uncommon for businesses or other organisations (like the police) to frame transgressions by employees or associated persons as being the product of a 'bad apple' when, in practice, they might be better understood as reflections of the structures of the corporation, such as the diffusion of decision-making or accountability across the division of labour, and the corresponding policies, culture, and social dynamics that empower and incentivise those in particular roles to engage in a criminal act. However, as discussed in Chapter 6, white-collar crimes are more complex and multi-faceted than structure alone, as several other capacities must also come together for a white-collar crime to occur.

This structure in relation to transnational corporate bribery represents the isolation of just one 'building block' of how we can begin to explain white-collar crime commissioning. Of course, the objects in this structure will also co-exist in several other social structures that mutually reinforce one another. For instance, the occupier of the briber position might also be embedded in other social arrangements, such as governmental advisor or other prestige executive and non-executive roles. Whilst these other social arrangements are not necessary for bribery, they represent the contingencies of everyday life that may contribute to decisions to bribe, such as where the financial incentives generated for the briber through organisational rewards may provide an opportunity to expand their private property ownership. Structures can and do overlap and shape each other, but we must analyse empirically the specific combinations of contingently necessary relations to help us understand the particular mechanisms that provide the conditions for individuals to offend. This reinforces the complexity of the social world and of explanations of white-collar offending.

In terms of the organisation of transnational public bribery, the necessary structure at the centre of such arrangements will be contingently connected to

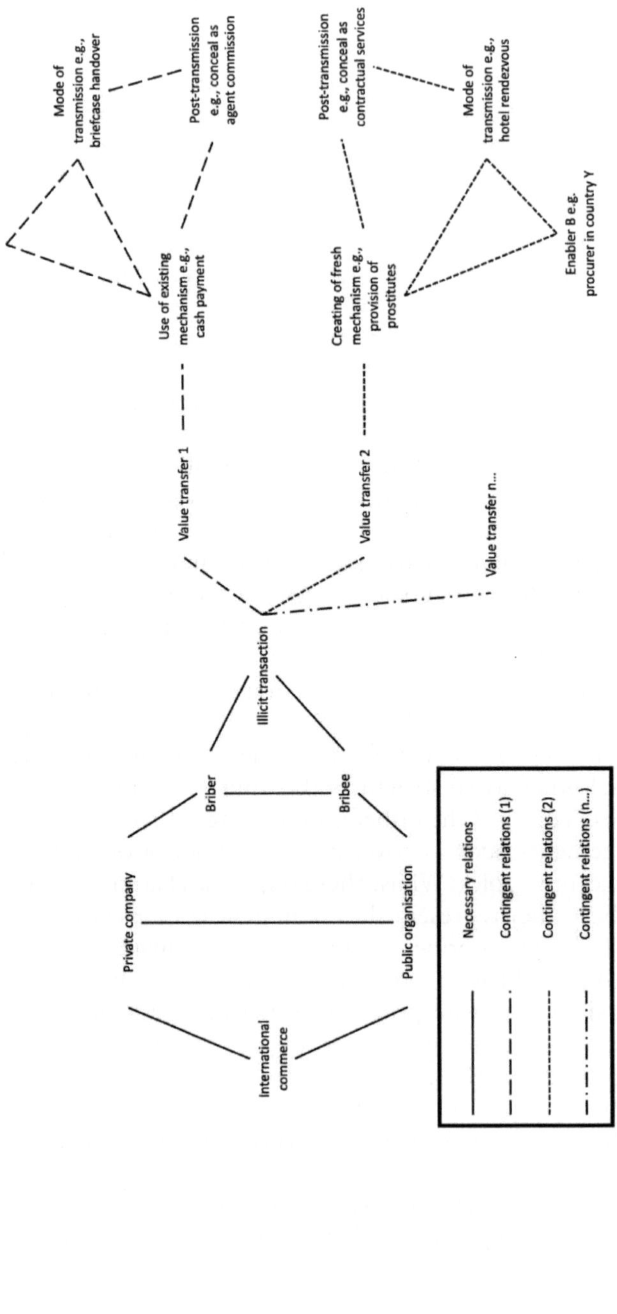

Figure 7.2 Connecting Transnational Public Bribery Structures

other structures. Figure 7.2 depicts such connections. For instance, how the illicit transaction is organised in any given bribery exchange varies but always involves some form of actual or promised value transfer, now or (where trust between the parties exists) in the future. In one case, the actors involved may make use of existing mechanisms for such bribery, such as the payment of cash (pathway 1). To do this, they may recruit agent or enabler *A* in country *X* to make this payment on their behalf. The agent then arranges to meet with the public official or a representative and hand over the cash directly. The bribers would then need to conceal this transaction in the company accounts, stating, for instance, that the funds were for the agent's commission for legitimate work. But whether the bribery is organised in this way or not is contingent on the necessary relations that constitute the bribery. Furthermore, each of these further organisational dynamics will be part of other necessary and contingent structures. For instance, cash payments presuppose the existence of banks and enduring currency markets.

Alternatively, the actors involved may pursue another approach to inducing public officials. For instance, they may choose to identify a new mechanism for gaining an advantage, such as the provision of prostitutes for public officials as they visit the company's country (pathway 2). In this case, a different enabler (*B*), such as a pimp or procurer, may be needed to set up the arrangement, including identifying a discreet location where the rendezvous can take place (with or without electronic recording). These further dimensions presuppose the existence of other structures, such as illicit sex markets, that, in turn, will inhere necessary structures. The bribers would again need to conceal such costs in the company accounts (e.g., provision of contractual services). We could go on to identify a broader array of potential value or financial transfer mechanisms through which the corruption can take place, but each of these is contingent and context specific.

A key issue is that as social scientists, we are not able to isolate particular structures and carry out systematic experiments of cause and effect in the same way that those in the natural sciences would. This has implications for empirical research into the causal relations and mechanisms of white-collar crimes. We might be able to ask particular offenders about which factors influenced their behaviours, but this is beset with obstacles, as respondents might confuse or conflate the impact of different structures, even if they believe they are telling us the truth (or *their* truth) about what happened. For instance, a senior business executive might blame governmental or regulatory bureaucracy rather than the demands and aspirations of capitalist tendencies for incentivising lower-level employees to engage in bribery, and go on to reproduce this issue through their own actions within the business. That is, creating policies geared towards circumventing bureaucracy that are conducive environments for criminal or unethical behaviour, rather than creating alternative rewards structures that might promote law-compliant ones. With this in mind, the next section considers how we can pursue research that goes about connecting these building blocks and structures to the coming together of particular mechanisms, or scripts, and the white-collar crimes that may follow.

Connecting 'Building Blocks' to Mechanisms and Events

As discussed in Chapter 6, and mentioned earlier, the building blocks or structures that generate white-collar crimes are not directly observable to academics through empirical research. Instead, a process of abstraction is required to identify and think about what forms these structures might take and what influence they have on how people and organisations, including white-collar and corporate offenders, behave. We can then question what it is about these structures that might lead to white-collar offending that can, in turn, be empirically observed and analysed, though many instances in which undetected white-collar crimes happen or do not happen remain a problem for our theorising (and for policy judgments about the effectiveness of controls). For instance, what is it about capitalist or socialist interests specifically that might lead to potential and actual discrimination against particular groups by businesses or organisations, and why might this vary across contexts or cultures? There have been protests by a range of individuals, corporations, third-sector NGOs and charities, and even jurisdictions against de-risking/de-banking. These have taken place in elite G7 economies, in China and Russia, and in the poorer countries of the Global South, as regulators and, to a lesser extent, prosecutors pressurise financial institutions to risk rate their customers and applicants for money laundering and terror financing. This has accelerated with North Korea, Iran, Ukraine, and Magnitsky economic sanctions policies which have led to evasion via corporate fronts and third-party countries, in turn leading to open-source intelligence tracking (OSINT) by bodies such as BellingCat to help check the movement of sanctioned oil and minerals, even if such tracking does not itself control the evasion.

For realists, the social world is a layered, complex, and open system, and the critical realist approach suggests reality is stratified into three domains: the empirical, the actual, and the real. This means we can distinguish between the 'real', where structures that have properties that can activate mechanisms that can affect other structures exist; the 'actual', where the events and their effects have been caused; and the 'empirical', where actual events and effects can be or have been observed and experienced. By making connections between underlying structures, the mechanisms they produce, and the events that take place, we can develop a concrete understanding of white-collar crimes. Figure 7.3 represents the connections between these different levels of analysis: that is, between the abstract and the concrete, and between generative structures, causal mechanisms, and white-collar crime events.

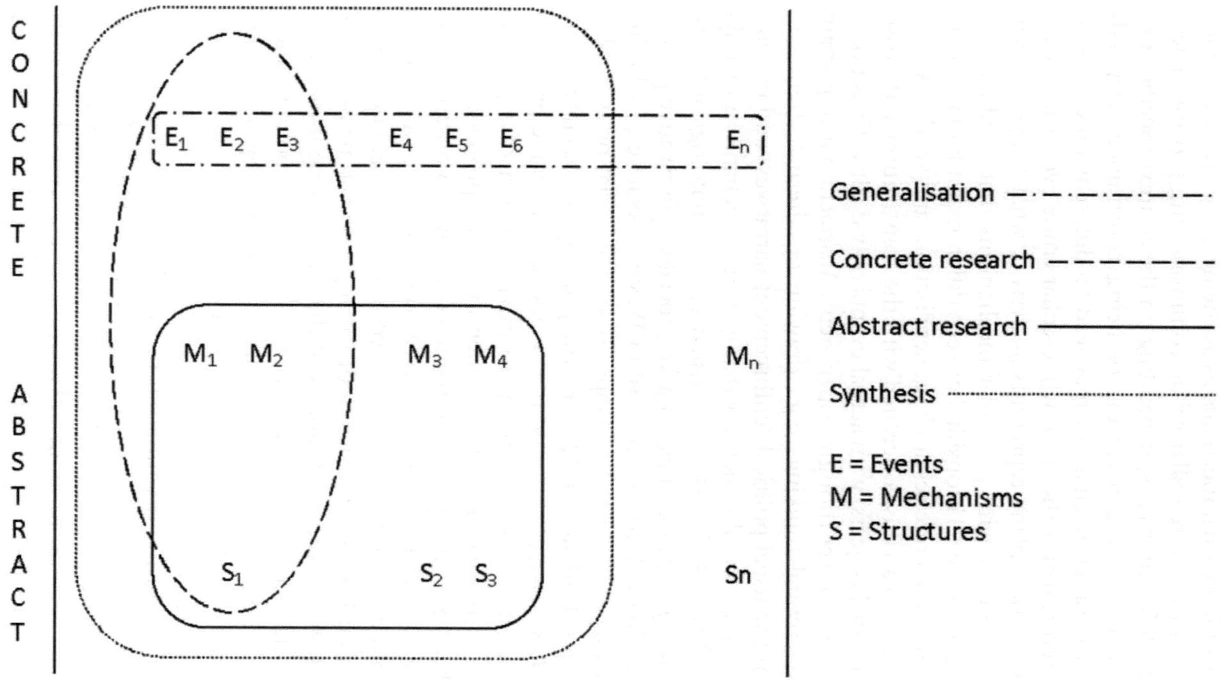

Figure 7.3 Types of Research[1]

1 Adapted from: *Method in Social Science: A Realist Approach*. Revised 2nd edition by A. Sayer, Copyright (Routledge @ 2010), p. 237. Reproduced by permission of Taylor & Francis Group.

The horizontal plane represents the varying structures (S) and mechanisms (M) that may be present in the commissioning, or unfolding, of white-collar crime events (E). As we discussed in Chapter 2 on scripts, we can think of the coming together of individual mechanisms as the necessary requirements, or scripts and tracks, of the white-collar crime commissioning process. These mechanisms produce different events, depending on the context-specific conditions that may lead to a crime occurring or being constrained. Depending on the context, the same mechanism may lead to different outcomes or white-collar crime events, whilst the same white-collar crime events may have different causes. The vertical plane represents analysis of what happens when particular structures combine with particular mechanisms that produce particular events and visualises the relationship between different kinds of research: that is, abstract research, concrete research, generalisation, and synthesis.

At the abstract level, research is concerned with the constitution and possible ways of acting of social objects, with actual events only dealt with as possible outcomes: that is, it involves thought experiment. Abstraction is important as it counters self-referential thinking (e.g., drawing on alternate frames of reference rather than the usual political/enforcement narratives) and encourages researchers to identify social structures that generate mechanisms or ways of acting (Edwards, 2016: 993–994). For instance, in criminological terms, we might point to the significance of free market, socially conservative politics and structures in shaping cultures of control in Western societies, including the shift towards managerial (including impression-managerial or symbolic) responses to crime (see Garland, 2002), or how processes of 'securitisation' (see Buzan et al., 1998) have come to dominate liberal democratic principles and enable authoritarian state interventions to expand as part of a punitive and populist turn. In other words, it entails identifying the processes, structures, and/or mechanisms through which white-collar and corporate crimes are commissioned or unfold. Or we might point to the absence of resources for serious fraud enforcement authorities, or, conversely, the abundance of resources directed towards treating drugs or other 'organised crime problems' as criminal justice issues and the implications of these enforcement prioritisation mechanisms for the occurrence and/or organisation of corporate fraud.

In contrast, concrete research analyses actual events and objects as 'unities of diverse determinations' that have been isolated and examined through abstract research (Sayer, 2010: 236): that is, empirical analysis of how particular mechanisms combine in the organisation of specific white-collar and corporate crimes in certain contexts. In terms of concrete research, in Chapter 2, we looked at market manipulation and saw that the coming together of the mechanisms of (i) calculated positioning and identification of co-collaborators, (ii) recruitment of these actors, (iii) manipulation, and (iv) recompense and solicitation were necessary for the rigging of the LIBOR rate, but whether or not these different mechanisms were actually activated or realised depended on suitable contingent conditions, such as the paradox in regulatory and organisational actors' acting as both 'capable guardians' and facilitators of misconduct. Under different conditions, the market manipulation may not have happened at all, or may have been detected earlier. As far as we are aware, some commercial businesses and individuals did not participate in this rigging even though they both objectively had these opportunities and were aware that they did. In other cases, there might be 'inner circle' people and firms who are in the scam, but outer circle ones who are not invited to participate. Similarly, in other cases of market manipulation, the mechanisms that need to come together may be different to those in the specific case analysed by Jordanoska and Lord (2020). (See Chapter 2.) Structures such as the emergence of finance capitalism and trading relations, amongst others, could be identified to inform an understanding of the necessity of these particular mechanisms or scripts. We can see this elsewhere also. For instance, Tudor's (2019) analysis of investment fraudsters in the UK drew attention to consumer capitalism as a motivator of such frauds: the fraudsters relied on, and feared losing, their financial wealth and lifestyles around consumer goods that formed how they constructed their identities.

Generalisation seeks regularities and common properties at the level of the empirical, where events can be observed, in turn providing more superficial than 'deep' analysis, such as searching for particular features or attributes of the singular notions of 'white-collar crime' and 'corporate crime'. For instance, if we examine the issue of generalisation in relation to the concepts of white-collar crimes, the dominant approaches to the concept are to approach the phenomenon through either an offender-based or offence-based lens, each of which is defined in terms of seemingly generalisable common properties or features. For example, the attributes of *the* white-collar offender pertain to a particular 'high social status' or ostensible 'respectability' (including possible 'psychopathy'), whilst the attributes of *the* offence pertain to particular processes such as an 'abuse of trust', 'dishonesty or deception', and so on. Whilst these approaches point to the value in understanding particular offenders and their methods, they also remain preoccupied with over-simplifying, and theoretically reducing, white-collar crime to a single expression, and identifying 'it' in the cases analysed, rather than looking at the organisation of very specific activities through particular scripts and networks, and appreciating the variation of the coming together of these factors in different places and times, how this organisation evolves over time, and what this tells us about the actual commissioning of white-collar crimes (cf. Edwards, 2016; Edwards and Levi, 2008).

Synthesis aims to combine abstract and concrete research with generalisations covering various constitutive structures, mechanisms, and events. This might take the form of comparing different case studies of white-collar crime in terms of how they are organised and determining whether there are overlaps or interdependencies between the organisation of different white-collar crimes. Such synthesis remains the most underdeveloped but can be beneficial for pointing to the connections between white-collar crimes. For instance, tax evasion benefitting high–net worth individuals may be carried out in isolation to generate illegal savings and, in turn, represent the coming together of structurally generated scripts and events, but it might also be a precursor to investments in insider dealing, such as using funds saved for bribing 'insiders' or for buying stocks on the back of receiving non-public corporate information, which, in turn, may feed into systematic corporate manipulation of financial markets (or, alternatively, merely a source of additional income/wealth). The potential for interconnectedness of formally different white-collar and corporate crimes, or what has been referred to as 'poly-criminality' in relation to organised crime (as conventionally construed), has not been extensively addressed in the research field, with the possible exception of money laundering, where it is intimately connected with all major 'predicate offences'. However, in terms of white-collar crime reduction, it has great potential, as key regular mechanisms can be identified as vulnerable points for intervention against varied crime types. We see these issues raised in the discourse around 'enablers': that is, those actors with skill sets and abilities, sometimes (but not always) with professional qualifications such as lawyers, to offer services to enable varying forms of serious crime. We see value in analysing how different elements of the crime scripts intersect: for instance, how the organisation of an investment fraud may overlap with the organisation of a drug trader via a shared interlocutor or shared service, such as the creation of a 'mailbox company' in Panama. These have been characterised evocatively by Bullough (2022) as the role of professional services in the UK as 'butler to the world', though we would add that the UK certainly does not have a monopoly on butlering services, and many such services are outsourced to or develop independently in other jurisdictions.

With these various research approaches in mind, a programme of research into the organisation of white-collar and corporate crimes that aims to generate fuller explanatory accounts ought to have three key dimensions. (See Edwards and Levi, 2008: 383.) First, abstract research that uses conceptual analysis to identify and isolate in thought the causal mechanisms that potentially, or most plausibly, produce particular manifestations of white-collar and corporate crimes. Second, concrete research that analyses how these mechanisms come together in specific contexts and then aims to substantiate the actual existence of the mechanisms identified and determine other mechanisms that may be at play. This second dimension also includes searching for counter-examples that might qualify or refine the propositions or hypotheses about the interconnectedness or combinations of mechanisms. Third, synthesis of the insights and findings from the first two dimensions, abstract and concrete research, informed by patterns and regularities of the organisation of white-collar crimes extracted through generalisation to also inform an understanding of the interrelationships and interdependencies of organisational aspects of the commissioning, or unfolding, of different white-collar crimes, in turn avoiding an event orientation in white-collar crime research that may obscure overlaps and thus explanations.

Theranos Case Study

To flesh this framework out further, in this section, we examine the case of Theranos to demonstrate how research on the organisation of such white-collar crimes can be synthesised. In January 2022, following a 15-week trial, Elizabeth A. Holmes, the former CEO, was found guilty by a jury in the US of one count of conspiracy and three counts of wire fraud relating to the multi-million-dollar scheme to defraud investors in Theranos, Inc. (but was not found guilty of defrauding patients). In July 2022, Ramesh 'Sunny' Balwani, the former company president, was also convicted of conspiracy and wire fraud on 12 counts, including defrauding investors and patients in relation to Theranos's operations. Theranos was a blood-testing company that Holmes had founded in 2003. She claimed Theranos had developed an analyser (the Theranos Sample Processing Unit, also known as 'Edison') that could undertake clinical tests based on small blood samples and, in turn, produce more accurate and more reliable results more quickly than conventional methods when detecting diseases such as cancer and diabetes. However, as the press release from the US Attorney's Office, Northern District of California, indicates, '[t]he evidence submitted during the trial demonstrated Holmes knowingly made materially false representations to investors and potential investors about the analyzer' (USAO, California, Northern: website.[2]) That is, Holmes knew the analyser was not as accurate, reliable, or swift as claimed; did not perform all the claimed blood tests; and, in some cases, did not compete with other more conventional machines. Holmes even used these existing machines, bought from third parties, to perform blood testing for Theranos. Theranos was propelled by claims from Mr. Balwani and Ms. Holmes that their technology could cheaply and quickly run more than 200 health tests using a proprietary finger-prick device that required just a few drops of blood. Their trials showed that the company managed to use its proprietary device for just 12 types of patient tests. Thousands of patients received inaccurate blood tests, including false HIV results, false miscarriages, and false cancer diagnoses.[3]

A central part of the criminal cases was that Holmes also misrepresented Theranos's financial condition and future prospects to investors, claiming high revenues would be generated when she knew these would only be negligible. False claims were also made by Holmes with regards where the machine 'Edison' was being used (e.g., on battlefields), as well as Theranos's financial and contractual relationships with the US Department of Defence, and fabricated endorsements from major pharmaceutical companies, amongst other misrepresentations. Following a series of reports in the *Wall Street Journal* in 2015 by

2 https://www.justice.gov/usao-ndca/pr/theranos-founder-elizabeth-holmes-found-guilty-investor-fraud

3 https://fortune.com/2022/01/04/theranos-elizabeth-holmes-human-cost-fraud-faulty-blood-test-patients/

John Carreyrou that questioned whether the 'Edison' machine did what was claimed, Theranos went bankrupt in 2018. At one point, Theranos was valued at US$9 billion and thought of as a leader in biotech. Holmes was sentenced to nearly 11 years' imprisonment (later reduced to 9 years), and Balwani was sentenced to nearly 13 years' imprisonment, and they were both banned for 90 years from working for any entity that receives federal healthcare funding.[4] After being allowed bail pending unsuccessful appeals, they were both in relatively civilised prisons by June 2023.[5] Holmes celebrated her 40th birthday in Federal Prison Camp Bryan in Texas with her husband, young children, and parents,[6] with further pictures of her friendship with another US female celebrity fraudster in jail.

The framework described here can be used to identify key structures, mechanisms, and events in the Theranos case. Starting with the process of abstraction, we might think about what the (social) world must have looked like for Holmes and Balwani to have been able to undertake this fraud. That is, which structures and conditions needed to be in place for them to organise and commission the fraud the way they did? Which mechanisms needed to come together? As mentioned earlier, we can think about the significance of US-style market capitalism, the 'American dream', the (de-)regulatory landscape, the privatisation of health services and products, the aspirational-individualist culture that encourages risk taking for material gain (e.g., 'fake it till you make it', emulating Apple's Steve Jobs), and so on. The hyper-localisation of those values among venture capitalists in Silicon Valley is also salient, though it has been suggested that the accumulation of frauds among start-ups *may* have generated a culture change in risk management there subsequent to the Theranos and FTX cases.[7] We might abstract which of these we considered to be of most significance (with a view to reviewing and refining these abstractions if our concrete research suggests we were wrong) and start by developing the building blocks of our Theranos analysis. Figure 7.4 outlines the structural relations of the Theranos-Holmes structure, illustrating the connections between large (e.g., US venture capitalism) and small structures (e.g., CEO-company), and drawing attention to the contingent background of Holmes. We can refer to this as structure 1 (S1).

4 https://thehill.com/policy/healthcare/4418691-elizabeth-holmes-banned-from-federal-health-programs-90-years/#:~:text=She%20will%20not%20be%20able,programs%2C%20also%20for%2090%20years

5 https://www.nytimes.com/2022/12/07/technology/sunny-balwani-theranos-sentenced.html; https://www.wsj.com/articles/theranos-founders-former-deputy-and-boyfriend-to-be-sentenced-today-11670395861; https://www.wsj.com/articles/elizabeth-holmes-is-sentenced-to-11-25-years-in-prison-for-defrauding-theranos-investors-11668809805?mod=series_theranos

6 https://www.dailymail.co.uk/news/article-13047253/Theranos-fraudster-Elizabeth-Holmes-beaming-celebrates-birthday-visit-family.html?ico=authors_pagination_desktop

7 https://www.nytimes.com/2023/04/15/business/silicon-valley-fraud.html

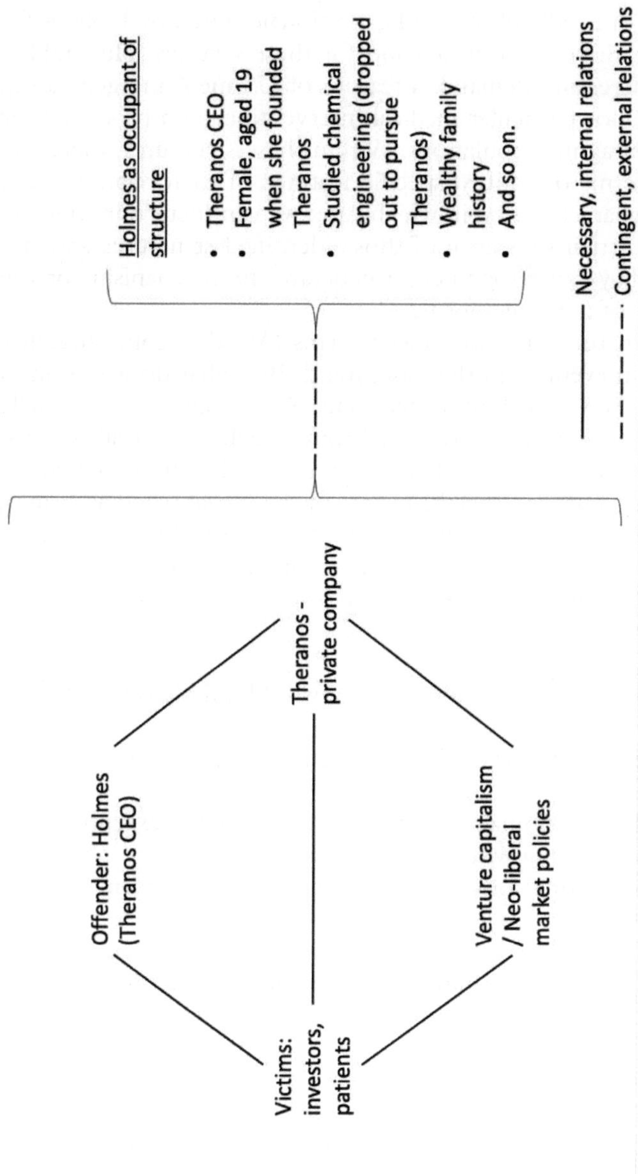

Figure 7.4 A Theranos Building Block (Structure 1)

We can also begin to think about the connections between building blocks: that is, other structures. Figure 7.5 identifies some other structures (and there will be more not identified here [Sn]) that have shaped the conditions in which Holmes could pursue her venture. We can argue social structural trends relating to venture capitalism (S1), the privatisation of healthcare (S2), and increased consumer spending on healthcare (S3) as potentially more significant than the role of needle phobia (S4), a rationale stated by Holmes for starting the company, driving social demand for these services (plus publicity for this start-up increasing demand, a feature of US medicine generating demand from patients for particular medical interventions and products), or perhaps the impacts of aging populations. Within these structures, there will be contingencies in terms of context-specific features of each relation, such as company or actor characteristics, in which case, we can focus our concrete research towards the actual substance of those identified structures and aim to understand how they came together to generate the mechanisms or the particular crime script of the Theranos fraud.

These structures, in turn, generate mechanisms (M) that come together and can lead to certain events – in this case, fraud. But what do we mean in the social sciences when we speak of mechanisms? A mechanism is essentially the way of acting or working of a structured thing, such as a social process, that, in turn, possesses causal powers that, when activated or triggered, act in a way that leads to or generates specific events in the world, such as crimes, when amenable conditions are present. (See Sayer, 2010.) Mechanisms possess causal powers and causal constraints. (See Chapter 6.) For instance, the script (see Chapter 2) of the Theranos fraud involved the coming together of the following mechanisms:

M1: Developing technology (that could never or would not plausibly in Theranos's lifetime work)
M2: Making (false) representations to investors and potential investors to gain capital
M3: Creating a façade of legitimacy by recruiting respectable executives and clinical staff, and contracting with major companies
M4: Deceiving clients by using conventional technologies to perform required services
M5: Making (fabricated) claims about technology uptake and usage
M6: Using legal/financial tools to minimise potential public disclosures
M7: Deriving and benefiting from personal and business (financial and status) gains

These structures and mechanisms combined to generate a major fraud event (E1) in a specific context that lacked sufficient and timely regulatory oversight and intervention, and was enabled through the collusion with the company president (Balwani), and an eagerness to praise entrepreneurialism (e.g., named by *Forbes* as a successful young female billionaire), amongst others. Had the

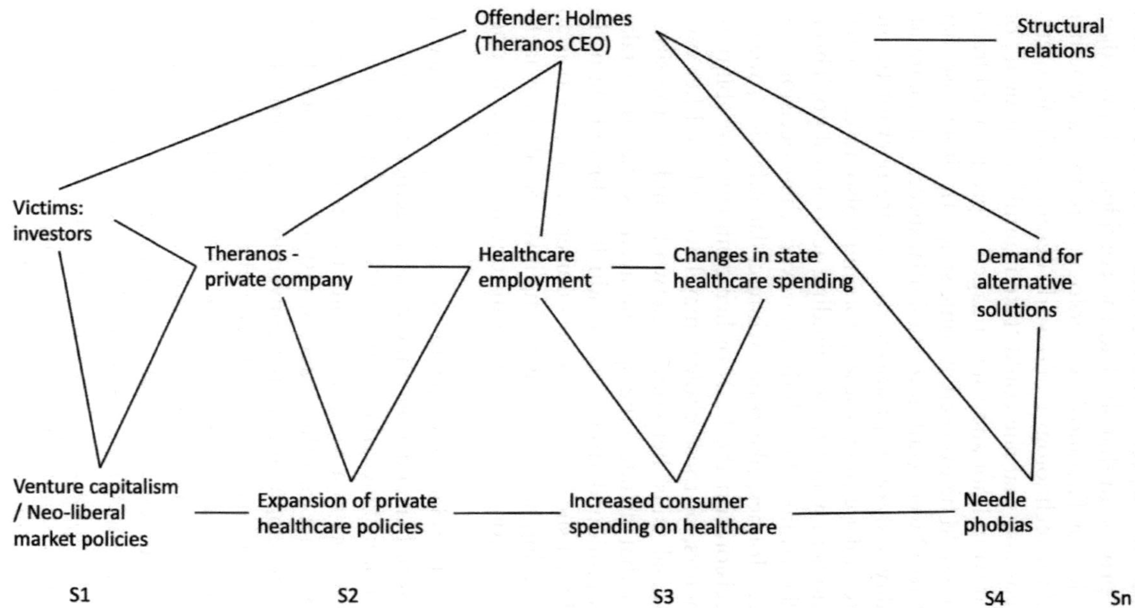

Figure 7.5 Social Structures Underpinning the Theranos Fraud

conditions under which these mechanisms came together been different – for instance, had Balwani been an ethical, prosocial actor who countered or did not encourage his then lover Holmes, or if greater regulatory scrutiny of the medical claims took place – then instead, the fraud might have been stopped (E2). Of course, as discussed in Chapter 6, the capacities of Holmes were also key in the commissioning process in that she had the confidence, knowledge, and skill to persuade outsiders of Theranos's technology. It is unclear whether Holmes ever truly believed the technology could work, despite medical experts advising that it was unlikely, and that she could 'fake it until she made it', or whether she always knew it would not and thus engaged in pre-planned fraud that she must have known would be exposed at some stage. In either case, her personality and personal 'story' were central to the initial success of the fraud. That said, whilst personality and/or dispositional factors are relevant to the commissioning of all white-collar crimes, these actors must also make situated decisions about the directions in which their offending actions will go. This is the case with all white-collar crimes, though the context of these decisions can vary greatly. For instance, Holmes, like other white-collar offenders, would have made procedural decisions on the basis of her confidence or ability to persuade/deceive those actors, or these choices may have reflected her own perceived technical and social skills, her contact network, and/or the situations she found herself in that dictated the specific avenues she could take. The decline of more old-fashioned stresses on gradually achieved status in favour of legendary rapid tech successes by (some) university drop-outs is an important reflection of changing belief systems among investors about what to look for as indicators of stellar commercial projects in contemporary enterprise societies.

Thus, the mechanisms identified here can be seen as being necessary to the Theranos fraud, but whether and how they came together was contingent on specific contexts. For instance, the ability of Holmes to gain access to wealthy and influential investors in a form of 'affinity fraud', which rolled up others reassured by the presence of other 'savvy investors' to provide funds for start-up and company development, source conventional equipment that could undertake bloods tests to maintain the façade of the Edison machines, present data publicly that could neutralise any prospective regulatory scrutiny, and so on, are all contingencies that shaped and provided the conditions for these mechanisms to occur 'successfully'. This, of course, also suggests where vulnerabilities in the fraud commissioning process might occur that might be suitable and plausible intervention points by enforcement authorities, regulators, or other bodies and actors, such as better regulation or licensing of conventional blood testing machines or greater procedural transparency with private medical healthcare providers.

This synthesis of research there encourages us to think about the potential structures and mechanisms that combine to generate a context in which particular types of fraud can occur, and then empirically analyse the mechanisms to better understand how certain events came about. We can then analyse whether such structures and mechanisms may appear in other analogous frauds to build explanations and start to generalise about common features whilst recognising the context specificity of their organisation. In the next section, we consider research designs that can help us undertake such concrete research.

Research Designs for Researching Organisation

To inform this programme further, in this section, we explore different designs for researching the organisation of white-collar crimes. Thinking through the research strategies outlined here is important for clarifying the value of the organisational perspective presented in this book. This next section considers designs for researching organisation and conducting theoretically informed concrete research. More specifically, we consider the implications of the organisational perspective for intensive and extensive research designs. (See Sayer, 2010: 242–243; see also Edwards and Levi, 2008, on the organisation of serious crimes.) According to Sayer (2010: 242), the distinction between intensive and extensive research designs is more than a question of depth versus breadth, as the two types of design ask different sorts of questions, aim to produce different types of accounts, use different techniques and methods, define their objects and boundaries differently, and have different limitations. (See Table 7.1.)

Intensive research is concerned with causal questions, identifying how some causal processes work in a particular case or a small number of cases, and understanding what produced a certain change and/or what the agents actually did. For example, studies of how internal bank actors organised the manipulation of financial markets in particular organisational environments shaped by the structure and functionality of particular financial markets (Jordanoska and Lord, 2020), or how contemporary cases of insider dealing are organised as a product of a legacy of particular legal and business structures and mechanisms (Zeng, 2021). Extensive research aims to identify some regularities, common patterns, and/or distinguishing features of a population, and, more specifically, questioning how widely certain characteristics or processes are distributed or represented within such populations. For example, studies of the criminal career characteristics and sociodemographic profile of convicted white-collar offenders (van Onna et al., 2014), or the personality traits these offenders and whether they constitute an identifiable sub-set of psychopaths. (See Babiak and Hare, 2007; Benson and Manchak, 2012) However, as Sayer (2010: 242–244) notes, intensive and extensive questions 'are widely conflated and confused, particularly when researchers pose ambiguous questions such as 'how much of the variation of *y* can be explained by *x*?' and rely on patterns and regularities in events as guides to causality'. For instance, extensive research that claims to 'test' or 'falsify' causal links, but is limited to superficial analysis of observable events only – that is, actual identified manifestations of white-collar crimes – does not engage with the 'real', unobservable structures that generate the mechanisms and conditions have the causal power to lead to

Table 7.1 Intensive and Extensive Research on the Organisation of White-Collar Crimes

	Intensive	*Extensive*
Research question	*How does a process work in a particular case or small number of cases?* • e.g., procedural aspects of embezzlement in public organisations. *What produces a certain change?* • e.g., why do white-collar actors alter their behaviours? *What did the agents actually do?* • e.g., how do white-collar actors interact; what are the daily 'routine' activities in which their criminal acts are embedded?	*What are the regularities, common patterns, and distinguishing features of a population?* • e.g., business organisations, social groups. *How widely are certain characteristics or processes distributed or represented?* • e.g., where do businesses or groups operate and in which markets?
Relations	*Substantial relations of connection* • i.e., how do people interact; what meaning do they give concepts; etc.?	*Formal relations of similarity* • i.e., which common features exist across groups of people/across situations and locations?
Type of groups studied	*Causal groups interacting in social contexts* • i.e., individuals relate to each other.	*Taxonomic groups* • i.e., individuals share similar attributes.
Type of account produced	*Contextualised insight* *Causal explanations of the production of certain objects or events, though not necessarily representative ones* *Structural analysis (of necessary/contingent relations)* • e.g., how do white-collar actors relate to each other and to licit actors with whom they interact?	*Descriptive 'representative' generalisations lacking in explanatory penetration* • e.g., about the risks posed by white-collar criminal actors. *Correlations and relationships*
Typical methods	*Study of individual agents in their causal contexts (e.g., observing organisational environments), interactive interviews (e.g., with offenders/victims), ethnography (e.g., immersing in the way of life), case studies* *Qualitative analysis*	*Surveys of population or representative sample (e.g., law enforcement agencies), content analyses (e.g., of police and court files), standardised interviews (e.g., with offenders/victims)* *Statistical analysis (quantitative)*

(*Continued*)

Table 7.1 (Continued)

	Intensive	*Extensive*
Limitations	*Actual concrete patterns and contingent relations are unlikely to be 'representative', 'average', 'generalisable'* • i.e., focus on discrete businesses or actors). *Necessary relations discovered will exist wherever their features are present* • e.g., causal powers of objects are generalisable to other contexts as they are necessary features of these objects.	*Although representative of a whole population, they are unlikely to be generalisable to other populations at different times and places* • e.g., identified risks or intelligence for harm reduction of white-collar crimes. *Problem of ecological fallacy in making inferences about individuals from aggregate data* Limited explanatory power
Appropriate tests	Corroboration	Replication

or inhibit (in whole or part) white-collar crimes taking place. In these terms, it is a theoretical failure to limit the building of concepts and theories to actual events that are observed, neglecting to incorporate analysis of mechanisms that could potentially lead to white-collar crimes occurring (or not occurring); causal *potential*, not just causal actuality, is also important, as are the structures and mechanisms that create such causal powers. So, it is not just a question of uncovering more of the 'dark figure of white-collar crime', but also of reviewing opportunities that could have become white-collar crimes but did not.

Extensive research questions are geared towards focusing on taxonomic groups in which individual members share similar attributes but do not need to actually connect or interact with each other. That is, there are formal relations of similarity between the individuals, but it is the features of the population, rather than the individuals per se, that are of interest, and, in turn, how these formally differ from other groups. For instance, studies that aim to understand the race or ethnicity of offenders convicted of different types of white-collar offences and their occupational access. (See Benson et al., 2021.) Intensive research questions aim to understand the substantial relations of connection between interacting actors and their groups: that is, the ways in which individuals, whether they are similar or different, relate to each other structurally or causally. Specific individuals, and their properties, are of interest, as is the mode or nature of their connection to others. Causality is analysed by examining these actual connections between individuals and their groups, rather than the aggregation of formal relations that characterise a taxonomic class. For example, Lord et al. (2017) analysed the interactions between cooperating actors, their motivations, organisational environments, market pressures, and the ways in which the routine activities of the business enterprise provided opportunities as part of ready-made structures for fraud in the food and drink industry. It is important to make connections between the social structural drivers or pre-conditions of white-collar and corporate crimes (e.g., the production and reproduction of trading dysfunctionality in the soft drinks market, along with the ownership structures that dominate and shape the market, as in the earlier case), and the situational or proximate conditions in which particular forms of fraud or crime manifest (e.g., intentionally changing the 'best before' dates on bottles). Doing so helps us understand and explain the contingently necessary mechanisms and relations of the white-collar crime commission process.

In terms of typical methods used, extensive research aims to produce descriptive and inferential statistics through surveys of populations and representative samples, content analyses, or standardised interviews, and is more quantitative in approach. Intensive research aims to study individual agents in their causal contexts, making use of mainly qualitative methods, such as interactive interviews, ethnography, and case studies, to inform a structural and causal analysis. That said, the distinction between intensive and extensive research does not equate to the distinction between qualitative and quantitative strategies, as intensive research may, for instance, make use of survey methods, and vice versa. More generally, though, extensive research aims to produce descriptive, representative generalisations, seeking to understand correlations and relationships but often lacking explanatory penetration. Whilst extensive research may produce accounts that are representative of a whole population, such accounts will be unlikely to be generalisable to other populations in other geo-historical places at different times. Consequently, explanatory power is limited, and there is a risk of ecological fallacy, or of making inferences about individuals from aggregate data. Intensive research generates contextualised insights through structural analysis of the necessary and contingent social relations of the crime commission process, in turn developing causal explanations of the production of white-collar crimes in particular contexts that may not necessarily be representative or generalisable. That said, the identification of necessary relations of particular white-collar crime structures and mechanisms are likely to exist wherever the phenomena to which they relate are present.

Given the corresponding features of intensive and extensive research, it is likely much can be gained from switching between these strategies in a research programme into white-collar crime. For instance, an intensive study into the practices of actors in a particular business organisation or institution that used interviews to gain insight into the procedural aspects of information sharing in relation to mergers and acquisitions would first seek to corroborate these insights by speaking to other informed actors in the organisation. However, to test whether these same practices were emergent in other similar organisations, a switch to extensive research to test for replication would be needed. The key point is that intensive and extensive research strategies play different roles that can complement rather than compete with each other, both offering different insights and accounts that can be mutually beneficial: that is, bringing together an understanding of the formal relations of similarity or dissimilarity with an understanding of the causal, structural, and substantial relations of connection.

Mixed-Strategy Research

With any programme of research, the selected strategy and methods ought to be determined by the research questions identified, in turn ensuring that there is a logical consistency from the research questions through the research strategy, research design, research methods, and data collection and analysis. Following on from the earlier discussion, however, what might a mixed intensive-extensive strategy research programme look like, and what is the benefit of pursuing this? Proposing to mix or combine research strategies and/or methods in social science, criminology specifically, is not new, with various concepts and terms used to describe related approaches emerging, such as 'triangulation',[8] 'combining methods', and 'multiple methods' (Timans

8 Triangulation is a term defined in various ways but generally used to refer to the corroboration of findings and inferences through varied research methods.

et al., 2019: 193). In general terms, '[m]ixed methods research is formally defined . . . as the class of research where the researcher mixes or combines quantitative and qualitative research techniques, methods, approaches, concepts or language into a single study' (Burke Johnson and Onwuegbuzie, 2004: 17). The social sciences have seen a rapid increase in the number of publications mentioning 'mixed methods' in the title or abstract, indicating the increasing discourse around such approaches since 2006 (Timans et al., 2019: 194–195).

When researchers opt for mixed-strategy, mixed-methods research, they

> need to have a clear sense of the logic and purpose of their approach and of what they are trying to achieve, because this ultimately must underpin their practical strategy not only for choosing and deploying a particular mix of methods, but crucially also for linking their data analytically.
> (Mason, 2006: 3)

For instance, different research questions imply different units of analysis (e.g., individuals, organisations, cities, institutions, nation-states), different time-spans (e.g., instantaneous to long periods), different analytical foci (e.g., at micro, meso, and macro levels), and variation in required observations (e.g., of individual instances, representative samples, or entire populations) with a view to qualitative, quantitative, or mixed/combined data analysis. (See Maggetti et al., 2013: 53.) Correspondingly, there are varied 'formal' typologies or approaches to mixed-strategy or mixed-method research but few actual concrete examples of how integration has occurred (Bryman, 2006). Bryman (2006: 98–99) explains the different aspects of multi-strategy approaches as follows:

- Process: sequential or simultaneous data collection?
- Priority: are the quantitative or qualitative data prioritised?
- Function: is the integration of data intended for triangulation, explanation, or exploration?
- Stage: when does the multi-strategy research occur (research question formulation, data collection, data analysis, data interpretation)?
- Strand: are there one or multiple data strands?

The logic and rationale that underpin the research choices and decisions to pursue mixed-method strategy are fundamental. Mason (2006) identifies six common strategies for mixing approaches in social science research: (i) Mixing methods for a close-up illustration of a bigger picture, or for background (rhetorical logic); (ii) Mixing methods to ask and answer differently conceived or separate questions (parallel logic); (iii) Mixing methods to ask questions about connecting parts, segments, or layers of a social whole (integrative logic); (iv) Mixing methods to achieve accurate measurement through triangulation (collaborative logic); (v) Mixing methods to ask distinctive but intersecting questions (multi-dimensional logic); and (vi) Mixing methods opportunistically (no intrinsic logic). (See Jordanoska and Lord, 2022, for an application of these strategies to compliance research.)

Attempts to add breadth or depth, or embellish intensive with extensive, and vice versa, represent a *rhetorical logic* as the intention is embellishment rather than the combination being a core part of the argument. For example, this might involve research driven by extensive, quantitative logic using large-N surveys to identify patterns or regularities in the implementation of anti-fraud policies across businesses, with a selection of business case studies to provide context, despite not being a primary objective and adding little to the core arguments. Such embellishment is straightforward but has limited explanatory value due to the lack of multi-method dialogue, with a tendency to polarise strategies (i.e., quantitative over qualitative and vice versa).

Attempts to pose different questions related to the same phenomenon but with no analytical connection represents a *parallel logic* as, whilst there is a presence of intensive and extensive strategy, these are not part of an integrative overall argument. For example, a project on banks' compliance with anti–money laundering (AML) regulations that inheres two discrete streams of research, one surveying AML compliance breaches by banks (an aggregation of the people who made or failed to make the sanctioned decisions), the other scrutinising decisions by bank employees to de-risk (i.e., to get rid of) clients: these are related concerns that lack analytical integration as data may not be connected across the research questions.

Attempts to mix intensive and extensive strategies to ask coherent questions about connecting parts of a social phenomenon whereby there is a predetermined, agreed, and clear sense that the separate parts are parts of a whole, represents an *integrative logic* as each method or strategy is rationally suited to the phenomenon, with the combination adding meaning. For example, research with an overarching intention to inform in what ways and under which conditions medical frauds are organised might be done by integrating an analysis of enforcement or regulator case file investigative data with semi-structured interviews with those implicated and with those tasked with investigating. This directly links data from constituent parts of the project for a fuller explanation using different methods, but it has potential for fragmentation if research questions across the projects are not clear and agreed on.

Attempts at mixing intensive and extensive strategies and methods in pursuit of triangulation support accurate measurement from different vantage points in pursuit of validation represent a *collaborative logic* as different forms of data and methods corroborate the object of inquiry or each other. For example, in pursuit of a more 'scientific' precision in the measurement of food frauds, triangulation may be involved to increase rigour as researchers first design a scale for statistically modelling levels of tolerance of food adulteration by individual business employees as part of the processing of minced beef products, and then follow this up with ethnographic research in a processing plant to gain deeper insights into why individuals tolerate these practices. However, different methods or approaches do not always corroborate each other straightforwardly, whilst the skill sets and predilections of researchers and expectations of funding bodies and journals may limit opportunities for such corroboration.

Attempts to ask distinctive but intersecting intensive and extensive research questions have a collective (rather than integrative) approach that brings together different disciplines, frames of reference, and epistemological/ontological positions to develop intersectional ways of thinking and seeing with a *multi-dimensional logic*, and where the distinctive (and competing) strengths and potential are allowed to flourish, social complexity can be appreciated. For example, a project on corporate tax frauds that does not leave questions of the enforcement of criminal and regulatory laws to criminologists, the construction of social norms on tax compliance to sociologists, questions of economic rationality or cost-benefit analysis to economics, or questions of corporate decision-making to organisational psychologists, but instead brings these perspectives together, allows disciplinary tensions to flourish rather than be subsumed by the agendas or intentions of others. This can encourage multi-dimensional insights and enhance social-scientific explanation, but there is a risk that such projects are instead badged and bracketed off/isolated as 'interdisciplinary' rather than just accepted as good social science.

Opportunistic mixing of strategies and methods has no intrinsic logic as this is done by chance rather than design, meaning careful evaluation is required as to potential benefits. For instance, a study into how organisational cultures may be conducive to health and safety violations at work is serendipitously offered a dataset on employee perceptions of occupational health that was not initially part of the research strategy.

Ensuring that the research aims and logic of using mixed-strategy research approaches is key, and this requires designing in the approach at an early stage. Often, research strategies align with intensive and extensive approaches to research, as discussed earlier, although there are varying ways of mixing or combining methods and strategies in white-collar and corporate crime research. The strategies discussed here are shaped by practical (e.g., possessing inadequate research skills), political (e.g., power, status, and imbalances between researchers, teams, and disciplines), and resource (e.g., constraints of funding) issues (Mason, 2006: 11–12). Similarly, barriers to implementing 'genuinely integrated' mixed-methods research have been identified, including the expectations of different audiences, methodological preferences, the structure of research projects, the role of timelines, skills specialisms, the nature of the data, bridging ontological divides, and the problem of exemplars (Bryman, 2007: 12–20). Mixed strategy research should appeal to scholars of white-collar and corporate crime, as the mixing of intensive and extensive research enables the transcending of traditional objectivist-interpretivist divides, framing research in line with conceptions of social realities that are stratified and emergent and in line with integrated agency-structure accounts, and the foregrounding multi-dimensional causal tendencies. (See Sayer, 2010; Gorski, 2013.) Sometimes, in the course of research, further opportunities may come up involving different research questions and methods, but what we are arguing is that care needs to be exercised that these issues are properly connected theoretically rather than just being added together.

Conclusion

Throughout the course of this book, we have provided an analytical framework for an (not 'the') organisational perspective on white-collar and corporate crimes. The framework has social-scientific benefits, in that it provides for fuller explanatory accounts of white-collar and corporate crimes by integrating an understanding of the connections between the real (i.e., the underlying generative structures and causal mechanisms that, when activated, lead to particular white-collar crime events), the actual (i.e., the occurrence of particular white-collar crime events), and the empirical (i.e., the experiences we have of those white-collar crime events that occur) dimensions of these behaviours. The framework provides for a more concrete conception of the multi-faceted mechanisms, relations, and conditions that lead to these crimes, rather than searching for causality within the domain of the 'actual' (as we see with many positivist accounts) or denying that the domain of the 'real' exists at all, even in principle (as we see with many interpretivist accounts). Recent methodological and conceptual developments, such as we see with crime script and social network analysis, have provided a way of undertaking empirical research that illuminates the necessary relations of particular white-collar crimes that are structurally generated, and their connections to contingent, context-specific situations and environments. The framework has clear policy and practice benefits, in that we can aim to identify the necessary relations between different white-collar crimes and, in turn, inform an understanding of the actual commissioning process or unfolding of white-collar and corporate crimes, the structures that generate these, and thus the development of better-informed strategic interventions. This has further potential where there are interdependencies and overlaps between different white-collar and corporate crimes. However, as with all concrete research approaches, what we can feasibly do in our research is shaped by various intrinsic and extrinsic factors. For instance, in intrinsic terms, our individual research competencies and limitations, our disciplinary and geographical constraints, and our skill sets to be able to understand certain kinds of analysis restrict what we can do alone (or in teams). In extrinsic terms, we are constrained by the funding we can obtain to cover our research time (historically challenging in the field of white-collar crimes) and the policy environment that marginalises our areas of interest.

In addition to the more traditional qualitative and quantitative methods associated with intensive, ad extensive, or mixed research strategies described here, research data has also been accessed from novel sources. For instance,

Soltes (2016) corresponded with offenders via letters whilst they were in prison, before going on to visit them in person, to better understand why these offenders 'did it'. Hunter (2015) analysed the written autobiographical accounts of offenders to understand how they attempted to avoid reoffending post-punishment. There are an increasing number of serious journalistic accounts of the genesis of scandals and cover-ups, some of which have been mentioned in this book (e.g., Enrich, 2018; Wylie, 2020; Wallis, 2021; Blackhurst, 2023; Carreyrou, 2023; McCrum, 2023; Verity, 2023). There are also broader-ranging texts on Grand Corruption (Belton, 2021; Burgis, 2020) and on the professional services sector that primarily focus on the UK (Bullough, 2022) but can be applied – with contextualisation that emphasises their different histories and different socio-legal professional frameworks (e.g., Levi, 2022 on lawyers) – to the rest of the world. Open democracy advocates and NGOs also offer datasets that can be used as part of intensive and extensive research, such as information on company formation over time, criminal and regulatory violations of corporations, and so on. Thus, there is much data out there that can inform our research.

The organisational perspective and corresponding research approach recognises that the knowledge we produce on white-collar and corporate crimes might be wrong. For instance, processes of abstraction to identify structures that generate mechanisms that must come together for the commissioning, or unfolding, of white-collar and corporate crimes are liable to be incorrect as it is only by following concrete research that their causal powers can be determined. Therefore, we may have to engage in critical reflection before, during, and after the research process and identify alternative structures on mechanisms that may instead have causal powers. This would constitute an adaptive approach to building theory iteratively through abstraction of potential causes and analysing empirically how they come together to create events in particular contexts, before then adapting and refining explanations as the research validates, falsifies, or modifies the initial propositions. The research process can involve both intensive and extensive research strategies or a combination of these to better understand the realities of white-collar and corporate crimes. It follows, then, that

> [R]ealists are methodological pluralists. Instead of privileging certain designs for deducing crime, for example from the outcomes of experimentation, or inducing crime through the insights of ethnography, realists admit the use of a plethora of research designs so long as they contribution to the adaptation and refinement of concrete conceptions of crime.
>
> (Edwards, 2015: 27)

Approaching research into white-collar and corporate crimes in this way allows us to determine or infer which explanatory accounts are more or less defensible and of practical use. It also allows us to reflexively interrogate the methods we use to collect data on white-collar and corporate crime phenomena and identify, to the greatest extent defensible, which factors are able to produce particular outcomes. These processes are fundamental to producing and building robust concepts and theories on the organisational aspects of white-collar and corporate crime commissioning.

8 Reflecting on an Organisational Perspective

Introduction

We end with some reflections. Readers who have made it this far, having worked through the organisational perspective and its key components in order, might be wondering where the framework fits within existing theorising on white-collar and corporate crimes. In the book, we have not engaged significantly with dominant theoretical perspectives that help us understand why individuals and/or organisations engage in crimes, though individual, organisational, or social-structural levels of abstraction are relevant to the various components of our framework. Similarly, we do not cover areas such as attitudes to and social and political movements against white-collar and corporate crimes, or engage in depth either with qualitative, case-study-oriented research, or with more quantitative, survey-based research, that provides empirical insights into the nature, extent, and scope of white-collar and corporate crimes. There is much out there that enhances our understanding of the structures, drivers, conditions, mechanisms, and relations of white-collar and corporate crime offending, and, in our view, the organisational perspective offers fresh ideas for thinking about how we may fruitfully theorise, conceptualise, and research white-collar and corporate crimes. We are beginning an intellectual journey, and many questions still remain, but we hope you will agree that focusing on organisation offers a novel framework for interpretation which complements rather than supplanting the array of existing ones.

In this concluding chapter, we consider four issues: (i) Accounting for change (over time and place), (ii) Implications of an organisational perspective for regulation and control, (iii) White-collar and corporate crimes in digital economies and societies, and (iv) Problematising the unresolved. These issues have appeared in various parts of the book, sometimes explicitly but at other times merely implied.

Accounting for Change (Over Time and Place)

If it is not clear yet, in this book, we have drawn attention to the multi-faceted nature of white-collar and corporate offending, arguing that only by thinking

DOI: 10.4324/9781315100227-8

through the context-specific 'unity of diverse determinations' (Edwards, 2015: 26) can we begin to develop concrete insights into causal accounts of these behaviours. Successionist causal accounts (e.g., that excessive greed is the root cause of frauds by business or, as per Cressey's (1953) account – replicated and critiqued by Klenowski and Copes (2013) – that *only* the combination of non-shareable problems and culturally available rationalisations causes embezzlement by executives (as these are repeatedly observed relationships)) are superficial, stuck at the level of what we can observe some of the time. It also is arguably tautological, if greed – a moral rather than analytical label – becomes 'excessive' if and only if it leads to crime. Some defenders of capitalism might assert that greed is good, provided it is constrained by obedience to law (though some contend this constraint only applies morally when the laws are 'sensible'). But recognising the multi-faceted nature of white-collar offending is not satisfied solely by multi-factorial accounts, as these may fail to distinguish what is necessary from what is contingent, and how what is contingently necessary varies over time and place. Building theory to make sense of combinations of factors, why some identified causal mechanisms are activated only some of time, why some conditions restrict the coming together of key factors at other times, and so on, is necessary to move beyond description to explanation.

Some might question at what point we begin to disregard the multiple factors or variables that have been thought to shape offending behaviour. The complexity of the social world does not permit a comprehensive, or exhaustible, incorporation of all factors with causal potential, so we must embrace the fact that our accounts are fallible and subject to inaccuracies, but open to refinement and the pursuit of fuller and more objective explanatory accounts over time. We build and adapt theory and explanations as we identify or abstract in thought what propositions represent the key context-specific determinations of different white-collar crimes. By doing this, we engage in a process referred to as retroduction, whereby we refine and adapt our conceptions of white-collar crimes to rationally identify and judge the more plausible accounts, or to develop knowledge that is increasingly 'practically adequate' (Sayer, 2010). This approach is distinguishable from approaches more closely aligned to either deduction or induction. The more concrete research we undertake on white-collar crimes, the more likely it is we can begin to establish common referents or generalisable insights.

Away from theory building, and in terms of the societal treatment of white-collar and corporate crimes, we frequently see that such crimes are treated in a static way, as if their relative unimportance is inevitable. However, if we look across the globe, we see how in some countries, such as Brazil, China/Hong Kong, Malta, Romania, Singapore, South Korea, and many others, societal (and criminal justice) treatment of business crimes (or at least *some* business and governmental crimes) does indeed change over time, not always in the same direction. But how do we account for such societal change and for its absence at other places and times? Sometimes external scandals and criminal justice interventions by other countries (historically, most commonly, the US as 'the world's police officer') can override local impunity (as in insider trading, FIFA corruption and sports doping scandals, and violations of Iranian and Russian sanctions). Sometimes (but far from often), internal democratic revolts occur to overthrow corrupt political regimes, as in Malta, Romania, Slovakia, and Peru. The role of external national actors, international bodies (especially EU, FATF, IMF, and OECD), independent media organisations, and international consortia of them can often be important but can be subject to allegations of economic, political, and personal partiality, and are not usually successful against politically and economically powerful countries. (Though allegations can be true or false, independent of the motives of the accusers.) Understanding how scandals unfold and their subsequent impacts (or lack thereof) on societal or state appetites for responding to the behaviours associated with them is of great sociological interest, and can tell us something about how change can occur.

Such societal changes are (re)shaped in many ways. For example, 'moral entrepreneurs' – that is, those who consider themselves representatives of world society who ostensibly promote social justice – may place fairness and transparency as central values, and much law transforming formerly 'lawful but awful' legal behaviour (see Passas, 2005) into 'white-collar crime' is the result of such moral entrepreneurship, combined with practical politics. High-level or 'grand' corruption, including political corruption, is exemplified by the creation of international frameworks such as the UN Convention Against Corruption and the OECD Anti-Bribery Convention, alongside a rise in non-state private and civil society attempts at reducing corruption, however imperfectly measured. The latter include the Council of Europe's GRECO evaluations, some of the work done by Global Witness and Transparency International, and the Partnership Against Corruption Initiatives. We have also seen a substantial rise in corruption research and scholarship in academia – most of it outside criminology departments – that aims to better understand, measure, and provide mitigations or even solutions to 'the' corruption problem globally (or, as we would prefer to consider them, to *some* corruption problems). Although there is more transnational scholarship (and transnational investigative journalism) than there used to be, white-collar criminologists still tend to be national (or over-global) in their empirical orientation, and country coverage is patchy. Elsewhere, political and business elites may endeavour to preserve their own interests through legal changes and resistance to others, and technocrats may seek to introduce rational oversight by enhancing bureaucracies and evaluations, both 'mutual' and by professional secretariats (Levi and Gilmore, 2002). It is important to recognise the array of personal, institutional, and social objectives.

This makes us consider what it would take to create big shifts in both the organisation of white-collar crimes (e.g., the scripts, networks, finances, geographies, etc.) and the societal treatment of white-collar crimes (e.g., reduced public indignation, increased political will, major regulatory change).

In terms of both issues, we might have expected that key transformational events, such as major data leaks including the Panama and Paradise papers, have affected how white-collar crimes are organised and how societies view those involved. In terms of organisation, very little has discernibly changed, as global financial structures and arrangements that provide confidentiality to criminals and (a flexible construct) 'bad' actors endure, meaning that the risks for those making use of contrived financial structures remain low. In terms of societal response, despite some initial outrage and virtue signalling by the authorities, large-scale enforcement activity did not materialise, yet public attitudes measured remained disapproving. This is consistent with the arguments of Levi (2009) that moral panics about white-collar crimes are difficult to sustain and tend to be managed down by governments fearful of heavy controls that might discourage business, unless they can be assured by monitoring bodies.

But we cannot simply expect big shifts to occur on the back of major scandals and events that we as criminologists consider *ought* to be disruptive. It is important to research and understand small and big shifts in attitudes towards, and regulatory responses to, white-collar and corporate crimes and scandals to inform how geographical and historical factors affect (or fail to affect) change over time in different ways. As Braithwaite (2016: 17) has noted, '[t]he community of corporate crime scholars must complement overly cross-sectional meta-analyses with a search for the historical shifts that in short spaces of time effect transformative change'. Opinions will vary on what constitutes a micro and what a big shift or 'transformation' in attitudes or regulation; they will also vary on which shifts, or transformations, are most significant (and to what, to whom, and where). But the broader question is what might generate more substantial attitudinal or regulatory changes as we seek to reduce white-collar and corporate offending, or (more plausibly) particular forms thereof. How might such shifts in control and global movements change the organisational dynamics of white-collar offending? Or, as has been alleged in relation to anti–money laundering measures (Halliday et al., 2020; Van Duyne et al., 2018), were they never designed to have or likely to have a major impact on underlying crime phenomena?[1] The formal application of money laundering legislation to the proceeds of 'all crimes' allows for flexibility in including action against white-collar crimes, but it is very difficult to pin down how it is applied to any particular sub-set of criminal activity or any set of professional 'enablers', such as lawyers, and what its white-collar and other crime reduction effects are (Levi et al., 2018; Levi, 2020, 2022). For Braithwaite (2016: 10), '[t]he nature of regulatory capitalism is that there are big turning points, often associated with crisis, that infrequently produce chunks of change'. We could consider which future crises – a term of art – might plausibly reshape the

1 For the avoidance of doubt, this does not mean that countries did not want or expect money laundering controls to reduce particular forms of crime or 'organised crime'.

response to white-collar crimes, what it would take to make that happen, and how could we identify it if it did or did not happen.

Tombs and Whyte (2020) argue that corporate crimes have been conventionalised or normalised, via a symbiotic relationship between states and corporations. Consequently, regulatory systems can (or will) only partially control rather than resolving the proliferation of criminal and harmful corporate behaviours, as powerful groups seek to neutralise radical change and conserve or further their own interests. Slapper and Tombs (1999: 141) argued that the 'structural necessities of contemporary capitalism' require the prioritisation of profit, leading to amoral calculations on the part of corporations, and this shapes the extent to which such crime is seen as more or less acceptable. As we have argued elsewhere,

> While this may be persuasive to many readers, such a perspective over-predicts criminality as economic markets are relatively stable, as ethical and morally responsible corporate policies can be profitable, and as notable legal and regulatory improvements (under consumer and worker and sometimes NGO and international political pressure) have been made to govern business criminality.
>
> (Levi and Lord, 2023: 488)

Not all vehicle manufacturers developed cheat devices on emissions as the VW group and some others did in 'diesel gate': why not? In temporal terms, why do some corporations offend only ephemerally and not on an ongoing basis? We must therefore look beyond unitary regulatory regimes at the national level to examine the variations that exist across different jurisdictions where there are divergences in the nature, extent, and scope of corporate offending and regulatory responses, to better understand when small or big shifts in attitudes and regulatory responses actually lead to significant changes in societal responses and/or levels of offending or don't. This is an ongoing analytical exercise to make sense of stasis and dynamics, and reasonable people can differ on how significant a change something is.

Implications of an Organisational Perspective for Regulation and Control

Throughout this book, we have focused on what an organisational perspective can bring in terms of helping us understand how white-collar and corporate crimes occur in the ways they do. At times, we have implied how such an approach can inform regulation and control, whether this be in terms of constructing scripts to identify points of intervention, building networks to see which actors play different roles across the scenes of the crime commissioning process, focusing on the finances and money flows as a plausible route to situational intervention, examining how different jurisdictions might offer opportunities for organising white-collar crimes, or exploring how the capacities of actors, alongside social structures, lead to opportunities being realised or not in different contexts. In this section, we engage more explicitly with the implications of our 'organisational framework' for regulation and responses. For instance, what does a structural analysis alongside a situational analysis imply for regulation and enforcement? How can we re-envisage what these sorts of white-collar and corporate crimes might have looked like in a different regulatory and criminal justice setting? What are the implications of an organisational perspective and an analysis of the white-collar crime commissioning processes for reducing such offending and/or the associated harms?

As with the nature and organisation of white-collar offences, offenders, and victims, we emphasise that regulatory, 'polic*ing*' (not just police, including the private sector), and criminal justice infrastructures, strategies, responsibilities, and responses are similarly diverse. The control response to white-collar and corporate crimes is highly pluralised, with the history of business regulation characterised by the creation of specialist bodies outside traditional 'police' authorities, and numerous state authorities involved in the investigation and prosecution of different white-collar and corporate crimes. For instance, we see authorities with responsibilities spread across a range of legal areas, including but beyond the criminal law (i.e., spanning administrative and civil law also), such as tax, health and safety, food safety and standards, environmental (including pollution), financial services, Social Security payments, and so on. In the UK, these include government and arms-length licensed regulatory authorities and bodies, including the Financial Conduct Authority (FCA), Prudential Regulation Authority (PRA), HM Revenue and Customs (HMRC), Health and Safety Executive (HSE), Environment Agency (EA), the Insolvency Service, the Solicitors Regulation Authority (SRA), and many other regulators of the professions formally under the superintendence for some purposes of the Office for Professional Body Anti-Money Laundering Supervision (OPBAS); law enforcement authorities – including the Serious Fraud Office (SFO), National Crime Agency (NCA), and economic and specialist crime units within police forces: for example, primarily the City of London Police (CoLP) Economic Crime Directorate (Doig and Levi, 2021); and international agencies, including the European Fraud Office (OLAF), the European Public Prosecutor's Office (EPPO), Europol, and Interpol. Much variation exists within the US. The FBI (including its IC3 internet complaints center fraud reporting process), the New York Department of Financial Services, the Manhattan District Attorney's Office, and the US (Federal) Department of Justice (DoJ) are the principal criminal investigation and prosecution bodies. However, the Securities and Exchange Commission (SEC), the US Secret Service (for counterfeiting and payment card fraud), and the Federal Trade Commission also have oversight of fraud and cartel abuses, and there are a plethora of regulators with enforcement powers. In federal systems (including Australia, Germany, and the US), there are usually state as well as federal criminal investigation bodies. Civil law tends to have more unified systems, in which white-collar crimes are dealt with in the same ways as others, but they may be decentralised and under pressure to deal with large numbers of cases, generating delays and shortcuts. We also see forms of 'meta-regulation' (see Grabosky, 2017) that invoke the question of how the regulators are regulated and by whom.

We know that within these varied areas of business regulation, criminal prosecution is rarely pursued, even where there is scope to do so, and we have seen competing ideologies advocating more 'punitive' (assuming this means an escalation of criminal law sanctioning) crime control and criminal justice responses, in contrast to more compliance-oriented, responsive, and risk-based approaches to regulation. Here we see scarce regulatory resources targeted away from (recidivist) corporates that willingly cooperate with regulators and seemingly aim to reform and reduce future non-compliance, with multiple state and non-state actors forming part of regulatory landscape. Those on the political left – including some NGOs – have critiqued responsive, risk-based forms of business regulation on the basis that prosecution rates are low, and such regulation reinforces and reproduces dominant neoliberal ideological approaches to business. In any case, such complex, plural, and dynamic regulatory relations, beyond the state or 'multi-centred governance' regimes, inevitably inhere power asymmetries as tensions exist between 'aspirant governors' (e.g., state, corporate, civil society) as they aim to confront illicit actors in partnership to realise their own agendas (Edwards, 2016).

In the UK, there can be private prosecutions of corporate and individual defendants whose costs, if successful, may fall on the public but otherwise will be paid for by the individuals or groups contracting them. Not formally part of either criminal justice or regulatory systems is civil litigation – usually but not always by private sector firms or individuals. The financial implications can be very substantial and normally aim for compensation, though the legal costs involved for the losing party in the UK (less in the US, where the loser does not have to pay the winner's costs as well as their own) can, in practice, count as a penalty. To give one example, in March 2024, a criminal trial began in Denmark of Sanjay Shah, who, after a lengthy legal struggle, was extradited from Dubai in relation to an alleged $1.3 billion tax refund fraud against Denmark, and in April 2024, a parallel civil trial began in London of similar highly complex issues.[2] In discussions about sanctions, criminologists generally ignore (and sometimes appear to be ignorant of) regulatory penalties, but those do potentially raise similar issues of proportionality and effectiveness, as do criminal penalties, especially since corporations cannot be imprisoned by the criminal courts either.[3] The appointment of corporate monitors

2 'He told the Danish court last month that his hedge fund merely exploited a legal loophole and did nothing wrong. "It was like a ballet", he said of the co-ordinated trading his firm and others undertook to obtain the tax refunds. Two former British employees of Shah's fund, Anthony Patterson, and Guenther Klar, were given prison sentences of eight and six years, respectively, by Danish courts earlier this year for their roles in the scheme.' *Financial Times*, 15/4/24.

3 See, e.g., https://competition-policy.ec.europa.eu/index/fines_en. The largest GDPR fines in Europe to 2024 are Meta Platforms Ireland Ltd. – €1.2 billion (2023); Amazon

by the court – often as part of a corporate plea agreement – may (or may not) incapacitate or reform corporate misconduct.

Irrespective of these ideological debates, a key 'problem' or 'challenge' with the regulation and control of white-collar and corporate crime is that we have very little knowledge of or robust data about what actually works in reducing these behaviours and their harms in different contexts, whether full-blown criminal law enforcement or other forms of justice, or what mixes of variously legal or extra-legal mechanisms, as well as networks of state and non-state authorities and actors, can and do contribute to harm reduction in intended ways. For instance, notable systematic reviews on corporate crime deterrence (Simpson et al., 2014; Schell-Busey et al., 2016) point to the low quality of evidence on 'what works', but find some support for the multiple-instruments approach to deterrence (e.g., legal, regulatory, extra-legal tools). If our underlying objective or philosophy is to reduce offending behaviours, then we need to think about generating before and after data that can inform an understanding of which regulatory mixes reduce harms and offending. Our concern is how an organisational perspective can contribute to this discussion. We outline key areas next in line with the order of this book.

First, analytical focus on the organisation of specific white-collar and corporate offences implies that each crime has its own context-specific 'script' constituted of particular combinations of necessary and contingent relations. These, in turn, can be corroborated through concrete research into particular white-collar and corporate crime cases to build theories and insights about the corresponding contingently necessary relations. Through repeated empirical investigations, these scripts and relations can be refined and validated, reaching a point at which more general insights about what is necessary for a range of similar crimes can be identified. Of course, each case is unique in terms of the combination of factors that come together (or the 'tracks' of the offending), and some may be highly exceptional – which is an important thing to acknowledge – but we can look at different levels of abstraction to see where common factors or mechanisms are in play in a similar way. For instance, the Wirecard fraud was organised differently to the VW fraud; however, we can see commonalities in the necessary relations across other accounting frauds similar to Wirecard, or across other emissions frauds similar to VW. A focus on how such frauds are organised in particular contexts or situations does not exclude an analysis of the wider generative conditions of those behaviours, such as global or transnational commercial structures, ambitions to defeat competitor businesses/individuals, or overseas market differentials. This, in turn, can inform intervention efforts by varied state or non-state regulators, in terms of legal gaps, auditing gaps, regulatory points of failure, business and 'market'

Europe – €746 million (2021); Meta Platforms, Inc. – €405 million (2022); Meta Platforms Ireland Ltd. – €390 million (2023); and TikTok Ltd – €345 million (2023).

failures, and so on, that can then assist in preventing a larger number of similar frauds or offences from taking place.

Second, analytical focus on the organisation of specific white-collar and corporate offences implies a need to understand the networks, relations, and interactions of actors involved across the offending scripts, as well as their interactions and relations with victims and 'regulators', and the routinised and/or necessary nature of these across different 'scenes' of analogous crime scripts. For instance, in the LIBOR market manipulation case, we saw how actors with certain positions in banks needed to interact to negotiate how the rates would be influenced and how an absence of capable guardians or credible overseers in these situations and environments was part of the coming together of the conditions needed for the rate rigging to be accomplished. Understanding these actor relations and interactions can help us identify critical points of intervention within the structure and dynamics of conspiratorial criminal networks, including those networks that involve inadvertent enablers who are 'just doing their job' without being knowing criminal conspirators.[4]

Third, analytical focus on the organisation of specific white-collar and corporate offences implies a need to understand the finances that are needed before, during, and after white-collar crime commission. For instance, if we understand how much money is required to invest in the equipment needed to fabricate a virtual currency for the purposes of a pyramid scheme fraud, or to form and service companies through which to transfer funds for this, or to pay accountants, lawyers, or financial advisors to invest the monies generated in physical assets, and so on, we can begin to build insights into the operational and infrastructural costs of white-collar crimes, or the business model required. Focusing on the entire money component of white-collar crime organisation, and not just the proceeds generated, allows us to identify the necessary and contingent operational and infrastructural costs of similar and different crime types. Costs are case and context specific, but recognising and identifying what, how, where, and why certain costs are needed enhances our understanding of money flows. For instance, if the management of finances as part of the white-collar crime process cannot be done via legitimate financial institutions already known to/holding accounts for offenders and their businesses, then what must offenders do to conceal, control, and/or convert their illicit finances? This can be useful for intervening with the points of intersection/

4 There is usually an element of interpretation in judging what was in lawyers' or other professionals' minds when acting for clients. There are objective features like compliance with anti–money laundering regulations, but the boundaries of legal professional privilege mean that measures to require recording of interactions applied in the financial sector cannot be applied there. On the other hand, by February 2024, banks and brokers had paid $2 billion in fines to US regulators for failing to prevent 'off the books' unrecorded business communications on WhatsApp and other media by a chain of major banks ('Brokers' Texting Violations Nets Another $81 Million in Fines for SEC', *Wall Street Journal*, 12 February 2024). Normally, none of these recordings would be available to researchers.

overlap between legitimate and illegitimate, or formal and informal financial management.

Fourth, inherent in much of this is an understanding of the dynamics of the scripts, networks, and finances, and their corresponding physical and digital locations. This implies the need to understand the relationship between the organisation of offending behaviours and their geo-spatial conditions over time. Which factors or conditions influence or even determine why a white-collar crime may be organised entirely domestically or have a 'beyond-national' dimension? For instance, we can look to the international, transnational, multinational, or global aspects of the offending behaviours, identifying how offenders and their networks make the most of the features offered by different jurisdictions, whether this relates to regulatory gaps, a wealth of potential victims, a mechanism for circumventing investigation and prosecution, or something else. Yet when the internet-connected systems or digital technologies more generally form part of offending processes, then any such offending almost inevitably takes on a beyond-national component, as emails, financial transactions, encrypted forums, internet searches, and so on, are likely to go via servers in other jurisdictions, particularly (but not only) when offenders look to conceal their IP addresses. Globalisation may have generated new opportunities for cross-border organisation, but offenders do not always use these; if not, then why not? Is it merely a lack of expert knowledge, or is this globalisation unnecessary for those crimes and offenders? As Levi and Soudijn (2020) have observed, though some laundering is very complex, laundering only *needs* to be as complicated as controls force it to be. If we can understand what drives decisions to organise of white-collar crimes across different spaces or jurisdictions, or not, we may be able to develop more impactful interventions.

Finally, whether a script can be accomplished or how a white-collar crime is organised depends on the capacities of the individuals involved; their knowledge, skills, personalities, and so on, all contribute to how offenders can commit different kinds of behaviours that contribute to different kinds of white-collar crime. For instance, to manipulate a market, an offender needs to possess knowledge of the market and the skills to be able to manipulate it, or have access to those who do, whilst also possessing the confidence to do so, particularly when concealing their illicit behaviour from others. In some circumstances, they may also need to be authorised by a regulator, a fact which inhibited Italian American Mafia groups who wanted to engage in 'pump and dump' schemes but were forced to search for others outside their trust/power relationships – in practice, Russians – who were willing to work with them for those purposes. If we can understand the different types of expertise, knowledge, and skills needed to carry out different elements of the crime commission process, we can better understand the features of different network positions in the scripts, and this can be useful when investigating these crimes.

Law enforcement, regulators, and prosecutorial authorities will benefit from constructing more detailed accounts of the processes and conditions germane to different white-collar crime types, but that is not to say that prosecution or formal regulatory sanctions should be the primary response to these behaviours. For instance, if we instead think in terms of a reduction of the harms associated with different kinds of white-collar and corporate crimes over time, this incorporates a wider array of legal and extra-legal mechanisms aimed at developing pro-social behaviours and reducing future harms, although this does not exclude repressive approaches. For example, it is long recognised that public responses are alone insufficient at dealing with white-collar and corporate crimes, and we have seen the emergence of varied private sector crime reduction initiatives, but we can also look to the role of civil society and transparency rules in the 'regulation' of white-collar and corporate crimes. That said, though there may remain tensions between measures that have maximum impact and those that can be resourced in house or between cooperating bodies, intervention measures of any sort ought to target and prioritise those critical points of vulnerability to have the greatest impact against those behaviours that generate the greatest harm (alone and in the aggregate). However, especially but not only given scarce resources, it may not always be cost effective to target the most important harms, meaning regulatory actors may rationally resort to a pursuit of more readily achievable 'successes' as part of their activity mix.

White-Collar and Corporate Crimes in Digital Economies and Societies

Most, if not all, contemporary white-collar and corporate crimes have a digital or internet-connected dimension, whether this relates to the commission of the criminal acts, the before or after management of the finances of the offending, or the inherent embeddedness of white-collar crimes in digital economies and societies. For instance, the device usage across time and place of white-collar offenders (e.g., making use of start-up FinTechs offering payment transfer services to conceal identities), the reliance on internet-connected systems to undertake white-collar offences (e.g., manipulating clients or members of the public generally using fake online identities), or the misuse of new technologies, such as AI or algorithm-based tools to exploit markets), all reflect the changing contexts of white-collar and corporate offending. It is perhaps mundane to draw attention to the digital aspects of white-collar and corporate crimes, as this is the dominant form of society and socio-economic relations in 2023. Digital systems, 'cyber', internet connectivity, and so on, are a daily part of social (and criminal) life. Technological changes over time have always altered opportunities for, and the organisation of, different types of offending, including white-collar and corporate crimes. In the very near future, the 'new' population of white-collar and corporate criminals will have grown up without ever knowing of a non-digital set of social systems. Digitally dependent and enabled economies have not only sped up or altered offending scripts but also generated entirely new forms of white-collar crimes.

Yet even with the digital component, the fundamental questions we must ask of their organisation remain the same. (See Box 8.1.) As discussed in Chapter 2, if we think through the processes or 'scripts' through which white-collar crimes occur, we can better understand the impact of digital technologies.

Box 8.1 The Process of Digitally Enabled/Dependent and Other Crimes for Gain

1. See a situation as a 'financial [crime] opportunity'.
2. Obtain whatever finance (digital or other) is needed to commit the crime.
3. Find – whether in person or online – people willing and able to offend (if necessary for the crimes contemplated and/or if not part of a 'criminal organisation' or looser network where personnel are already available).
4. Obtain any equipment/data needed to offend.
5. Neutralise immediate operational/enforcement risks, including concealing cyber/digital footprint.
6. Carry out offences in domestic and/or overseas locations with or without physical presence in jurisdiction(s), made possible by internet-connected systems.
7. Convert, where necessary (e.g., where goods rather than money are obtained on credit), products of crime into money or other usable (digital) assets.
8. Find people, places, and crypto media willing to store proceeds (and perhaps transmit and conceal their origin, otherwise known as money laundering).
9. Decide which jurisdiction(s) offer the optimal balance between social/physical/digital comfort and the risk of asset forfeiture/ criminal justice sanctions.
10. Neutralise law enforcement by technical skill (including cyber knowledge), by corruption, and/or legal arbitrage, using legal obstacles to enforcement operations and prosecutions, which vary between states. Indifference to or even active support for suspects in any one state or sub-state arena along the criminal supply chain may suffice to neutralise an investigation, and staffing inadequacies – competence and numbers – as well as corruption may be the cause of official inaction.

Source: Adapted from Levi, 2023: 481

The scripts of white-collar crimes may not require all these procedural elements, as it may not be necessary for offenders to neutralise operational risks, or to convert the products of their crimes, as we discussed in Chapter 2. But they must recognise a situation as an opportunity, for instance, and know how to go about making the most of it, or be able to recruit or instruct someone who does. (Some of the time – perhaps especially but not exclusively in a corporate context – offenders have to convince themselves that what they are doing is not really a crime but an opportunity for profit making that is outside the usual practices but not criminal.) Whilst the digital context of all ten elements might be contingent (most white-collar crimes do not need a digital aspect, except insofar as most financial transfers are now digital) and may be explicit or implicit in the crime commission process, we can still think through how the digital shapes or is reshaping how offenders go about some white-collar crimes.

What is different about white-collar and corporate crimes in digital societies? In what ways have patterns of white-collar and corporate crime offending and victimisation changed alongside the digital revolution? First, the capacities of actors in positions to undertake white-collar and corporate crimes are increasingly digital, as they require increased knowledge and skills relating to the internet, smart devices, electronic money, and so on, and their relations to others are increasingly though seldom exclusively digital. Second, the routine activities of these actors reflect wider patterns of business that similarly have seen increases in digital technological innovation, datafication, and hyperconnectivity. Actors must engage regularly with digital systems as part of workplace practice, and this, in turn, shapes how they recognise different criminal opportunities. Third, as with other forms of crime, many white-collar crimes can now be cyber/digital enabled or assisted, changing the organisational dynamics of these behaviours in terms of the 'tools of the trade' or the nature of the data available. For instance, offenders can more easily make use of global commercial systems, or reach 'victims' instantaneously in close or faraway places, or access complex 'big data' for criminal purposes. They can also use AI for fakes not easily detectable by non-specialist or even quite knowledgeable members of the public. Fourth, we now also see cyber/digitally dependent white-collar crimes, such as the hacking of competitor information systems, or the use of malware and ransomware, to gain advantage. Though the continuing role of the non-digital world in offline and hybrid crimes can be understated or ignored by cyber specialists, further research is needed in this space to better understand the changing dynamics of white-collar and corporate crimes and evolving digital economies and societies, including how the role of cyber or digital technologies varies across different types of white-collar and corporate crime (e.g., from financial crimes to health and safety violations), as well as how and why involved actors place trust in digital tools as part of their commission of crimes.

Problematising the Unresolved

It is clear that our framework leaves varying issues and 'problems' unresolved. For instance, researchers in our field generally acknowledge the conceptual convergences and divergences that exist, such as the overlaps and intersections between (organised) white-collar and corporate crimes and classical 'organised crimes', white-collar and corporate crimes and cybercrimes (the former nowadays are invariably underpinned by digital systems which did not exist in Sutherland's era), or phenomena that permeate all the categories, such as flows of illicit finance and money laundering, which was not specifically criminalised anywhere until the mid-1980s and not until this century in ways that related to white-collar crimes. Some of the boundaries between these related categories are dissolving, in both social-scientific and policy discourse, as we become more aware of the nature of the acts and the actors involved; hence, we view white-collar and corporates crimes as organised. For instance, many white-collar offenders do not inadvertently stray, but – whatever their internal justifications – knowingly engage systematically and entrepreneurially in crimes for gain over time. In addition, the denotation of what the subject matter encompasses shifts over time. For example, so-called 'green crime' now encompasses the harmful activities of state and of a range of corporate actors great and small, and continues to be an emerging area of interest. Sutherland would not have envisaged that so many new lines of inquiry would fall within scope of the definition he loosely set out to differentiate from the crimes that most criminologists then and now research and make the centrepiece of what they (and politicians) call 'crime' or 'neighbourhood crime', which excludes frauds and cybercrimes as well as corporate crime, though many online as well as offline fraud victims become victims in their homes and local area.[5] Thus, as mentioned in the introduction, the questions remain of what criteria we can properly use when distinguishing legal from illegal organisational acts, and whether we include in our construct all acts in which corporations great and small, long-term functioning or merely nominal 'front companies', are used as tools in crime. This goes far beyond the questions Tappan raised about whether unprosecuted cases 'are' crimes, to include large swathes of illegal drugs and human trafficking activities that use businesses at some stage of the supply chain in their ongoing enterprise activities.

Relatedly, the types of white-collar crime that become the focus of (new) legislation and/or enforcement and regulatory agendas change over time and place, yet it is not always clear what drives these legal and policy shifts, and the amount of expert socio-legal attention in different countries – especially

5 'Neighbourhood crime . . . consists of vehicle related theft, domestic burglary, theft from the person (including pickpocketing) and robbery of personal property' (HMG 2021, Chapter 2). This *Beating Crime Plan* does contain a chapter on fraud and cybercrimes, but our point is that it is incorrectly not viewed as 'neighbourhood crime'.

non-Anglophone ones – to consider these also varies. The symbolic battle over criminalisation, in law and practice, has preoccupied many white-collar criminologists, but assessing the overall 'sanction ability' of businesses by administrative, civil, and criminal mechanisms requires a broader expertise and analytical lens than is generally available in any one person or research group.

Finally, and perhaps most notably, we expect our framework will be unsatisfactory for those with a more prominent 'critical criminological' approach to researching and theorising white-collar and corporate crime. It is common in this field for the foregrounding of extrinsically political ideological accounts when investigating white-collar and corporate crimes, drawing attention to the macro-economic policies of nation-states and supranational groupings, or to the privileging of anti-capitalist, anti-neoliberal (and the varying conceptions of these terms) ideologies, to highlight the structural dysfunctionalities that exist within liberal democratic societies. We are sympathetic with these positions, similarly finding problematic the often intentional but also taken-for-granted exclusion of corporate and white-collar crimes by crime control policies in neoliberal capitalist societies, where low prosecution rates and preferences for negotiating with elite offenders reinforce societal imbalances and the 'real social order'. The organisation of capitalism has undoubtedly led to a regulatory framework that lowers the risks for corporate offenders of being dealt with punitively, though levels of offending across similarly organised cultures vary. (And pre-industrial, pre-capitalist societies handled very few cases of elite offenders except for treason, while proclaimedly communist societies have not obviously prioritised health and safety or human rights over economic growth). That said, the factors mentioned here are all structures, mechanisms, and conditions that can be incorporated into our capacities model (see Chapter 6) and our approach to researching organisation. (See Chapter 7.) But rather than privilege these issues, we integrate them as part of the building of concrete conceptions of white-collar crimes that may or may not identify them as key drivers. We are also more interested in variations in offending and control rates than is generally displayed in structuralist critical criminology accounts.

Even given the effort that we have put into exposition of crime scripts and other features of our proposed analytical models, there remain issues of how far we can generalise from the limited case studies and data. Dutch criminologists have led the way in individual and life-course white-collar criminology, using administrative as well as criminal justice data. In terms of new and promising lines of inquiry in corporate crime research and theory, we see innovation relating to life-course analysis of corporate and organisational entities, or their 'criminal (and non-criminal) careers', to help us understand how and why companies continue (or don't) to offend despite personnel changing or enduring. There are major data challenges when it comes to such longitudinal analysis. But given the under-explored particularities of Dutch corporate and financial services culture – a part-Calvinistic former colonial power with some differences from the British 'Butler to the World' (Bullough, 2022) history and networks – can we read across to other countries in the Global North and South? Indeed, are those categories of 'North' and 'South' not far too homogenised for the real differences between the countries historically placed in those categories? Even within the BRICS countries – initially, Brazil, Russia, India, China, and South Africa, but now also including Egypt, Ethiopia, Iran, and the United Arab Emirates – is it plausible that there is commonality in white-collar crime and a big difference from G7 countries, which are themselves varied? How does the US's more federalist polity create problems for tackling fraud, money laundering, and corporate regulation, given very different state regimes as well as variations in federal policies and legislation over time? Revelations in December 2022 about the paucity of IRS resources to audit then-President Trump's tax affairs and about the shortage of UK resources to investigate COVID loan frauds (Levi and Smith, 2022; National Audit Office, 2022, 2023; PAC, 2023) tell us something important about priorities, but is that sufficient to generalise about either offending rates or the control processes over time and place?

Final Remarks

This brings us to the end of this book. We set out to explore how we can re-constitute our approach to analysing and empirically investigating the *organisation* of white-collar and corporate crimes, with a view to building fuller theoretical and empirical accounts. We demonstrated how we can produce and systematise knowledge within a conceptual and analytical framework concerned with understanding *how* such crimes are organised, *why* they are organised as they are, *who* gets involved in them as primary offenders and as facilitators, and the 'real' factors that shape these *organisational dynamics* over time in particular contexts and under varying conditions. The book is primarily for critical social scientists, including, but not limited to, criminologists, sociologists, and socio-legal, business, economics, and political studies scholars, who have an interest in theorising about and empirically investigating white-collar and corporate crimes, or in understanding empirical approaches to analysing such behaviours, or other types of crime. Although the content is intellectually and, at times, linguistically challenging, the book will also interest practitioners and policymakers keen to learn more about how and why these crimes are organised as they are.

Our organisational perspective focuses on the proximal and distal social arrangements and relations that contribute to the emergence of white-collar crime opportunities and their structures. We highlighted the *necessary* mechanisms, processes, and conditions that form part of the white-collar crime commissioning process, and their associated *contingent* relations that come together in specific contexts to enable (or restrict) the capacities to offend. That is, we go beyond multi-factorial accounts of offending, to distinguish causal mechanisms or factors that are *necessary* for these crimes to occur from those which are merely contingent, and, in turn, allow us to identify what is contingently necessary over time and place. Scripts, networks, finances, geographies, and capacities are key to understanding these dynamics of offending, as are the enduring structural and societal configurations that produce and reproduce these relations. Asking such questions about what is contingently necessary helps us move beyond describing relevant factors with causal potential to explaining why certain factors contributed to any given case of white-collar crime occurring, helping us capture the contingencies of everyday life. Making connections between the mechanisms, relations, structures, and conditions outlined here implies a requirement for combining both abstract thinking and empirical analysis to gain insight into what are complex sets of social relations and organisational dynamics. In our view, thinking in terms of 'organisation' is important for how we build theory on white-collar and corporate crimes, how we develop convincing explanatory accounts of associated behaviours, and how we contribute to operational and policy discourse by enabling motivated controllers to do so with a clearer appreciation of the likely effects of their interventions.

It is our aim with this book to build upon and move beyond current academic debates, to provide a comprehensive, evidence-based, and realist analysis of the organisation of white-collar and corporate crimes. We have aimed to offer fresh ways of thinking intellectually about the multi-faceted nature of crime commission, and whilst our framework does not provide a 'formula' that all should follow, it does allow interested readers to dip into particular chapters to enhance or supplement their research, or perhaps challenge (or reaffirm) their own ways of thinking. We have unashamedly made the case for foregrounding complexity and the multi-faceted factors that shape white-collar and corporate offending to encourage us to think also about variations in the nature, organisation, and levels of offending across contexts and cultures and over time.

Bibliography

Albanese, J. (2014) *Organized Crime: From the Mob to Transnational Organized Crime*. 7th edition. New York: Routledge. Available at: https://doi.org/10.4324/9781315721477.

Alonso Berbotto, A. and Chainey, S. (2021) 'Theft of Oil from Pipelines: An Examination of Its Crime Commission in Mexico Using Crime Script Analysis', *Global Crime*, 22(4), pp. 265–287. Available at: https://doi.org/10.1080/17440572.2021.1925552.

Aziani, A., Ferwerda, J. and Riccardi, M. (2022) 'Who Are Our Owners? Exploring the Ownership Links of Businesses to Identify Illicit Financial Flows', *European Journal of Criminology*, 19(6), pp. 1542–1573.

Babiak, P. and Hare, R.D. (2007) *Snakes in Suits: When Psychopaths Go to Work*. 1st edition. New York: Regan Books.

Baker, W.E. and Faulkner, R.R. (1993) 'The Social Organization of Conspiracy: Illegal Networks in the Heavy Electrical Equipment Industry', *American Sociological Review*, 58(6), p. 837. Available at: https://doi.org/10.2307/2095954.

Baker, W.E. and Faulkner, R.R. (2003) 'Diffusion of Fraud: Intermediate Economic Crime and Investor Dynamics*', *Criminology*, 41(4), pp. 1173–1206. Available at: https://doi.org/10.1111/j.1745-9125.2003.tb01017.x.

Baker, W.E. and Faulkner, R.R. (2004) 'Social Networks and Loss of Capital', *Social Networks*, 26(2), pp. 91–111. Available at: https://doi.org/10.1016/j.socnet.2004.01.004.

Balleisen, E. (2018) *Fraud – An American History from Barnum to Madoff*. Princeton, NJ: Princeton University Press.

Bartlett, J. (2022) *The Missing Cryptoqueen*. Available at: https://www.penguin.co.uk/books/442256/the-missing-cryptoqueen-by-bartlett-jamie/9780753559581 (Accessed: 16 March 2023).

Bellotti, E., Spencer, J., Lord, N. and Benson, K. (2020) 'Counterfeit Alcohol Distribution: A Criminological Script Network Analysis', *European Journal of Criminology*, 17(4), pp. 373–398. Available at: https://doi.org/10.1177/1477370818794870.

Belton, C. (2021) *Putin's People: How the KGB Took Back Russia and then Took on the West*. London: Harper Collins.

Benson, K. (2020) *Lawyers and the Proceeds of Crime: The Facilitation of Money Laundering and Its Control*. 1st edition. Abingdon; Oxon; New York, NY: Routledge, 2020 (Series: The Law of Financial Crime | Based on Author's Thesis (Doctoral-University of Manchester, 2016) Issued Under Title: The Facilitation of Money Laundering by Legal and Financial Professionals: Routledge). Available at: https://doi.org/10.4324/9781315179735.

Benson, M.L. and Cullen, F.T. (2018) 'Subterranean Values, Self-Deception, and White-Collar Crime', in T.G. Blomberg et al. (eds) *Delinquency and Drift Revisited*. London: Routledge, pp. 99–124.

Benson, M.L. and Madensen, T.D. (2007) 'Situational Crime Prevention and White-Collar Crime', in H.N. Pontell and G. Geis (eds) *International Handbook of White-Collar and Corporate Crime*. New York: Springer, pp. 609–626.
Benson, M.L. and Manchak, S.M. (2012) 'The Psychology of White-Collar Offending', in Oxford Handbooks Editorial Board (ed.) *Oxford Handbook Topics in Criminology and Criminal Justice*. Oxford University Press. Available at: https://doi.org/10.1093/oxfordhb/9780199935383.013.008.
Benson, M.L. et al. (2021) 'Race, Ethnicity, and Social Change: The Democratization of Middle-Class Crime*', *Criminology*, 59(1), pp. 10–41. Available at: https://doi.org/10.1111/1745-9125.12261.
Benson, M.L. et al. (2024) *White-Collar Crime: An Opportunity Perspective*. 4th edition. London: Routledge.
Benson, M.L., Feldmeyer, B., Gabbidon, S.L. and Chio, H.L. (2021) 'Race, Ethnicity, and Social Change: The Democratization of Middle-Class Crime', *Criminology*, 59(1), pp. 10–41.
Benson, M.L., Madensen, T.D. and Eck, J.E. (2009) 'White-Collar Crime from an Opportunity Perspective', in S.S. Simpson and D. Weisburd (eds) *The Criminology of White-Collar Crime*. New York: Springer, pp. 175–193. Available at: https://doi.org/10.1007/978-0-387-09502-8_9.
Benson, M.L., Van Slyke, S.R. and Cullen, F.T. (2016) 'Core Themes in the Study of White-Collar Crime', *The Oxford Handbook of White-Collar Crime*, 1, pp. 1–24.
Bichler, G. et al. (2019) 'The Impact of Civil Gang Injunctions on Networked Violence Between the Bloods and the Crips', *Crime & Delinquency*, 65(7), pp. 875–915. Available at: https://doi.org/10.1177/0011128717739607.
Blackhurst, C. (2023) *Too Big to Jail*. Pan Macmillan. Available at: https://www.panmacmillan.com/authors/chris-blackhurst/too-big-to-jail/9781529065077 (Accessed: 23 May 2023).
Blokland, A., Kluin, M. and Huisman, W. (2021) 'Life-Course Criminology and Corporate Offending', in B. van Rooij and D.D. Sokol (eds) *The Cambridge Handbook of Compliance* (Cambridge Law Handbooks). Cambridge: Cambridge University Press, pp. 684–704. Available at: https://doi.org/10.1017/9781108759458.047.
Blumer, H. (2009) *Symbolic Interactionism: Perspective and Method*. Berkeley, CA: University of California Press.
Bonger, W.A. (1916) *Criminality and Economic Conditions*. Boston MA: Little, Brown.
Borgatti, S.P. and Everett, M.G. (2000) 'Models of Core/Periphery Structures', *Social Networks*, 21(4), pp. 375–395. Available at: https://doi.org/10.1016/S0378-8733(99)00019-2.
Borgatti, S.P., Everett, M.G. and Johnson, J.C. (2013) *Analyzing Social Networks*. Los Angeles, CA: SAGE.
Bouchard, M. (2007) 'On the Resilience of Illegal Drug Markets', *Global Crime*, 8(4), pp. 325–344. Available at: https://doi.org/10.1080/17440570701739702.
Box, S. (1983) *Power, Crime and Mystification*. London: Routledge. Available at: https://www.routledge.com/Power-Crime-and-Mystification/Box/p/book/9780415045728 (Accessed: 16 February 2023).
Braithwaite, J. (1985) 'White Collar Crime', *Annual Review of Sociology*, 11, pp. 1–25.
Braithwaite, J. (2016) 'In Search of Donald Campbell', *Criminology & Public Policy*, 15(2), pp. 417–437. Available at: https://doi.org/10.1111/1745-9133.12198.
Bright, D. et al. (2017) 'Criminal Network Vulnerabilities and Adaptations', *Global Crime*, 18(4), pp. 424–441. Available at: https://doi.org/10.1080/17440572.2017.1377614.
Bright, D.A. and Delaney, J.J. (2013) 'Evolution of a Drug Trafficking Network: Mapping Changes in Network Structure and Function Across Time', *Global Crime*, 14(2–3), pp. 238–260. Available at: https://doi.org/10.1080/17440572.2013.787927.

Bright, D.A. et al. (2015) 'Networks within Networks: Using Multiple Link Types to Examine Network Structure and Identify Key Actors in a Drug Trafficking Operation', *Global Crime*, 16(3), pp. 219–237. Available at: https://doi.org/10.1080/17440572.2015.1039164.

Brivati, B. (2022) *Icarus the Life and Death of the Abraaj Group*. Biteback Publishing. Available at: https://www.politicos.co.uk/products/icarus-the-life-and-death-of-the-abraaj-group-by-brian-brivati (Accessed: 22 May 2023).

Bryman, A. (2006) 'Integrating Quantitative and Qualitative Research: How Is It Done?', *Qualitative Research*, 6(1), pp. 97–113. Available at: https://doi.org/10.1177/1468794106058877.

Bryman, A. (2007) 'Barriers to Integrating Quantitative and Qualitative Research', *Journal of Mixed Methods Research*, 1(1), pp. 8–22.

Bullough, O. (2022) *Butler to the World*. London: Profile Books.

Burgis, T. (2020) *Kleptopia*. London: William Collins.

Buzan, B., Wæver, O. and Wilde, J. de (1998) *Security: A New Framework for Analysis*. Boulder, CO: Lynne Rienner Publishers.

Campana, P. (2016) 'Explaining Criminal Networks: Strategies and Potential Pitfalls', *Methodological Innovations*, 9. Available at: https://doi.org/10.1177/2059799115622748.

Campana, P. and Varese, F. (2013) 'Cooperation in Criminal Organizations: Kinship and Violence as Credible Commitments', *Rationality and Society*, 25(3), pp. 263–289. Available at: https://doi.org/10.1177/1043463113481202.

Campbell, L. (2015) 'Legislative Comment – The Offence of Participating in Activities of Organised Crime Group: Section 45 of the Serious Crime Act 2015', *Archbold Review*, 10, pp. 6–9.

Carley, K.M. (2003) 'Dynamic Network Analysis', in *Dynamic Social Network Modeling and Analysis: Workshop Summary and Papers*. Washington, D.C.: National Academies Press, pp. 133–145. Available at: https://doi.org/10.17226/10735.

Carreyrou, J. (2023) *Bad Blood*. Pan Macmillan. Available at: https://www.waterstones.com/book/bad-blood/john-carreyrou/9781035006779 (Accessed: 23 May 2023).

Carreyrou, J. (2023) *Bad Blood: Secrets and Lies in a Silicon Valley Startup*. London: Picador.

Carrington, P.J. (2011) 'Crime and Social Network Analysis', in *Sage Handbook of Social Network Analysis*. London: SAGE, pp. 236–255.

Carrington, P.J., Scott, J. and Wasserman, S. (eds) (2005) *Models and Methods in Social Network Analysis* (Structural Analysis in the Social Sciences). Cambridge: Cambridge University Press. Available at: https://doi.org/10.1017/CBO9780511811395.

Chiu, Y.-N., Leclerc, B. and Townsley, M. (2011) 'Crime Script Analysis of Drug Manufacturing in Clandestine Laboratories: Implications for Prevention', *British Journal of Criminology*, 51(2), pp. 355–374. Available at: https://doi.org/10.1093/bjc/azr005.

Clark, S. and Louch, W. (2023) *The Key Man*. London: Penguin. Available at: https://www.penguin.co.uk/books/316807/the-key-man-by-louch-simon-clark-and-will/9780241988947 (Accessed: 16 February 2023).

Clarke, R.V. (2012) 'Opportunity Makes the Thief. Really? And So What?', *Crime Science*, 1(1), p. 3. Available at: https://doi.org/10.1186/2193-7680-1-3.

Clarke, R.V. and Cornish, D.B. (1985) 'Modeling Offenders' Decisions: A Framework for Research and Policy', in M. Tonry (ed.) *Crime and Justice: An Annual Review of Research* (vol. 6). Chicago, IL: University of Chicago Press, pp. 147–185.

Clarke, R.V.G. and Cornish, D.B. (eds) (1983) *Crime Control in Britain: A Review of Policy Research*. Albany, NY: State University of New York Press.

Clinard, M.B. and Yeager, P.C. (1980) *Corporate Crime*. New York: Free Press.

Clinard, M.B., Quinney, R. and Treviño, A.J. (2019) *Clinard and Quinney's Criminal Behavior Systems*. 4th edition. Abingdon, Oxon: Routledge.

Cohen, L.E. and Felson, M. (1979) 'Social Change and Crime Rate Trends: A Routine Activity Approach', *American Sociological Review*, 44(4), pp. 588–608. Available at: https://doi.org/10.2307/2094589.

Collins, H. and Evans, R. (2007) *Rethinking Expertise*. Chicago, IL: University of Chicago Press.

Collins, H.M. and Evans, R. (2002) 'The Third Wave of Science Studies: Studies of Expertise and Experience', *Social Studies of Science*, 32(2), pp. 235–296. Available at: https://doi.org/10.1177/0306312702032002003.

Collins, H.M. and Evans, R. (2007) *Rethinking Expertise*. Chicago, IL: University of Chicago Press.

Cornish, D. (1994) 'The Procedural Analysis of Offending and Its Relevance for Situational Prevention', *Crime Prevention Studies*, 3, pp. 151–196.

Cornish, D.B. and Clarke, R.V. (2003) 'Opportunities, Precipitators, and Criminal Decisions: A Reply to Wortley's Critique of Situational Crime Prevention', *Crime Prevention Studies*, 14, pp. 41–96.

Cressey, D. (1953) *Other People's Money: A Study in the Social Psychology of Embezzlement*. Glencoe, IL: Free Press.

Cressey, D.R. (1950) 'The Criminal Violation of Financial Trust', *American Sociological Review*, 15(6), pp. 738–743. Available at: https://doi.org/10.2307/2086606.

Croall, H. (2001) *Understanding White Collar Crime* (Crime and Justice). Buckingham: Open University Press.

Crossley, N. et al. (2015) *Social Network Analysis for Ego-Nets*. Sage. Available at: https://doi.org/10.4135/9781473911871.

David Whyte, N. (2014) 'Regimes of Permission and State-Corporate Crime', *State Crime Journal*, 3(2), pp. 237–246. [Preprint]. Available at: https://doi.org/10.13169/statecrime.3.2.0237.

Davies, J. (2021) 'Labour Exploitation and Posted Workers in the European Construction Industry', in N. Lord et al. (eds) *European White-Collar Crime: Exploring the Nature of European Realities*. Policy Press. Available at: https://doi.org/10.1332/policypress/9781529212327.003.0010.

de Korte, L.R. and Kleemans, E.R. (2022) 'Contract Killings: A Crime Script Analysis', *Trends in Organized Crime*, 25, pp. 130–143. Available at: https://doi.org/10.1007/s12117-021-09411-4.

Department of Justice. (2017) *Second Superseding Indictment. No. 2: 16-cr-20394*. United States District Court Eastern District of Michigan Southern Division. Available at: https://www.justice.gov/opa/press-release/file/924401/dl?inline.

Dicken, P. (2014) *Global Shift: Mapping the Changing Contours of the World Economy*. 7th edition. Thousand Oaks, CA: SAGE.

Diviák, T. (2020) *Criminal Networks: Actors, Mechanisms, and Structures*. PhD thesis. Rijksuniversiteit Groningen.

Diviák, T. and Lord, N. (2022) 'Tainted Ties: The Structure and Dynamics of Corruption Networks Extracted from Deferred Prosecution Agreements', *EPJ Data Science*, 11(1), p. 7. Available at: https://doi.org/10.1140/epjds/s13688-022-00320-2.

Diviák, T., Dijkstra, J.K. and Snijders, T.A.B. (2019) 'Structure, Multiplexity, and Centrality in a Corruption Network: The Czech Rath Affair', *Trends in Organized Crime*, 22(3), pp. 274–297. Available at: https://doi.org/10.1007/s12117-018-9334-y.

Doig, A. and Levi, M. (2021) *Frauds and Financial Crimes: Trends, Strategic Responses and Implementation Issues in England and Wales*. London: Routledge. ISBN 1032015322.

Duijn, P.A.C. and Sloot, P.M.A. (2015) 'From Data to Disruption', *Digital Investigation*, 15, pp. 39–45. Available at: https://doi.org/10.1016/j.diin.2015.09.005.

Edelhertz, H. (1970) *The Nature, Impact and Prosecution of White-Collar Crime*. Washington, DC: US Department of Justice.

Edwards, A. (2015) 'Realist Criminology: Adam Edwards reviews Roger Matthews' Latest Book', *Criminal Justice Matters*, 99(1), pp. 26–27. Available at: https://doi.org/10.1080/09627251.2015.1026570.

Edwards, A. (2016) 'Actors, Scripts, Scenes and Scenarios: Key Trends in Policy and Research on the Organisation of Serious Crimes', *Oñati Socio-Legal Series*, 6(4). Available at: https://papers.ssrn.com/abstract=2875318 (Accessed: 20 December 2022).

Edwards, A. and Levi, M. (2008) 'Researching the Organization of Serious Crimes', *Criminology & Criminal Justice*, 8(4), pp. 363–388. Available at: https://doi.org/10.1177/1748895808097403.

Enrich, D. (2018) *The Spider Network: The Wild Story of a Maths Genius, a Gang of Backstabbing Bankers, and One of the Greatest Scams in Financial History*. Ebury Publishing. Available at: https://www.abebooks.co.uk/9780753557501/Spider-Network-Wild-Story-Maths-0753557509/plp (Accessed: 23 May 2023).

Europol (n.d.) 'Intellectual Property Crime', *Europol Website*. Available at: https://www.europol.europa.eu/crime-areas/intellectual-property-crime#:~:text=Intellectual%20property%20crime%20is%20committed,artistic%20works%2C%20for%20commercial%20gain.

Ewing, J. (2017) *Faster, Higher, Farther: The Inside Story of the Volkswagen Scandal*. Bantam Press.

Farrall, S. and Karstedt, S. (2020) *Respectable Citizens – Shady Practices: The Economic Morality of the Middle Classes* (Clarendon Studies in Criminology). Oxford and New York: Oxford University Press.

FATF. (2011) *Laundering the Proceeds of Corruption*. Paris: Financial Action Task Force, p. 54.

Felson, M. and Boba, R. (2010) *Crime and Everyday Life*. 4th edition. Thousand Oaks, CA: SAGE. Available at: https://doi.org/10.4135/9781483349299.

Felson, M. and Eckert, M. (2019) *Crime and Everyday Life: A Brief Introduction*. 6th edition. Los Angeles, CA: SAGE.

Findley, M.G., Nielson, D.L. and Sharman, J.C. (2022) 'Testing the Effectiveness of Targeted Financial Sanctions on Russia: Law or War?' Available at: https://bahamasamlconference.centralbankbahamas.com/documents/2024-03-26-15-21-56-Findley-Nielson-SharmanFinancial-Sanctions-on-Russia.pdf.

Fisse, B. and Braithwaite, J. (1993) *Corporations, Crime, and Accountability* (Theories of Institutional Design). Cambridge: Cambridge University Press.

Fligstein, N. and Roehrkasse, A.F. (2016) 'The Causes of Fraud in the Financial Crisis of 2007 to 2009: Evidence from the Mortgage-Backed Securities Industry', *American Sociological Review*, 81(4), pp. 617–643.

Freeman, L.C. (1978) 'Centrality in Social Networks Conceptual Clarification', *Social Networks*, 1(3), pp. 215–239. Available at: https://doi.org/10.1016/0378-8733(78)90021-7.

Friedrichs, D.O. (1996) *Trusted Criminals: White Collar Crime in Contemporary Society*. Belmont: Wadsworth.

Friedrichs, D.O. (2007) 'White-Collar Crime in a Postmodern, Globalized World', in *International Handbook of White-Collar and Corporate Crime*. New York: Springer, pp. 163–184.

Galvin, M.A., Logan, M. and Snook, D.W. (2022) 'Assessing the Validity of White-Collar Crime Definitions Using Experimental Survey Data', *Journal of Experimental Criminology*, 18(3), pp. 665–693. Available at: https://doi.org/10.1007/s11292-020-09455-6.

Garland, D. (2002) *The Culture of Control: Crime and Social Order in Contemporary Society*. 1st edition. Oxford: Oxford University Press.

Geis, G. (2016) 'The Roots and Variant Definitions of the Concept of "White-Collar Crime"', in S.R. Van Slyke, M.L. Benson and F.T. Cullen (eds) *The Oxford Handbook of White-Collar Crime*. Oxford: Oxford University Press. Available at: https://doi.org/10.1093/oxfordhb/9780199925513.013.2.

Gilbert, J. (2024) 'Scripting Mortgage Fraud for the Motion Picture: "Fraud and Its Interrelationship with the Financial Services Sector in the UK"', *Journal of Economic Criminology*, 5. [Preprint]. Available at: https://www.sciencedirect.com/science/article/pii/S2949791424000368 (Accessed: 24 July 2024).

Gilbert, J. (forthcoming) *Mortgage Fraud and Financial Crime: A Qualitative and Comparative Approach to Regulation in the UK and US*. London: Routledge.

Gilmour, N. (2023) 'Crime Scripting the Criminal Activities of Money Laundering – Holistically', *Journal of Money Laundering Control*, 26(3), pp. 594–608. Available at: https://doi.org/10.1108/JMLC-09-2020-0109.

Gimenez-Salinas, F.A. (2014) 'Illegal Networks or Criminal Organizations: Power, Roles and Facilitators in Four Cocaine Trafficking Structures', in C. Morselli (ed.) *Crime and Networks* (Criminology and Justice Studies Series). New York: Routledge, pp. 131–148.

Gladkova, E. (2021) 'Food Production Harms in the European Context: The EU as an Enabler or a Solution?', in N. Lord et al. (eds) *European White-Collar Crime: Exploring the Nature of European Realities*. Policy Press, p. 0. Available at: https://doi.org/10.1332/policypress/9781529212327.003.0008.

Goodall, O. (2019) *Beyond Wildlife Crime: Realist Social Relations Crime Scripts of the Illegal Taking of Deer*. Phd. Cardiff University. Available at: https://orca.cardiff.ac.uk/id/eprint/125648/(Accessed: 16 February 2023).

Gorski, P.S. (2013) 'What Is Critical Realism? And Why Should You Care?', *Contemporary Sociology: A Journal of Reviews*, 42(5), pp. 658–670. Available at: https://doi.org/10.1177/0094306113499533.

Gould, R.V. and Fernandez, R.M. (1989) 'Structures of Mediation: A Formal Approach to Brokerage in Transaction Networks', *Sociological Methodology*, 19, pp. 89–126. Available at: https://doi.org/10.2307/270949.

Grabosky, P. (1995) 'Counterproductive Regulation', *International journal of the Sociology of Law*, 23(4), pp. 347–369.

Grabosky, P. (2009) 'Globalization and White-Collar Crime', in S.S. Simpson and D. Weisburd (eds) *The Criminology of White-Collar Crime*. New York: Springer, pp. 129–151.

Grabosky, P. (2017) 'Meta-Regulation', in P. Drahos (ed.) *Regulatory Theory: Foundations and Applications*. Canberra: ANU ePress, pp. 149–161. Available at: https://doi.org/10.22459/RT.02.2017.09.

Györy, C. (2019) 'Gaining Edge: Criminology of Financial Crimes in the Age of Cyborg Finance', in *Presented at the European Society of Criminology Annual Conference 2019*. Ghent.

Halliday, T., Levi, M. and Reuter, P. (2020) 'Why Do Transnational Legal Orders Persist? The Curious Case of Anti-Money Laundering', in Gregory Shaffer and Ely Aaronson (eds) *Transnational Legal Ordering of Criminal Justice*. Cambridge University Press. pp. 51–83. ISBN 978-1-108-83658-6.

Hancock, G. and Laycock, G. (2010) 'Organized Crime and Crime Scripts: Prospects for Disruption', in K. Bullock, R.V.G. Clarke, and N. Tilley (eds) *Situational Prevention of Organised Crimes* (Crime Science Series). Portland: Willan Publishing.

HMG. (2021) 'Beating Crime Plan. Fewer Victims, Peaceful Neighbourhoods, Safe Country', *HM Government*. Available at: https://assets.publishing.service.gov.uk/media/6135f34ed3bf7f05b7bcb54e/Crime-plan-v10.pdf.

Holt, T.J. and Lee, J.R. (2022) 'A Crime Script Analysis of Counterfeit Identity Document Procurement Online', *Deviant Behavior*, 43(3), pp. 285–302. Available at: https://doi.org/10.1080/01639625.2020.1825915.

Hou, D. and Skeie, D. (2014) *LIBOR: Origins, Economics, Crisis, Scandal, and Reform* (Staff Report No. 667). Federal Reserve Bank of New York.

Huisman, W. and van Erp, J. (2013) 'Opportunities for Environmental Crime: A Test of Situational Crime Prevention Theory', *British Journal of Criminology*, 53(6), pp. 1178–1200. Available at: https://doi.org/10.1093/bjc/azt036.

Hunter, B. (2015) *White-Collar Offenders and Desistance from Crime: Future Selves and the Constancy of Change*. London: Routledge. Available at: https://www.taylorfrancis.com/books/mono/10.4324/9781315760575/white-collar-offenders-desistance-crime-ben-hunter (Accessed: 11 January 2023).

Hutchings, A. and Holt, T.J. (2015) 'A Crime Script Analysis of the Online Stolen Data Market: Table 1', *British Journal of Criminology*, 55(3), pp. 596–614. Available at: https://doi.org/10.1093/bjc/azu106.

International Trademark Association. (2024) 'Fact Sheet: Protecting a Trademark. Counterfeiting (Intended for a non-legal audience', *International Trademark Association Website*. Available at: https://www.inta.org/fact-sheets/counterfeiting-intended-for-a-non-legal-audience/

Jofre, M. et al. (2021) 'Money Laundering and the Detection of Bad Companies: A Machine Learning Approach for the Risk Assessment of Opaque Ownership Structures', in *Research Paper for the 2021 Bahamas AML Conference*. Available at: https://bahamasamlconference.centralbankbahamas.com/2021.

Johnson, R.B. and Onwuegbuzie, A.J. (2004) 'Mixed Methods Research: A Research Paradigm Whose Time Has Come', *Educational Researcher*, 33(7), pp. 14–26. Available at: https://doi.org/10.3102/0013189X033007014.

Jordanoska, A. and Lord, N. (2020) 'Scripting the Mechanics of the Benchmark Manipulation Corporate Scandals: The "Guardian" Paradox', *European Journal of Criminology*, 17(1), pp. 49–64.

Jordanoska, A. and Lord, N. (2022) 'Mixing and Combining Research Strategies and Methods to Understand Compliance', in M. Rorie and B. van Rooij (eds) *Measuring Compliance*. Cambridge: Cambridge University Press, pp. 241–263. Available at: https://www.cambridge.org/core/books/abs/measuring-compliance/mixing-and-combining-research-strategies-and-methods-to-understand-compliance/4C87616CD5C8F9595630E0AB0322B578 (Accessed: 30 June 2023).

Kagan, R. and Scholz, J. (1984) 'The "Criminology of the Corporation" and Regulatory Enforcement Strategies', in K. Hawkins and J.M. Thomas (eds) *Enforcing Regulation* (Law in Social Context Series). Boston: Kluwer-Nijhoff.

Katz, J. (1980) 'The Social Movement Against White-Collar Crime', *Criminology Review Yearbook*, 2, pp. 161–184.

Kleemans, E.R. and Van de Bunt, H. (1999) 'The Social Embeddedness of Organized Crime', *Transnational Organized Crime*, 5, pp. 19–36.

Klenowski, P.M. and Copes, H. (2013) 'Looking Back at Other People's Money: A Qualitative Test of Cressey's Classic Hypothesis of Trust Violating Behavior', *Journal of Qualitative Criminal Justice & Criminology*, 1(1), pp. 1–27. Available at: https://doi.org/10.21428/88de04a1.9f45b3c4.

Klerks, P. (2001) 'The Network Paradigm Applied to Criminal Organizations: Theoretical Nitpicking or a Relevant Doctrine for Investigators? Recent Developments in the Netherlands', *Connections*, 24(3), pp. 53–65.

Koblenz, M., Labbate, K. and Turner, C. (2014) 'LIBOR: Everything You Ever Wanted to Know But Were Afraid to Ask', *The Journal of Business, Entrepreneurship & the Law*, 6(2). Available at: https://digitalcommons.pepperdine.edu/jbel/vol6/iss2/4.

Koschade, S. (2006) 'A Social Network Analysis of Jemaah Islamiyah: The Applications to Counterterrorism and Intelligence', *Studies in Conflict & Terrorism*, 29(6), pp. 559–575. Available at: https://doi.org/10.1080/10576100600798418.

Krebs, V.E. (2002) 'Mapping Terrorist Networks', *Connections*, 24(3), pp. 43–52.

Langton, L. and Piquero, N.L. (2007) 'Can General Strain Theory Explain White-Collar Crime? A Preliminary Investigation of the Relationship Between Strain and Select

White-Collar Offenses', *Journal of Criminal Justice*, 35(1), pp. 1–15. Available at: https://doi.org/10.1016/j.jcrimjus.2006.11.011.

Lazega, E. and Snijders, T.A.B. (eds) (2016) *Multilevel Network Analysis for the Social Sciences*. Cham: Springer International Publishing. Available at: https://doi.org/10.1007/978-3-319-24520-1.

Leclerc, B., Wortley, R. and Smallbone, S. (2011) 'Getting into the Script of Adult Child Sex Offenders and Mapping out Situational Prevention Measures', *Journal of Research in Crime and Delinquency*, 48(2), pp. 209–237. Available at: https://doi.org/10.1177/0022427810391540.

Levi, M. (2007) 'The Organization of Serious Crimes', in M. Maguire, R. Morgan, and R. Reiner (eds) *The Oxford Handbook of Criminology*. 4th edition. Oxford: Oxford University Press Inc.

Levi, M. (2008) *The Phantom Capitalists: The Organization and Control of Long-Firm Fraud*. Revised 2nd edition. Aldershot and Hampshire: Burlington.

Levi, M. (2009a) 'Financial Crimes', in M. Tonry (ed.) *The Oxford Handbook of Crime and Public Policy*. New York: Oxford University Press, pp. 223–246.

Levi, M. (2009b) 'Suite Revenge?: The Shaping of Folk Devils and Moral Panics About White-Collar Crimes', *British Journal of Criminology*, 49(1), pp. 48–67. Available at: https://doi.org/10.1093/bjc/azn073.

Levi, M. (2013) 'Legitimacy, Crimes, and Compliance in "the City": De Maximis Non Curat Lex?', in J. Tankebe and A. Liebling (eds) *Legitimacy and Criminal Justice: An International Exploration*. New York: Oxford University Press, pp. 157–177. ISBN 978-0-19-870199-6.

Levi, M. (2015) 'Money for Crime and Money from Crime: Financing Crime and Laundering Crime Proceeds', *European Journal on Criminal Policy and Research*, 21(2), pp. 275–297. Available at: https://doi.org/10.1007/s10610-015-9269-7.

Levi, M. (2016) 'Globalisation, Locale and Bankruptcy Fraud: A Historical Exploration', in G. Antonopoulos (ed) *Illegal Entrepreneurship, 'Organised Crime' and Social Control: Essays in Honour of Professor Dick Hobbs*. New York: Springer, pp. 37–56. ISBN: 978-3-319-31606-2.

Levi, M. (2019) 'Theoretical Perspectives on White Collar Crime', in Henry Pontell (ed) *Oxford Research Encyclopedia of Criminology and Criminal Justice*. New York and Oxford: Oxford University Press. Available at: https://doi.org/10.1093/acrefore/9780190264079.013.266.

Levi, M. (2020) 'Evaluating the Control of Money Laundering and Its Underlying Offences: The Search for Meaningful Data', *Asian Journal of Criminology*, 15(4), pp. 301–320. Available at: https://doi.org/10.1007/s11417-020-09319-y.

Levi, M. (2022) 'Lawyers as Money Laundering Enablers? An Evolving and Contentious Relationship', *Global Crime*, 23(2), pp. 126–147.

Levi, M. (2023) 'Pandemics and Fraud: Learning from the Coronavirus Pandemic and Its Antecedents', in R.G. Smith et al. (eds) Palgrave Macmillan Cham, pp. 31–56. Available at: https://doi.org/10.1007/978-3-031-29107-4_3.

Levi, M. and Gilmore, W. (2002) 'Terrorist Finance, Money Laundering and the Rise and Rise of Mutual Evaluation: A New Paradigm for Crime Control?', in M. Pieth (ed) *Financing Terrorism*. Dordrecht: Kluwer, pp. 87–114. ISBN 1-4020-1152-0.

Levi, M. and Lord, L. (2023) 'White-Collar and Corporate Crime', in A. Liebling, L. McAra, and S. Maruna (eds) *Oxford Handbook of Criminology*. 7th edition. Oxford: OUP.

Levi, M. and Lord, N. (2017) 'White-Collar and Corporate Crimes', in *The Oxford Handbook of Criminology*. 6th edition. Oxford: Oxford University Press.

Levi, M. and Maguire, M. (2004) 'Reducing and Preventing Organised Crime: An Evidence-Based Critique', *Crime, Law and Social Change*, 41(5), pp. 397–469. Available at: https://doi.org/10.1023/B:CRIS.0000039600.88691.af.

Levi, M. and Smith, R. (2022) 'Fraud and Pandemics', *Journal of Financial Crime*, 29(2), pp. 413–432.

Levi, M. and Soudijn, M. (2020) 'Understanding the Laundering of Organized Crime Money', *Crime and Justice*, 49(1), pp. 579–631.

Levi, M., Reuter, P. and Halliday, T. (2018) 'Can the AML/CTF System Be Evaluated Without Better Data?' *Crime, Law and Social Change*, 69(2), pp. 307–328. Available at: https://link.springer.com/content/pdf/10.1007%2Fs10611-017-9757-4.pdf.

Levi, M., & Soudijn, M. (2020) 'Understanding the Laundering of Organized Crime Money', in P. Reuter and M Tonry (eds) *Organizing Crime: Mafias, Markets, and Networks, Crime and Justice: An Annual Review of Research*. Chicago: University of Chicago Press Journals. pp. 579–631. Available at: https://www.journals.uchicago.edu/doi/10.1086/708047.

Lewis, M. (2015) *Flash Boys: A Wall Street Revolt*. New York: Norton.

Lord, N. (2014) *Regulating Corporate Bribery in International Business: Anti-Corruption in the UK and Germany* (Law, Crime and Culture). Farnham, Surrey: Ashgate.

Lord, N. (2015) 'Establishing Enforcement Legitimacy in the Pursuit of Rule-Breaking "Global Elites": The Case of Transnational Corporate Bribery', *Theoretical Criminology*, 20(3), pp. 376–399. Available at: https://doi.org/10.1177/1362480615605560.

Lord, N. and Broad, R. (2017) 'Corporate Failures to Prevent Serious and Organised Crimes: Foregrounding the "Organisational" Component', *The European Review of Organised Crime*, 4(2), pp. 25–52.

Lord, N. and Levi, M. (2015) 'Determining the Adequate Enforcement of Corporate and White-Collar Crimes in Europe', in J.G. van Erp, W. Huisman, and G. Vande Walle (eds) *The Routledge Handbook of White-Collar and Corporate Crime in Europe*. Oxford: Routledge, pp. 39–56.

Lord, N. and Levi, M. (2017) 'Organizing the Finances for and the Finances from Transnational Corporate Bribery', *European Journal of Criminology*, 14(3), pp. 365–389. Available at: https://doi.org/10.1177/1477370816661740.

Lord, N. et al. (2017) 'A Script Analysis of the Distribution of Counterfeit Alcohol Across Two European Jurisdictions', *Trends in Organized Crime*, 20(3–4), pp. 252–272. Available at: https://doi.org/10.1007/s12117-017-9305-8.

Lord, N. et al. (2020) *ScriptNet: An Integrated Criminological-Network Analysis Tool*. Manchester: University of Manchester.

Lord, N., Van Wingerde, L. and Levi, M. (2021) 'Corruption, Culture and Comparative Analyses Across Europe: Developing new Research Traditions', in N. Lord et al. (eds) *What Is "European" About White-Collar and Corporate Crime in Europe? A Collection of Essays*. Bristol: Bristol University Press, pp. 55–71.

Lord, N., Wingerde, K. and Campbell, L. (2018) 'Organising the Monies of Corporate Financial Crimes via Organisational Structures: Ostensible Legitimacy, Effective Anonymity, and Third-Party Facilitation', *Administrative Sciences*, 8(2), p. 17. Available at: https://doi.org/10.3390/admsci8020017.

Lord, N., Zeng., Y. and Jordanoska, A. (2022) 'White-Collar Crimes Beyond the Nation-State' in E. Erez and P. Ibarra (eds) The Oxford Encyclopedia of International Criminology, Oxford: Oxford University Press, pp. 1361–1385.

Lord, N.J., Campbell, L.J. and Van Wingerde, K. (2019) 'Other People's Dirty Money: Professional Intermediaries, Market Dynamics and the Finances of White-Collar, Corporate and Organized Crimes', *The British Journal of Criminology*, 59(5), pp. 1217–1236. Available at: https://doi.org/10.1093/bjc/azz004.

Lusthaus, J. et al. (2023) 'Cybercriminal Networks in the UK and Beyond: Network Structure, Criminal Cooperation and External Interactions', *Trends in Organized Crime*, 27, pp. 364–387. [Preprint]. Available at: https://doi.org/10.1007/s12117-022-09476-9.

Maesschalck, J. (2021) 'Using Grid-Group Cultural Theory to Assess Approaches to the Prevention of Corporate and Occupational Crime: The EU as a Natural Experiment', in N. Lord et al. (eds) *European White-Collar Crime: Exploring the Nature of European Realities*. Bristol: Bristol University Press, pp. 17–38.

Maggetti, M., Radaelli, C.M. and Gilardi, F. (2013) *Designing Research in the Social Sciences*. Los Angeles, CA; London: Sage.

Malm, A. and Bichler, G. (2011) 'Networks of Collaborating Criminals: Assessing the Structural Vulnerability of Drug Markets', *Journal of Research in Crime and Delinquency*, 48(2), pp. 271–297. Available at: https://doi.org/10.1177/0022427810391535.

Mason, J. (2006) *Real Life Methods Working Papers: Six Strategies for Mixing Methods and Linking Data in Social Science Research* (4/06). University of Manchester. Available at: https://core.ac.uk/download/pdf/229987619.pdf (Accessed: 12 April 2022).

Matthijsse, S., van't Hoff-de Goede, M. and Leukfeldt, E.R. (2023) 'Your Files Have Been Encrypted: A Crime Script Analysis of Ransomware Attacks', *Trends in Organized Crime*, pp. 1–27.

McCrum, D. (2019) 'Wirecard's Suspect Accounting Practices Revealed', *Financial Times*, 15 October. Available at: https://www.ft.com/content/19c6be2a-ee67-11e9-bfa4-b25f11f42901.

McCrum, D. (2022) *Money Men: A Hot Startup, A Billion Dollar Fraud, A Fight for the Truth*. London: Penguin.

McCrum, D. (2023) *Money Men*. Penguin. Available at: https://www.penguin.co.uk/books/444756/money-men-by-mccrum-dan/9780552178464 (Accessed: 23 May 2023).

Middleton, D. and Levi, M. (2015) 'Let Sleeping Lawyers Lie: Organized Crime, Lawyers and the Regulation of Legal Services: Table 1', *British Journal of Criminology*, 55(4), pp. 647–668. Available at: https://doi.org/10.1093/bjc/azv001.

Morgenthaler, E. and LeClerc, B. (2023) 'Crime Script Analysis of Drug Importation into Australia Facilitated by the Dark Net', *Global Crime*, pp. 1–26.

Morselli, C. (2009) *Inside Criminal Networks: 8 (Studies of Organized Crime, 8)*. New York: Springer.

Morselli, C. (2010) 'Assessing Vulnerable and Strategic Positions in a Criminal Network', *Journal of Contemporary Criminal Justice*, 26(4), pp. 382–392. Available at: https://doi.org/10.1177/1043986210377105.

Morselli, C. (2010b) *Inside Criminal Networks: 8 (Studies of Organized Crime, 8)*. New York: Springer.

Morselli, C., Giguère, C. and Petit, K. (2007) 'The Efficiency/Security Trade-off in Criminal Networks', *Social Networks*, 29(1), pp. 143–153. Available at: https://doi.org/10.1016/j.socnet.2006.05.001.

Morselli, C. and Roy, J. (2008) 'Brokerage Qualifications in Ringing Operations', *Criminology*, 46(1), pp. 71–98. Available at: https://doi.org/10.1111/j.1745-9125.2008.00103.x.

Nash, R., Bouchard, M. and Malm, A. (2018) 'Twisting Trust: Social Networks, Due Diligence, and Loss of Capital in a Ponzi Scheme', *Crime, Law and Social Change*, 69(1), pp. 67–89. Available at: https://doi.org/10.1007/s10611-017-9706-2.

National Audit Office. (2022). *Managing Tax Compliance Following the Pandemic, HC 957*. Available at: https://www.nao.org.uk/wp-content/uploads/2022/12/managing-tax-compliance-following-the-pandemic-report.pdf.

National Audit Office. (2023) *Report: Covid-19 Business Grant Schemes* (HC 1200). House of Commons.

Neilson, D. and Sharman, J. (2022) Signatures for Sale. *World Bank*. Available at: https://star.worldbank.org/publications/signatures-sale-how-nominee-services-shell-companies-are-abused-conceal-beneficial.

Nelken, D. (2010) *Comparative Criminal Justice: Making Sense of Difference* (Compact Criminology). London: SAGE.
Nelken, D. (2012) 'White-Collar and Corporate Crime', in M. Maguire, R. Morgan and R. Reiner (eds) *The Oxford Handbook of Criminology*. 5th edition. Oxford: Oxford University Press Inc.
OECD. (2007) *Bribery in Public Procurement: Methods, Actors and Counter-Measures*. OECD. Available at: https://doi.org/10.1787/9789264013964-en.
Oldenburg, P. (1987) 'Middlemen in Third-World Corruption: Implications of an Indian Case', *World Politics*, 39(4), pp. 508–535. Available at: https://doi.org/10.2307/2010290.
Oliver, K. (2014) *Covert Networks: Structures, Processes and Types* (Working Paper) Manchester: University of Manchester, Mitchell Centre, p. 24.
PAC. (2023) *PPE Medpro: Awarding of Contracts During the Pandemic*. London: House of Commons HC 1590.
Paoli, L. and Donati, A. (2014) *The Sports Doping Market*. New York: Springer.
Papachristos, A.V. and Bastomski, S. (2018) 'Connected in Crime: The Enduring Effect of Neighborhood Networks on the Spatial Patterning of Violence', *American Journal of Sociology*, 124(2), pp. 517–568. Available at: https://doi.org/10.1086/699217.
Parker, C. and Gilad, S. (2011) 'Internal Corporate Compliance Management Systems: Structure, Culture and Agency', *Explaining Compliance: Business Responses to Regulation*, pp. 170–195.
Parker, C. and Nielsen, V.L. (2011) 'Introduction', in C. Parker and V.L. Nielsen (eds) *Explaining Compliance: Business Responses to Regulation*. Edward Elgar Publishing, pp. 1–34.
Parker, C. and Vibeke, L.N. (2011) 'Introduction: from Regulation to Compliance', in C. Parker and L.N. Vibeke (eds) *Explaining Compliance: Business Responses to Regulation*. Cheltenham: Edward Elgar, pp. 1–33.
Passas, N. (1999) 'Globalization, Criminogenic Asymmetries and Economic Crime', *European Journal of Law Reform*, 1(4), pp. 399–423.
Passas, N. (2001) 'Globalization and Transnational Crime: Effects of Criminogenic Asymmetries', in P. Williams and D. Vlassis (eds) *Combating Transnational Crime: Concepts, Activities, and Responses*. London: Routledge.
Passas, N. (2005) 'Lawful but Awful: "Legal Corporate Crimes" &', *Journal of Socio-Economics*, 34(6), pp. 771–786.
Passas, N. and Goodwin, N.R. (eds) (2004) *It's Legal but It Ain't Right: Harmful Social Consequences of Legal Industries* (Evolving Values for a Capitalist World). Ann Arbor: University of Michigan Press.
Piquero, A.R. and Weisburd, D. (eds) (2010) *Handbook of Quantitative Criminology*. New York, NY: Springer. Available at: https://doi.org/10.1007/978-0-387-77650-7.
Piquero, N.L. and Benson, M.L. (2004) 'White-Collar Crime and Criminal Careers: Specifying a Trajectory of Punctuated Situational Offending', *Journal of Contemporary Criminal Justice*, 20(2), pp. 148–165. Available at: https://doi.org/10.1177/1043986204263770.
Piquero, N.L. and Weisburd, D. (2009) 'Developmental Trajectories of White-Collar Crime', in S.S. Simpson and D. Weisburd (eds) *The Criminology of White-Collar Crime*. New York, NY: Springer, pp. 153–171. Available at: https://doi.org/10.1007/978-0-387-09502-8_8.
Pontell, H.N. (2016) 'Theoretical, Empirical, and Policy Implications of Alternative Definitions of "Whitecollar Crime": "Trivializing the Lunatic Crime Rate"', in S. Van Slyke, M.L. Benson, and F.T. Cullen (eds) *The Oxford Handbook of White-Collar Crime* (The Oxford Handbooks in Criminology and Criminal Justice). 1st edition. Oxford: Oxford University Press, pp. 39–59.

Pontell, H.N. and Geis, G. (eds) (2007) *International Handbook of White-Collar and Corporate Crime*. Boston, MA: Springer US. Available at: https://doi.org/10.1007/978-0-387-34111-8.

Prechel, H. (2016) 'Organizational Political Economy and White-Collar Crime', in S. van Slyke, M. Benson, and F. Cullen (eds) *The Oxford Handbook of White-Collar Crime*. Oxford: Oxford University Press, pp. 294–325. Available at: https://doi.org/10.1093/oxfordhb/9780199925513.013.15.

Punch, M. (1996) *Dirty Business: Exploring Corporate Misconduct: Analysis and Cases*. London: SAGE.

Punch, M. (2011) 'The Organizational Component in Corporate Crime: Maurice Punch', in J. Gobert and A.-M. Pascal (eds) *European Developments in Corporate Criminal Liability*. Routledge, pp. 114–126. Available at: https://www.taylorfrancis.com/books/edit/10.4324/9780203819203/european-developments-corporate-criminal-liability-james-gobert-ana-maria-pascal

Pusch, N. and Holtfreter, K. (2021) 'Individual and Organizational Predictors of White-Collar Crime: A Meta-Analysis', *Journal of White Collar and Corporate Crime*, 2(1), pp. 5–23. Available at: https://doi.org/10.1177/2631309X19901317.

Ramaphosa Response. (2022) '*Response by President Cyril Ramaphosa to the Recommendations of the Judicial Commission of Inquiry into Allegations of State Capture, Corruption and Fraud*'. October 2022, Republic of South Africa. Available at: https://www.stateofthenation.gov.za/assets/downloads/State%20Capture%20Commission%20Response.pdf

Rodchenkov, G. (2020) *The Rodchenkov Affair: How I Brought Down Russia's Secret Doping Empire*. Random House.

Rorie, M.L. (ed.) (2020) *The Handbook of White-Collar Crime* (Wiley Handbooks in Criminology and Criminal Justice). Hoboken, NJ: Wiley-Blackwell.

Rose-Ackerman, S. (1999) *Corruption and Government: Causes, Consequences and Reform*. 1st edition. Cambridge University Press.

Ross, E.A. (1907) 'The Criminaloid', *The Atlantic Monthly*, 99(1), pp. 44–50.

Rothe, D. and Friedrichs, D.O. (2015) *Crimes of Globalization* (New Directions in Critical Criminology). Abingdon, Oxon: Routledge.

Savona, E.U. (2010) 'Infiltration of the Public Construction Industry by the Italian Organized Crime', in *Situational Prevention of Organised Crimes* (Crime Science Series, 1). Portland: Willan Publishing, pp. 1–6.

Savona, E.U., Giommoni, L. and Mancuso, M. (2013) 'Human Trafficking for Sexual Exploitation in Italy', in B. LeClerc and R. Wortley (eds) *Cognition and Crime: Offender Decision-Making and Script Analyses* (Crime Science Series). 1st edition. New York: Routledge.

Sayer, A. (2010) *Method in Social Science: A Realist Approach*. Revised 2nd edition. London and New York: Routledge.

Schell-Busey, N. et al. (2016) 'What Works?', *Criminology & Public Policy*, 15(2), pp. 387–416. Available at: https://doi.org/10.1111/1745-9133.12195.

Schrager, L.S. and Short, J.F. (1978) 'Toward a Sociology of Organizational Crime', *Social Problems*, 25(4), pp. 407–419. Available at: https://doi.org/10.2307/800493.

Schwartz, D.M. and (D.A.) Rouselle, T. (2009) 'Using Social Network Analysis to Target Criminal Networks', *Trends in Organized Crime*, 12(2), pp. 188–207. Available at: https://doi.org/10.1007/s12117-008-9046-9.

Scott, J. (1988) 'Trend Report Social Network Analysis', *Sociology*, 22(1), pp. 109–127.

Shapiro, S.P. (1990) 'Collaring the Crime, Not the Criminal: Reconsidering the Concept of White-Collar Crime', *American Sociological Review*, 55(3), pp. 346–365. Available at: https://doi.org/10.2307/2095761.

Shover, N. and Hochstetler, A. (2006) *Choosing White-Collar Crime* (Cambridge Studies in Criminology). Cambridge: Cambridge University Press.

Simpson, S.S. (2013) 'White-Collar Crime: A Review of Recent Developments and Promising Directions for Future Research', *Annual Review of Sociology*, 39(1), pp. 309–331. Available at: https://doi.org/10.1146/annurev-soc-071811-145546.

Simpson, S.S. et al. (2014) 'Corporate Crime Deterrence: A Systematic Review', *Campbell Systematic Reviews*, 10(1), pp. 1–105. Available at: https://doi.org/10.4073/csr.2014.4.

Skidmore, A. (2021) 'Using Crime Script Analysis to Elucidate the Details of Amur Tiger Poaching in the Russian Far East', *Crime Science*, 10(1), p. 16. Available at: https://doi.org/10.1186/s40163-021-00150-z.

Slapper, G. and Tombs, S. (1999) *Corporate Crime* (Longman Criminology Series). Harlow: Longman.

Smith, A. (1982) *The Wealth of Nations*. London: Penguin.

Smith, C.M. and Papachristos, A.V. (2016) 'Trust Thy Crooked Neighbor: Multiplexity in Chicago Organized Crime Networks', *American Sociological Review*, 81(4), pp. 644–667. Available at: https://doi.org/10.1177/0003122416650149.

Soltes, E. (2016) *Why They Do It: Inside the Mind of the White-Collar Criminal*. PublicAffairs. Available at: https://books.google.co.uk/books/about/Why_They_Do_It.html?id=wTfXCwAAQBAJ&redir_esc=y (Accessed: 11 January 2023).

Soothill, K., Humphreys, L. and Francis, B. (2013) 'Middle-Class Offenders as Employees – Assessing the Risk: A 35-Year Follow-Up', *Journal of Offender Rehabilitation*, 52(6), pp. 407–420. Available at: https://doi.org/10.1080/10509674.2013.813617.

Sparrow, M.K. (1991) 'The Application of Network Analysis to Criminal Intelligence: An Assessment of the Prospects', *Social Networks*, 13(3), pp. 251–274. Available at: https://doi.org/10.1016/0378-8733(91)90008-H.

Stevenson, R. and Crossley, N. (2014) 'Change in Covert Social Movement Networks: The "Inner Circle" of the Provisional Irish Republican Army', *Social Movement Studies*, 13(1), pp. 70–91. Available at: https://doi.org/10.1080/14742837.2013.832622.

Suchman, L.A. (1987) *Plans and Situated Actions: The Problem of Human-Machine Communication*. Cambridge: Cambridge University Press.

Sullivan, B.N., Haunschild, P. and Page, K. (2007) 'Organizations Non Gratae? The Impact of Unethical Corporate Acts on Interorganizational Networks', *Organization Science*, 18(1), pp. 55–70. Available at: https://doi.org/10.1287/orsc.1060.0229.

Sutherland, E.H. (1983) *White Collar Crime: The Uncut Version*. New Haven, CT: Yale University Press.

Svorken, M., Kvalvik, I. and Lord, N. (2023) 'Understanding the Organisational Structure of Fisheries Crime in Well-Regulated Fisheries', *Marine Policy*, 157, p. 105860. Available at: https://doi.org/10.1016/j.marpol.2023.105860.

Taylor, D. (2013) *Boardroom Scandal: The Criminalization of Company Fraud in Nineteenth-Century Britain*. Oxford: Oxford University Press.

Timans, R., Wouters, P. and Heilbron, J. (2019) 'Mixed Methods Research: What It Is and What It Could Be', *Theory and Society*, 48(2), pp. 193–216. Available at: https://doi.org/10.1007/s11186-019-09345-5.

Tombs, S. and Whyte, D. (2015) *The Corporate Criminal: Why Corporations Must Be Abolished* (Key Ideas in Criminology). Abingdon: Routledge.

Tombs, S. and Whyte, D. (2020) 'The Shifting Imaginaries of Corporate Crime', *Journal of White Collar and Corporate Crime*, 1(1), pp. 16–23. Available at: https://doi.org/10.1177/2631309X19882641.

Tompson, L. and Chainey, S. (2011) 'Profiling Illegal Waste Activity: Using Crime Scripts as a Data Collection and Analytical Strategy', *European Journal on Criminal Policy and Research*, 17(3), pp. 179–201. Available at: https://doi.org/10.1007/s10610-011-9146-y.

Toms, S. (2024) *Systems of Deceit: Financial Fraud and Scandal in the United Kingdom, 1700–2010*. London: World Scientific.

Tremblay, P., Talon, B. and Hurley, D. (2001) 'Body Switching and Related Adaptations in the Resale of Stolen Vehicles. Script Elaborations and Aggregate Crime Learning Curves', *British Journal of Criminology*, 41(4), pp. 561–579. Available at: https://doi.org/10.1093/bjc/41.4.561.

Tudor, K. (2019) 'Symbolic Survival and Harm: Serious Fraud and Consumer Capitalism's Perversion of the Causa Sui Project', *The British Journal of Criminology*, 59(5), pp. 1237–1253.

Turner, A. (2024) *Little Englanders: Britain in the Edwardian Era*. London: Profile Books.

US Department of Justice. (2022) *Co-Founder of Multi-Billion-Dollar Cryptocurrency Pyramid Scheme "OneCoin" Pleads Guilty*. Available at: https://www.justice.gov/usao-sdny/pr/co-founder-multi-billion-dollar-cryptocurrency-pyramid-scheme-onecoin-pleads-guilty (Accessed: 16 March 2023).

van de Bunt, H. (2010) 'Walls of Secrecy and Silence. The Madoff Case and Cartels in the Construction Industry', *Criminology & Public Policy*, 9(3), pp. 435–453. Available at: https://doi.org/10.1111/j.1745-9133.2010.00640.x.

van der Does de Willebois, E. et al. (2011) *The Puppet Masters: How the Corrupt Use Legal Structures to Hide Stolen Assets and What to Do About It*. World Bank. Available at: https://doi.org/10.1596/978-0-8213-8894-5.

Van Duyne, P.C., Harvey, J.H. and Gelemerova, L.Y. (2018) *The Critical Handbook of Money Laundering: Policy, Analysis and Myths*. New York: Springer.

Van Erp, J. and Levi, M. (forthcoming) *Naming and Shaming: Corporate Responsibility and Reputational Sanctions in Global Society*. Cambridge: Cambridge University Press.

Van Nguyen, T. (2022) 'The Modus Operandi of Transnational Computer Fraud: A Crime Script Analysis in Vietnam', *Trends in Organized Crime*, 25(2), pp. 226–247. Available at: https://doi.org/10.1007/s12117-021-09422-1.

van Onna, J.H.R. (2020) 'From the Avalanche to the Game: White-Collar Offenders on Crime, Bonds and Morality', *Crime, Law and Social Change*, 74(4), pp. 405–431. Available at: https://doi.org/10.1007/s10611-020-09899-x.

van Onna, J.H.R. et al. (2014) 'Criminal Trajectories of White-collar Offenders', *Journal of Research in Crime and Delinquency*, 51(6), pp. 759–784. Available at: https://doi.org/10.1177/0022427814531489.

Van Slyke, S., Benson, M.L. and Cullen, F.T. (eds) (2016) *The Oxford Handbook of White-Collar Crime* (The Oxford Handbooks in Criminology and Criminal Justice). 1st edition. Oxford: Oxford University Press.

Van Wingerde, K. (2015) 'The Limits of Environmental Regulation in a Globalized Economy. Lessons from the Probo Koala Case', in J.G. van Erp, W. Huisman, and G.V. Walle (eds) *The Routledge Handbook of White-Collar and Corporate Crime in Europe*. Oxford: Routledge, pp. 260–275.

Van Wingerde, K. and Lord, N.J. (eds) (2020) 'The Elusiveness of White-Collar and Corporate Crime in a Globalized Economy', in *The Handbook of White-Collar Crime* (Wiley Handbooks in Criminology and Criminal Justice). Hoboken, NJ: Wiley-Blackwell, pp. 469–483.

Varese, F. (2013) 'The Structure and the Content of Criminal Connections: The Russian Mafia in Italy', *European Sociological Review*, 29(5), pp. 899–909.

Vaughan, D. (1996) *The Challenger Launch Decision: Risky Technology, Culture, and Deviance at NASA*. Chicago, IL: University of Chicago Press.

Vaughan, D. (1998) 'Rational Choice, Situated Action, and the Social Control of Organizations', *Law & Society Review*, 32(1), pp. 23–62.

Vaughan, D. (2007) 'Beyond Macro- and Micro-Levels of Analysis, Organizations, and the Cultural Fix', in H.N. Pontell and G. Geis (eds) *International Handbook of*

White-Collar and Corporate Crime. Boston, MA: Springer, pp. 3–24. Available at: https://doi.org/10.1007/978-0-387-34111-8_1.

Verity, A. (2023) *Rigged: The Incredible True Story of the Whistleblowers Jailed After Exposing the Rotten Heart of the Financial System*. S.l.: Flint.

von Lampe, K. (2009) 'Human Capital and Social Capital in Criminal Networks: Introduction to the Special Issue on the 7th Blankensee Colloquium', *Trends in Organized Crime*, 12(2), pp. 93–100. Available at: https://doi.org/10.1007/s12117-009-9067-z.

Wallis, N. (2021) *The Great Post Office Scandal*. Bath Publishing Limited. Available at: https://bathpublishing.com/products/the-great-post-office-scandal (Accessed: 23 May 2023).

Wasserman, S. and Faust, K. (1994) *Social Network Analysis: Methods and Applications* (Structural Analysis in the Social Sciences, 8). Cambridge: Cambridge University Press.

Wasserman, S., Pattison, P. and Steinley, D. (2005) 'Social Networks', in *Encyclopedia of Statistics in Behavioral Science*. John Wiley & Sons, Ltd. Available at: https://doi.org/10.1002/0470013192.bsa720.

Weisburd, D. and Waring, E.J. (2001) *White-Collar Crime and Criminal Careers* (Cambridge Studies in Criminology). Cambridge: Cambridge University Press.

Weisburd, D. et al. (1991) *Crimes of the Middle Classes: White-Collar Offenders in the Federal Courts* (Yale Studies on White-Collar Crime). New Haven, CT: Yale University Press.

Weisburd, D., Wheeler, S., Waring, E. and Bode, N. (1991) *Crimes of the Middle Classes: White-Collar Offenders in the Federal Courts* (Yale Studies on White-Collar Crime). New Haven, CT: Yale University Press.

White, G. (2022) *The Lazarus Heist*. London: Penguin Business.

Whyte, D. (2014) 'Regimes of Permission and State-Corporate Crime', *State Crime Journal*, 3, p. 237.

Williams, A. (2021) *Deep Collusion: Bain and the Capture of South Africa*. Tafelberg Publishers Ltd.

Witness, G. (2013) *Anonymous Companies: How Hidden Company Ownership Is a Major Barrier in the Fight Against Poverty and What to Do About It*. London: Global Witness. Available at: https://cdn.globalwitness.org/archive/files/library/anonymous_companies4b.pdf (Accessed: 7 May 2022).

Wylie, B. (2020) *Bandit Capitalism*. Birlinn Ltd. Available at: https://birlinn.co.uk/product/bandit-capitalism/ (Accessed: 23 May 2023).

Zabyelina, Y.G. (2015) 'Reverse Money Laundering in Russia: Clean Cash for Dirty Ends', *Journal of Money Laundering Control*, 18(2), pp. 202–219. Available at: https://doi.org.manchester.idm.oclc.org/10.1108/JMLC-10-2014-0039.

Zagaris, B. (2015) *International White Collar Crimes: Cases and Materials*. 2nd edition. New York: Cambridge University Press.

Zanella, M. (2013) 'Script Analysis of Corruption in Public Procurement', in B. LeClerc and R. Wortley (eds) *Cognition and Crime: Offender Decision-Making and Script Analyses* (Crime Science Series). 1st edition. New York: Routledge.

Zeng, Y. (2021) *Scripting" Insider Dealing: The Abuse of Inside Information*. Unpublished doctoral thesis. University of Manchester.

Zhu, A. et al. (2017) 'Ponzi Scheme Diffusion in Complex Networks', *Physica A: Statistical Mechanics and its Applications*, 479, pp. 128–136. Available at: https://doi.org/10.1016/j.physa.2017.03.015.

Index

Note: Page numbers in *italics* indicate figures, **bold** indicate tables in the text, and references following "n" refer notes.